Library 2.0 and Information Management

Essays in Honour of Dr. Jalaja V.

Library 2.0 and Information Management

Essays in Honour of Dr. Jalaja V.

Edited by
Dineshan Koovakkai
T.M. Vasudevan

ATLANTIC
PUBLISHERS & DISTRIBUTORS (P) LTD

Published by

ATLANTIC

PUBLISHERS & DISTRIBUTORS (P) LTD

7/22, Ansari Road, Darya Ganj,
New Delhi-110002
Phones : +91-11-40775252, 23273880, 23275880, 23280451
Fax : +91-11-23285873
Web : www.atlanticbooks.com
E-mail : orders@atlanticbooks.com

Branch Office
5, Nallathambi Street, Wallajah Road,
Chennai-600002
Phones : +91-44-64611085, 32413319
E-mail : chennai@atlanticbooks.com

ISBN 978-81-269-1630-6

Printed in India at Nice Printing Press, A-33/3A, Site-IV, Industrial Area, Sahibabad, Ghaziabad, U.P.

Dr. Jalaja V.

Dr. Jalaja V.: A Biographical Sketch

Librarianship, teaching and nursing are said to be the three professions which are more suitable to women than other professions. If this is true, the post of library science teacher should be doubly suitable to women. However, in practice, at least in Indian universities, we see that women are less in number compared to men in the teaching and research departments of Library and Information Science. Especially in Kerala, women as teachers are rare in LIS departments of the universities. When women are there, they make the department of teaching and research a home of love and affection and mutual trust. Dr. Jalaja is a glorious example of such rare teachers in LIS.

Early Life and Education

Dr. Jalaja was born on 15th May, 1951 in a hamlet called Kadakkavoor blessed with lush green growth of plants and trees in the Chirayinkeezh Thalook of Trivandrum district. She had her school education in the SSPB High School, Kadakkavoor in 1966 and passed SSLC from there. She had her higher education first in the Government College for Women, Trivandrum and further in the Department of Mathematics and the Department of Library & Information Science of the University of Kerala. She took B.Sc. degree in Mathematics in 1971, M.Sc. degree in Mathematics in 1973 and B.L.I.Sc. degree in 1975. She did her Masters course in Library and Information Science from the prestigious University Department of Library Science of the University of Madras where there was an efficient team of library science teachers such as Prof. G. Bhattacharya, Prof. P. Gangadhara Rao and Prof. K.S. Raghavan. She did her M.L.I.Sc. from Madras University in 1979. She was awarded Ph.D. in 1995 from Calicut University. Her topic of research was the Bibliometric Analysis of Science Journals Published from India.

Entering into the Library Profession

Dr. Jalaja joined the Calicut University service as a library professional in January 1976. She worked in the Departments of Physics, Sanskrit and Psychology of the University of Calicut for about twelve and a half years as a library professional and gained experience in library organization and management and in various operations of technical processing. She maintained good personal contact with all faculty members, P.G. students and research scholars and took special interest in rendering personalized reference service to them.

As a Teacher of Library and Information Science

Dr. Jalaja joined the Department of Library & Information Science of the University of Calicut in August 1988 as a Lecturer when I was the Head of the Department. At this time it was easy for her to choose library management and reference service as her topics of teaching with her considerable experience as a library professional in various departments of the University of Calicut.

When the M.L.I.Sc. course was started in the Department in 1995, with her subject background in mathematics and statistics at M.Sc. level and bibliometrics in Ph.D., Dr. Jalaja could choose Research Methodology and Statistical Methods & Bibliometrics as her subjects for P.G. level teaching. She developed her skill in these areas of specialization and has made significant contributions. Dr. Jalaja became Reader in December 2000 and was designated as Associate Professor in 2006. After about 23 years of service as a teacher of Library and Information Science she retired on 31st May 2011 to lead a professionally active retired life. I acknowledge the good cooperation Dr. Jalaja had extended in all academic matters in the department until my retirement.

As a Research Guide

Eight persons have been awarded Ph.D. under the guidance of Dr. Jalaja, one is about to submit his thesis and many more are nearing completion. Dr. Jalaja has also guided about 150 M.L.I.Sc. and 5 M.Phil. dissertations.

As an Academician

As an academician Dr. Jalaja has made significant contributions. I retired in March 2004 when I had framed the syllabus for 2-year integrated M.L.I.Sc. in the capacity of Head of the Department and Chairman of Board of Studies in Library & Information Science. Then it was the job of Dr. Jalaja and her colleagues to implement this teaching programme which they carried out meticulously.

Later, when credit based M.L.I.Sc. teaching programme and integrated M.Phil.–Ph.D. programme were introduced, Dr. Jalaja had many challenges ahead as the Head of the Department with only a skeletal staff in the Department. However, she met all the challenges and organized these teaching programmes faultlessly. She revised the syllabi for M.L.I.Sc. integrated course and designed the curriculum for M.Phil. degree with the cooperation of her colleagues. As a person of good understanding it was easy for her to elicit the cooperation and support of her colleagues.

Dr. Jalaja was a counselor for IGNOU from the very beginning and continued it in the midst of her multiple academic programmes. She is a life member of several professional associations like ILA, IASLIC, KLA, and KELPRO.

Dr. Jalaja was a member of the Senate of the University of Calicut and worked as the member of the Academic Council and Faculty of Humanities and Chairman of the Board of Studies in Library & Information Science, University of Calicut.

She remained an active member of the Board of Studies in Library & Information Science in the universities of Kerala, Madras and Mysore. She was a research guide in Calicut University and Kerala Kalamandalam, in Kerala and also in Alagappa University and Karpagam University of Tamil Nadu. She was the resource person for the Academic Staff College of the Calicut and Kerala Universities. She worked as the Chairman of the Board of Examination of Calicut University and had been associated as a question paper setter and examiner in various other universities such as Kerala, Mysore and M.G. universities.

Publications in Library and Information Science

Dr. Jalaja was a member of the Editorial Board of the *Journal of Information Science* and *Kelpro Bulletin*. She is the author of about 25 research papers in journals and conference proceedings. In addition, she has edited a book entitled *Organisation Processing and Use of Information in the Digital Era*. She was a regular participant of national seminars and conferences.

Family Life

Dr. Jalaja is married to Sri S. Murleedharan, who retired as a Badminton Coach from the Physical Education Department of the University of Calicut. He is a coach of international reputation, who travels far and wide throughout the country and in foreign countries.

Dr. Jalaja is blessed with two daughters. The elder daughter Seema is a Homeopathic physician in the Kerala Government. The younger daughter Sumi is a faculty member of a prestigious fashion design institution in Delhi.

As a former colleague of Dr. Jalaja and a senior person in the realm of library science education, I extend my best wishes to her and I pray to God to give her a healthy long life.

Prof. Ulloor M. Parameswaran

Preface

Library and Information Science (LIS) is a dynamic subject and a noble profession which has the prime objective of informing and enlightening the people in various walks of life. We the practitioners have every right to be proud of being instrumental in the nation-building activities by providing the right information at the right time. It is the Library School which moulded us to be what we are now. We are all indebted to the LIS gurus who lit the lamp of knowledge in us that only enabled us to perform as successful LIS professionals and teachers.

Dr. Jalaja V., Associate Professor and Head, DLIS, University of Calicut is one such LIS guru who motivated us to earn knowledge and learn the skills of LIS profession. She, with her motherly affection, has always been supporting her innumerable students and others in the profession who are now holding different positions in India and abroad.

This book is a commemorative volume brought out on the eve of her retirement from the University of Calicut. Eminent LIS professionals and teachers have contributed to this volume. It is a collection of 26 scholarly articles written by well experienced practitioners in LIS and eminent teachers. The articles focus on the current developments in Library and Information Science and Information Technology.

The articles are grouped into seven parts. Part I Digital Library contains three articles on digital library software and the practical experience in Digital Library. Part II Web 2.0 and Information Professionals includes five articles covering the various tools and techniques and components of Web 2.0. Part III Library Professionals and Professional Associations contains three articles relating to role and professional requirements of LIS professionals and professional associations. Part IV Public

Libraries has two articles which are based on the practical experience and research study. Part V Information Users and User Studies contains six research papers on various information user groups and their use of a variety of information sources. Part VI Library Provisions and Access Possibilities with four papers discusses various modern information sources provided in the libraries and the tools and techniques related to them. Part VII The Open Source Philosophy contains three informative articles relating to various open source application possibilities.

There is no doubt that this volume will be a good contribution in the field of Library and Information Science and will add more information to the existing treasure of knowledge in LIS. We hope that the LIS community will receive this book wholeheartedly.

Dineshan Koovakkai
T.M. Vasudevan

Contents

PART V
INFORMATION USERS AND USER STUDIES

PART VI
LIBRARY PROVISIONS AND ACCESS POSSIBILITIES

PART VII

THE OPEN SOURCE PHILOSOPHY

PART I

DIGITAL LIBRARY

Building Digital Libraries Using Open Source Software: Introducing Greenstone

1

M.G. Sreekumar, R. Biju, T. Sunitha, P. Sreejaya and *Joshy Kuriakose*

1. Introduction

Libraries all over the world are in the constant business of providing their clientele nascent as well as legacy information and in the process they buy, subscribe, license and accumulate information in an unprecedented array of content categories or publication types, and in a rapidly proliferating mix of formats (digital as well as print). There is a great deal of cultural divide and philosophical deviation between the traditional information resources being handled by libraries for centuries now and the new genre of electronic and digital information being sourced and accessed. In the traditional paradigm, the books and journals bought and subscribed to by the libraries were naturally owned by them, allowing them to make the best use of the resources within the 'fair use' clause or principle. Whereas in the electronic publishing scenario all the traditional belief, approach and understanding about the digital documents that the library purchase/subscribe to, have a world of difference. Libraries get only a license to use the electronic information (books, journals, databases, software, etc.) while purchasing, and even this license is issued only for a prescribed period of time. Librarians at the same time, have the professional responsibility to assure uninterrupted as well as perpetual access to the information subscribed to by the library. Issues of copyright, intellectual property, and fair use are very much important to libraries.[1]

In the current practical library setting there is an amazing penetration of digital information through a variety of publication forms such as books (published as such or issued as accompaniment), journals, portals, vortals, reports, CBTs, WBTs, cases, databases, etc. The penetration level of electronic information in the special libraries and libraries belonging to centres of higher learning are supposed to be 70 percent as against their print counterparts. To make matters more complex the vast array of different formats, standards and platforms in which documents are published, pose a multiplicity of threats to the librarian who is supposed to be the custodian and service provider of these information products once it has found its way into the library. As librarians, we are sometimes the stewards of unique collections too.

2. Digital Libraries

Digital Libraries (DL) are now emerging as a crucial component of global information infrastructure, adopting the latest information and communication technology. Digital Libraries are networked collections of digital texts, documents, images, sounds, data, software, and many more that are the core of today's Internet and tomorrow's universally accessible digital repositories of all human knowledge. According to the Digital Library Federation (DLF, USA—http://www.dlf.org), "Digital libraries are organizations that provide the resources, including the specialized staff, to select, structure, offer intellectual access to, interpret, distribute, preserve the integrity of, and ensure the persistence over time of collections of digital works so that they are readily and economically available for use by a defined community or set of communities."

Currently in vast majority of instances, the concept 'Digital Library' is being practiced by and large loosely or even confused by many information systems. It is, therefore, imperative that the concept is properly understood so that there is no ambiguity while we progress with the work of designing or developing a digital library which is fully justified in the technical sense of the word. It is important that embarking on a digital library project is something which will take away substantial amount of time, energy, manpower and of course the hard earned money being pumped into it—be it for system development or towards development and maintenance of the collection, in a meaningful way. There is consensus all over that there exists a very large quantum of digital information, scholarly as well as trade, which are scattered and distributed throughout the Net and also being stored in numerous other databases and repositories spread across the world. Also there is an unprecedented technology support and availability of infrastructure for digital libraries.[2]

3. DL Features

Digital libraries offer new levels of access to broader audiences of users and new opportunities for library and information science field to advance both theory and practice.[3] They contain information collections predominantly in digital or electronic form. Electronic publications have some special management requirements as compared to printed document. They include infrastructure, acceptability, access restrictions, readability, standardization, authentication, preservation, copyright, user interface, etc.

Digital libraries do enable the seamless integration of the scholarly electronic information, help in creating and maintaining local digital content, and strengthen the mechanisms and capacity of the library's information systems and services. They increase the portability, efficiency of access, flexibility, availability and preservation of digital objects. Digital Libraries can help move the nation towards realizing the enormously powerful vision of 'anytime, anywhere' access to the best and the latest of human thought and culture, so that no classroom, individual or a society is isolated from knowledge resources. Digital library brings the library to the user, overcoming all geographical barriers.[4]

4. DL Software

Undoubtedly it is essential to have a robust and flexible digital collections management and presentation software for creating and delivering digital collections. The preservation of digital objects is currently intimately tied to software that presents those objects. Complete preservation of complex digital objects, especially, is likely to require preservation of the software needed to use those objects.[5] The complexity of the situation is that digital library technologies and contents are not static. Continual evolution and investment are required to maintain the digital library. Commercial digital library products are comprehensive and extensible enough to support this evolution, but in many cases they are beyond the reach of most of the libraries in India. Some of the popular commercial DL software in the Indian libraries are VTLS (http://www.vtls.com) from the international market and ACADO (http://www.transversalnet.com/acado/index.htm) as an Indian initiative. The latter is definitely less costlier when compared but still striving its best to get a critical mass of users. The whole lot of associated issues include initial purchase fee, licensing fee, upgrade fee, annual maintenance contracts (AMCs) and so on. The best available choice for the librarian now is to turn to an Open Source Software (OSS). OSS has grown tremendously in scope and popularity over the last several years, and is now in widespread use. The growth of OSS has gained the attention of research librarians and created new opportunities for libraries.[6] OSS is close to our hearts primarily for their free (or almost free) availability and the broad rights it awards to the consumer. According to Stallman and others at OSS, 'Free Software' uses the 'free' from 'freedom', not the one from 'free beer'.[7]

"OSS is software for which the source code is available to the end-user. The source code can be modified by the end-user. The licensing conditions are intended to facilitate continued re-use and wide availability of the software in both commercial and non-commercial contexts. The cost of acquisition to the end-user is often minimal. According to the proponents of OSS, 'Open source is a development methodology; free software is a social movement'. There are number of other notable features to OSS. Firstly, it has no secrets and the innards are available for anyone to inspect. It is not privately controlled and hence likely to promote open rather than proprietary formats. It is typically maintained by communities rather than corporations and hence bug fixes and enhancement are often frequent and free. It is usually distributed free of charge (developers make their money from support, training, and specialist add-ons; not marketing). It is also essential to clear up some of the misunderstandings about

OSS. Open source software may or may not cost money. The cost of ownership often bears little relation to the cost of acquiring a piece of software. 'Public domain' is something different. Open source software has a copyright holder and conditions of legal use. Open source software does not mandate exclusivity. One can use open source programs under Windows. Also one should not choose software solely on the basis of open source. Interoperability and open standards for data are equally important".[8]

According to Altman[9], for the library fraternity there are other set of reasons too for preferring OSS over commercial software. Long-term preservation, assurance of privacy, provision for auditing, facilitating community resources, and conformity to open standards are hallmarks of OSS. Since commercial software is usually distributed only as a binary that will run only on a single hardware platform (and often only under a single version of a particular operating system) commercial software is very difficult to preserve over the long run without developing hardware emulation (and possibly OS 'emulation', as well). OSS, in contrast, can often be recompiled, or at least ported, to new hardware and operating systems. In order to get a picture about the availability of OSS for digital library applications, it is encouraged to visit the directories of OSS projects, such as GNU [http://www.gnu.org/] and Sourceforge [http://www.sourceforge.net/] open source directory which lists over fifty-thousand projects, and the numbers continue to grow.

5. DL Objectives and Workflow

The primary objective of a digital library is to enhance the digital collection in a substantial way, by strategically sourcing digital materials, conforming to copyright permissions, in all possible standards/formats so that scalability and flexibility is guaranteed for the future and advanced information services are assured to the user community right from the beginning. The digital library should also be able to integrate and aggregate the existing collections and services mentioned above with an outstanding client interface. This implies that the digital library system should also have a strong collection interface capable of embracing almost all the popular digital standards and formats and software platforms, in line with the underlying digital library technologies in vogue. This is crucial in the case of multimedia integration, which is again important as we planned to also host a digital audio and video library as part of the core library collection. Emphasis should also be given to maximise the efficiency and effectiveness of the information access and retrieval capabilities of the system by deploying Resource Description Framework [RDF] supplemented with popular descriptive metadata standards. The Internet also possesses, in addition to its mammoth proprietary information base, an invaluable wealth and a vast collection of public domain information products such as databases, books, journals, theses, technical reports, cases, standards, newsletters etc., scattered and distributed across the world. This treasure should also be explored to its maximum for collection building, based on the source and quality. Standard workflow patterns are to be identified for the system which include 'content selection', 'content acquisition', 'content publishing', 'content indexing and storage', and 'content accessing and delivery'. The system should also concern about such related issues, viz., preservation, usage monitoring, access management, interoperability, administration and management, etc.

It is always desirable to have crosswalks between the digital catalogue of the library (OPAC) and the digital library, as the OPAC in most cases, acts as a stepping stone for effective information discovery in the library. It also facilitates a healthy bridging between the traditional and the digital library. MARC or any of its variant forms is the desired bibliographic standard recommended for the OPAC, for want of interoperability. Dublin Core [DCMI], MODS (Metadata Object Description Schema) or METS (Metadata Encoding and Transmission) are the recommended metadata format for the digital collection, and XML is the desired encoding scheme [XML]. The XML encoding schemas and the related DTDs (Document Type Definition) strengthen the digital library on strong footing and the XSL (Extensible Stylesheet Language) transformations acts as dynamic gateways between the diverse data streams and the HTML front-end.

6. Selection of the DL Software

The software selection based on set parameters is an uphill task, as the technology itself was still emerging only. In general, what is desirable is a system that is flexible enough to fit the current digital information system as above and to accommodate future migration. It should be robust in technical architecture as well as the content architecture. The system should address all major digital library related issues such as 'design criteria', 'collection building', 'content organisation', 'access', 'evaluation', 'policy and legal issues' including 'intellectual property rights'. That the system should be in a position to embrace almost all predominant and emerging digital object formats and capable of supporting the standard library technology platforms, should be the major focus. It should provide two important user interfaces: a public user interface for presentation and a metadata creation interface for administration. The system should also provide a powerful search engine and thc interface should be easy to navigate and there should be provision for customisation.

There are many digital library software available, proprietary as well as open source, and most of them conform to international standards. As mentioned earlier, VTLS and ACADO are the commercial ones available and popular in the Indian market. Some of the popular Open Source Softwares for digital libraries, which are in use internationally, are 'DSpace', 'Dienst', 'Eprints', 'Fedora', 'Greenstone', etc. In line with the subject thrust of this paper, the Greenstone features are discussed in this paper.

7. Developing Digital Libraries Using Open Source Software

Digital libraries do enable the creation of local content, strengthen the mechanisms and capacity of the library's information systems and services. They increase the portability, efficiency of access, flexibility, availability and preservation of content. A state-of-art Digital Library shall give a real boost to the library's modernization activities and its endeavours to launch innovative digital information services to the user community. Once the information is made digital, it could be stored, retrieved, shared, copied and transmitted across distances without having to invest any additional expenditure. Value added and pinpointed information at the click of the mouse will become a reality if there is a Library Portal to provide access to the invaluable collection hosted by the Digital Library.

World over there is increasing appreciation of the Open Access movement and the Open Source Software philosophies and for many a library it is a chosen decision, be it technical or financial reasons, not to go for a proprietary digital library software. One needs to evaluate some of the popular Open Source Software for digital libraries, which are in use internationally. 'Dienst', 'Eprints', 'Fedora', 'Greenstone', etc. are among the candidates for the preferred software. Obviously Greenstone outscores the group as a general purpose digital library software from the point of view of a multi-publication type, multi-format, multi-media and a multi-lingual practical digital library [Greenstone]. And once finalized, it could be formally adopted as the software for creating the digital library.

The Greenstone Digital Library Software (GSDL) is a top of the line and internationally renowned Open Source Software system for developing digital libraries, promoted by the New Zealand Digital Library project research group at the University of Waikato, led by Dr. Ian H. Witten, and is sponsored by the UNESCO. Greenstone software uses three more additional associated softwares namely, Java Run Time Environment (JRE), ImageMagick and Ghostscript. The software suite is available at the open source directory 'Sourceforge.Net'.

8. Greenstone Fact Sheet (www.greenstone.org)

Greenstone is a suite of software for building and distributing digital library collections. It is not a digital library but a tool for building digital libraries. It provides a new way of organizing information and publishing it on the Internet in the form of a fully-searchable, metadata-driven digital library. It has been developed and distributed in cooperation with UNESCO and the Human Info NGO in Belgium. It is open-source, multilingual software, issued under the terms of the GNU General Public License. Its developers received the 2004 IFIP Namur award for "contributions to the awareness of social implications of information technology, and the need for an holistic approach in the use of information technology that takes account of social implications".

There are presently two versions of Greenstone going around, Version 2 and 3, and they are generally represented as Greenstone2 and Greenstone3. The latest in Greenstone2 as on April 2011 is V.2.84 and that of Greenstone3 is V.04. Greenstone2 will be there for some more years, but ultimately Waikato/ Greenstone see that Greenstone3 will replace it.

8.1 Technical Features

8.1.1 Platforms

Greenstone runs on all versions of Windows, and Unix, and Mac OS-X. It is very easy to install. For the default Windows installation absolutely no configuration is necessary, and end users routinely install Greenstone on their personal laptops or workstations. Institutional users run it on their main web server, where it interoperates with standard web server software (e.g. Apache).

8.1.2 Interoperability

Greenstone is highly interoperable using contemporary standards. It incorporates a server that can serve any collection over the Open Archives Protocol for Metadata Harvesting (OAI-PMH), and Greenstone can harvest documents over OAI-PMH and include them in a collection. Any collection can be exported to METS (in the Greenstone METS Profile, approved by the METS Editorial Board and published at http://www.loc.gov/standards/mets/mets-profiles.html), and Greenstone can ingest documents in METS form. Any collection can be exported to DSpace ready for DSpace's batch import program, and any DSpace collection can be imported into Greenstone.

8.1.3 Interfaces

Greenstone has two separate interactive interfaces, the Reader interface and the Librarian interface. End users access the digital library through the Reader interface, which operates within a web browser. The Librarian interface is a Java-based graphical user interface (also available as an applet) that makes it easy to gather material for a collection (downloading it from the web where necessary), enrich it by adding metadata, design the searching and browsing facilities that the collection will offer the user, and build and serve the collection.

8.1.4 Metadata formats

Users define metadata interactively within the Librarian interface.

These metadata sets are predefined: Dublin Core (qualified and unqualified) , RFC 1807, NZGLS (New Zealand Government Locator Service), AGLS (Australian Government Locator Service). New metadata sets can be defined using Greenstone's Metadata Set Editor. "Plug-ins" are used to ingest externally-prepared metadata in different forms, and plug-ins exist for XML, MARC, CDS/ISIS, ProCite, BibTex, Refer, OAI, DSpace, METS.

8.1.5 Document formats

Greenstone basically supports all popular file formats and media. Plug-ins are also used to ingest documents. For textual documents, there are plug-ins for PDF, PostScript, Word, RTF, HTML, Plain text, Latex, ZIP archives, Excel, PPT, E-mail (various formats), source code. For multimedia documents, there are plug-ins for Images (any format, including GIF, JIF, JPEG, TIFF), MP3 audio, Ogg Vorbis audio, and a generic plug-in that can be configured for audio formats, MPEG, MIDI, etc.

9. User Base

9.1 Distribution

As with all open source projects, the user base for Greenstone is unknown. Tens of thousands of installations of Greenstone are estimated across world as is evidenced by the increasing volume of messages being exchanged in the various fora, especially the Greenstone E-lists. It is distributed on SourceForge, a leading distribution center for open source software.

9.2 Greenstone Example Collections

Examples of public Greenstone collections (see http:// www.greenstone.org for URLs) can be found at:

- Association of Indian Labour Historians, Delhi
- Auburn University, Alabama
- California University at Riverside
- Chicago University Library
- Detroit Public Library
- Gresham College, London
- Hawaiian Electronic Library
- Illinois Wesleyan University
- Indian Institute of Management Kozhikode (IIMK)
- Kyrgyz Republic National Library
- LeHigh University, Pennsylvania
- Mari El Republic, Russia
- National Centre for Science Information, Bangalore, India
- Netherlands Institute for Scientific Information Services
- New York Botanical Garden
- Peking University Digital Library
- Philippine Research Education and Government Information Network
- Secretary of Human Rights of Argentina
- Slavonski Brod Public Library, Slovenia
- State Library of Tasmania
- Stuttgart University of Applied Sciences
- Texas A&M University Center for the Study of Digital Libraries
- University of Illinois
- University of North Carolina Biblio. project
- Vietnam National University
- Vimercate Public Library, Milan, Italy
- Washington Research Library Consortium
- Welsh Books Council

10. Languages

One of Greenstone's unique strengths is its multilingual nature. The reader's interface is available in the following languages: Arabic, Armenian, Bengali, Catalan, Croatian, Czech, Chinese (both simplified and traditional), Dutch, English, Farsi,

Finnish, French, Galician, Georgian, German, Greek, Hebrew, Hindi, Indonesian, Italian, Japanese, Kannada, Kazakh, Kyrgyz, Latvian, Maori, Mongolian, Portuguese (BR and PT versions), Russian, Serbian, Spanish, Thai, Turkish, Ukrainian, Vietnamese.

The Librarian interface and the full Greenstone documentation (which is extensive) is in: English, French, Spanish, and Russian.

11. Training

Training is a bottleneck for widespread adoption of any digital library software. Greenstone's Waikato site http://www.greenstone.org; the Greenstone Wiki http://greenstone.sourceforge.net/wiki/index.php/GreenstoneWiki, and the Greenstone Support for South Asia http://greenstonesupport.iimk.ac.in give many training materials and guidance on the software. It is observed that Greenstone training and workshops are quite common in digital library conferences and seminar all over the world and this itself speaks volumes the importance of Greenstone.

12. E-mail Support

There are many E-Lists and E-Groups available for Greenstone support. For subscribing to the main Greenstone lists, visit https://list.scms.waikato.ac.nz/mailman/listinfo/greenstone-users for User's List (greenstone-users-request@list.scms.waikato.ac.nz) and https://list.scms. waikato.ac.nzmailman/listinfo/greenstone-devel for Developer's list. There is also an E-List for supporting the South Asian Greenstone users greenstonesupport@iimk.ac.in. You can join the South Asia Support E-List by filling the form at http://eprints.iimk.ac.in/mailman/listinfo/greenstonesupport.

13. Greenstone: Features

The salient features of Greenstone are basically taken from two of the official publications of the software development team appeared in D-Lib Magazine during the year 2001[10] and 2003.[11] Greenstone builds collections using almost popular and standard digital formats such as HTML, XML, Word, Post Script, PDF, RTF, JPG, GIF, JPEG, MPEG, etc. and many other formats which include audio as well as video. It is provided with effective full-text searching and metadata-based browsing facilities that are attractive and easy to use. Moreover, they are easily maintained and can be augmented and rebuilt entirely automatically. The system is extensible: software "plug-ins" accommodate different document and metadata types. Greenstone incorporates an interface that makes it easy for people to create their own library collections. Collections may be built and served locally from the user's own web server, or (given appropriate permissions) remotely on a shared digital library host. End users can easily build new collections styled after existing ones from material on the Web or from their local files (or both), and collections can be updated and new ones brought on-line at any time. The Greenstone Librarian Interface (GLI) is a Java based GUI interface for easy collection building. Greenstone software runs on a wide variety of platforms such as Windows, Unix/ Linux, Apple Mac, etc. and provides full-text mirroring, indexing, searching, browsing and metadata extraction. It incorporates an interface that makes it easy for institutions to create their own library collections. Collections could be built and served locally from the user's own web server, or (given appropriate permissions) remotely on a shared digital library host. The other set of features include OAI plug-in (introduced since the 2.40 version) and DCMI compliance, UNICODE based multi-lingual capabilities and a user-friendly multimedia interfacing [Unicode]. Furthermore, it has a powerful search engine 'Managing Gigabyte' Plus-Plus ('MG' PP) and metadata-based browsing facilities. A very interesting feature of Greenstone is its exhaustive set of well documented and articulated manuals (http://www.greenstone.org/ cgi-bin/library?e=p-en-docs-utfZz-8&a=p&p=docs) such as 'Installer's Guide', 'User's Guide', 'Developer's Guide', and 'From Paper to Collection' a document describing the entire process of creating a digital library collection from paper documents. This includes the scanning and OCR process and the use of the "Organizer". There is one more interesting documentation 'Inside Greenstone Collections' which clarifies most of the trickier parts of using Greenstone, especially dealing with configuration file for the collection in question.

The primary objective of any digital library will be to enhance the digital collection in a substantial way, by strategically sourcing digital materials, conforming to copyright permissions, in all possible standards/formats so that scalability and flexibility is guaranteed for the future and advanced information services and are assured to the user community right from beginning. The digital library has to be planned in such a way that it will integrate and aggregate the existing collections and services with an outstanding user interface. Accordingly, necessary strategies are to be adopted towards working out the digital library system. This implies that the digital library system should have a strong collection interface capable of embracing almost all the popular digital standards, digital formats and software platforms, in line with the underlying digital library technologies in vogue. This is crucial in the case of multimedia integration, which is again important as it is planned to host digital audio and video library as part of the core library collection.

14. Greenstone Installation

The GNU Public License version Greenstone can be downloaded from 'http://www.greenstone.org' or 'http://sourceforge.net/index.php'. You can download the binaries for Linux or Windows. The associated softwares such as Java Runtime Environment (JRE) and the Imagemagick also to be downloaded. A graphical tool is used for collection building and configurations and customization. This is called the Greenstone Librarian Interface (GLI) and it requires the Java Runtime Environment (JRE). The latest version pertaining to Volume 2 release of Greenstone as on December 2010 is V.2.83.

Installation

Here is what you need to do to install Greenstone:

- Select the language for this installation. We choose English
- Welcome to the Greenstone Digital Library Software Installer. It is recommended that you uninstall any previous installations of Greenstone2 before running this installer. Click <Next>

- License Agreement. Click <Accept>
- Choose location to install Greenstone. Leave at the default and click <Next>
- Components. Click the question mark button on the right of each component will display the description of this component in a popup window. Leave at the default (all components are selected) and click <Next>
- (For older installers you must now select collections. Leave at the default, Documented Example Collections, and click <Next>)
- Enable administration pages. Read the description on this page, if you check to enable, click <Next> to set admin password. Choose a suitable password and click <Next> (If your computer will not be serving collections online, the password doesn't matter)
- Click <Install> to start the installation. Click <Show Details> to show the details of this installation
- Files are copied across

15. Collection Building and Configuration

Greenstone used to have three modes for collection building, viz., Command Line, Web Interface and the Greenstone Librarian Interface (GLI). Among these GLI is the one getting more prominence as far as the librarian/information professionals are concerned.

15.1 Greenstone Librarian Interface (GLI)

The GLI (Greenstone Librarian Interface) was introduced recently, progressing with the version 2.4x. Soon the GLI got strengthened as well as popularized, and the Web Interface mode has been withdrawn temporarily, while it could also be reinforced if one wishes so. The GLI based collection building is quite easy and simple a method. Collection developers can activate the GLI software and use the 'Gather', 'Enrich', 'Design', 'Create', and the 'Format' panels for making, configuring, customizing and managing collections.

1. The 'Gather' Panel facilitates putting the relevant files from the 'workspace' to the 'collection building' area. The 'Enrich'

Panel explains how metadata is created, edited, assigned and retrieved, and how to use external metadata sources. Help for this is provided in the GLI Interface. The 'Design' Panel facilitates customising your interface, once your files are marked up with metadata. Using the Gather Panel, you can specify the fields that are searchable, allow browsing through the document, facilitate the languages that are supported, and provide the buttons that are to appear on the page. Help for this is provided in the GLI Interface. The Create Panel facilitates creation of your collection.

To build a typical collection, say 'MyTest' collection, first go to 'File' section, select 'New' and then give the collection name as 'MyTest'. Select OK from the panel and then you will get another panel popped up where you will select the appropriate Metadata Set. You may also give the description about the collection here. By default, the system will prompt Dublin Core metadata set. Click on OK button and you will get the collection create panel made ready for accepting the file(s).

The 'Gather' Panel is activated now. From the 'Workspace' provided, identify the document to be put in the collection by locating it in the local folder. Drag and drop the file to the Collection Area using the mouse. The necessary 'plugin' for the creation of the collection is to be tick marked and enabled in the 'Design' panel, which is the next step in the collection building process. If the collection has objects for which 'plugins' are not provided in the default set, a new dialog box for adding the required plugin will appear and it has to be the added to the default set.

2. Go to the 'Enrich' panel and give necessary values for the Dublin Core element sets.

Manage Metadata Sets—This feature allows you to add, configure and remove the Metadata Sets in your collection and what Elements they contain.

3. Design Panel. The next step is to give necessary values and arguments for the 'Design' panel which include [Note: GLI Design Panel's own language is used below (i) to (x), for want of clarity and to avoid any ambiguity in usage]:

(i) *General Options*—In this section, give the e-mail address of the 'collection creator', 'collection maintainer', 'collection title' (will be supplied by the system), collection folder (will be supplied by the system), Image file location for the Collection icon and the Image file location for the Document icon. Click on the Tick mark for making this collection publicly available.

(ii) *Document Plugins*—This section facilitates adding, configuring or removing plugins from your collection. To add one, choose it from the combobox and click 'Add Plugin'. To configure or remove one, select it from the list of assigned plugins and then: (i) Change its position in the plugin order by clicking on the arrow buttons (Note: The position of RecPlug and ArcPlug are fixed.), (ii) Configure it by clicking 'Configure Plugin', (iii) Remove it by clicking 'Remove Plugin'. Plugins are configured using a pop-up design area with a scrollable list of arguments. Enable arguments and enter or select values as necessary.

(iii) *Search Types*—Defining the search type is an advanced feature, only available when enabled (by checking the 'Enable Advanced Searches' box). Once enabled, further controls for selecting and changing the order of search types become available. See the 'Search Type Selection and Ordering' section of the 'Design' Panel for more information on this.

(iv) *Search Indexes*—The required number of searchable indexes the collection must have, is to be selected here. To add a new index, enter a unique name for the index, select material/metadata is to be indexed, and click 'Add Index'. If you wish to add all of the available sources so as to have indexes built on them, then click 'Add All'.

(v) *Partition Indexes*—This feature help to refine index creation. This facility is disabled in the GLI mode.

(vi) *Cross-Collection Search*—This feature facilitates cross-collection searching, where a single search is performed over several collections, as if all the collections were one. Specify (Tick Mark) the collections to include in a search by clicking on the appropriate collection's name in the list below. The current collection will automatically be included. [Note: If the individual collections do not have the same indexes (including sub collection partitions and language partitions) as each other, cross-collection searching will not work properly. The user will only be able to search using indexes common to all collections.]

(vii) *Browsing Classifiers*—This feature allows the AtoZ browsing of the collection and by default if takes the 'Dublin Core. Title'. You can more data elements in the AtoZ classify list as deem fit for the collection using this feature.

(viii) *Format Features*—The web pages you see when using Greenstone are not pre-stored, but are generated 'on the fly' as they are needed. Format commands are used to change the appearance of these generated pages. Some are switches that control the display of documents or parts of documents; others are more complex and require html code as an argument. To add a format command, choose it from the 'feature' list. If a True/False option panel appears, select the state by clicking on the appropriate button.

For example, to get the Cover Image displayed in the document while building the collection, go to the 'Choose Features' dropdown box and enable the 'DocumentIMages', i.e., make its value to True.

(ix) *Translate Text*—Use this feature to review and assign translations of text fragments in your collection. The translated text will appear in a different box in the browser.

(x) *Metadata Sets*—This feature allows you to add, configure and remove the Metadata Sets in your collection and what Elements they contain.

4. Now go to the 'Create' panel and click on the 'Build Collection'. Greenstone will start creating the collection. You can see the built collection by clicking on the 'Preview Collection'.

Please remember you have to save your collection development process from time to time. It is not mandatory that you need to comply with the entire set of formalities for building a collection in a single stretch. You can do it in different sessions too. What is important is saving the sessions from time to time. In the GLI mode of collection building, the various panels to be used are illustrated in Fig. 1.1.

5. Format Panel

(i) *General*—This section explains how to review and alter the general settings associated with your collection. First, under the "Format" tab, click "General". Here some collection wide metadata can be set or modified, including the title and description entered when starting a new collection. First are the contact e-mail addresses of the collection's creator and maintainer. The following field allows you to change the collection title. The folder that the collection is stored in is shown next, but this cannot be altered. Then comes the icon to show at the top left of the collection's "About" page (in the form of a URL), followed by the icon used in the Greenstone library page to link to the collection. Next is a checkbox that controls whether the collection should be publicly accessible. Finally comes the "Collection Description" text area as described in "Creating a New Collection".

(ii) *Search*—This section explains how to set the display text for the drop down lists on the search page. Under the "Format" tab, click "Search". This pane contains a table listing each search index, index level (for MGPP or Lucene collections), and index or language partition. Here you can enter the text to be used for each item in the various drop-down lists on the search page. This pane only allows you to set the text for one language, the current language used by GLI. To translate these names for other languages, use the Translate Text part of the Format view (see "Translate Text" feature in the Format panel).

(iii) *Format Features*—The web pages you see when using Greenstone are not pre-stored, but are generated 'on the fly' as they are needed. Format commands are used to change the appearance of these generated pages. Some are switches that control the display of documents or parts of documents; others are more complex and require html code as an argument. To add a format command, choose it from the 'feature' list. If a True/False option panel appears, select the state by clicking on the appropriate button.

For example, to get the Cover Image displayed in the document while building the collection, go to the 'Choose Features' dropdown box and enable the 'DocumentIMages', i.e., set its value to True.

(iv) *Translate Text*—Use this feature to review and assign translations of text fragments in your collection. The translated text will appear in a different box in the browser.

(v) *Cross-Collection Search*—This feature facilitates cross-collection searching, where a single search is performed over several collections, as if all the collections were one. Specify (Tick Mark) the collections to include in a search by clicking on the appropriate collection's name in the list below. The current collection will automatically be included. [Note: If the individual collections do not have the same indexes (including sub collection partitions and language partitions) as each other, cross-collection searching will not work properly. The user will only be able to search using indexes common to all collections.]

(vi) *Collection Specific Macros*—Under the "Format" tab, click "Collection Specific Macros". This view shows the contents of the collection's extra.dm macro file. This is where collection specific macros can be defined.

To learn more about macros, see Chapter 3 of the Greenstone *Developer's Guide*.

15.2 Hierarchy Structure

To create indexes for section and sub-section, the pre-requisite is that the document should be in HTML format. Therefore your collection files in other formats like PDF, Word, etc. are first to be converted into HTML format. Also in the Collection Configuration file (for GLI, in the Design Panel, in the Document Plugin section, while configuring the Arguments in the HTML Plugin, click and enable the 'description_tags'), the HTML plugin has to be modified to 'plugin HTMLPlug–description_tags'. Corresponding changes have to be made in the 'indexes' and the 'collectionmeta' lines. Obviously now the Source File has to be edited as a HTML file structure. For the section and sub-sections, you need to edit the source file as follows, giving XML tags as comments in the body of the HTML file. Fig. 1.1 below shows a hierarchy structured EBook.

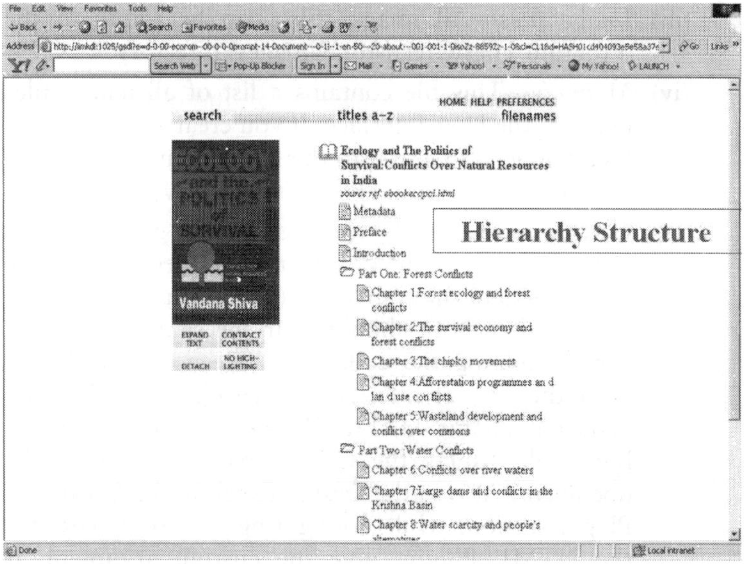

Fig. 1.1: An EBook with the Hierarchy Structure

15.3 Customization of User Interface (MyLibrary)

In order to change the look and feel of the Greenstone user interface, you need to work on the Collection Configuration (Collect.cfg) files. Customising the User Interface requires a certain degree of knowledge on HTML and some level of Web Designing skills are pre-requisites for this.

(i) *Collect.cfg*—This is the collection configuration file. You can find this file in the "Program Files\Greenstone\collect\etc" directory. Details on how to create this file can be found in the *Developer's Guide*, "1.5 Collection configuration file" and "2.3 Formatting Greenstone output".

(ii) *Macro files*—Macro files have an extension '.dm'. All macro files are stored in the "macros" directory. Details on how to create macros and macro files can be found in the *Developer's Guide* "2.4 controlling the Greenstone user interface".

(iii) *Image files*—All images files can be found in the 'Program Files\Greenstone\images' directory.

(iv) *Main.cfg*—This file contains a list of all macro files used for the User Interface. If you created a new '.dm' file, you need to add it to this file. The main.cfg file is stored in the "Program Files\Greenstone\etc" directory.

(v) *Getting the Cover Image*—For you to get the Cover Image of your input document, you need to put the image file and the source file (document) into a single folder. They both should bear the same name also. While building the collection, Greenstone will take both the files to "Program Files\Greenstone\collect\<collection name>\archives\Hash". The collection thus built will display the Cover Image along with the document. Also in the Design Panel, in the Document Plugin section, while configuring the Arguments for the HTML Plugin, give the custom argument as 'cover_image'.

(vi) *Getting the Collection Icon*—Click on Design panel <-General Option-> URL to home page icon (Browse for image and locate it).

(vii) *Getting Header Image for the Digital Library*—To get the header image which says MyLibrary banner in the DL head, create the graphic file (preferably a GIF file), name it as 'gsdlhead.xxx' and then replace it with the file available in 'Program Files\Greenstone\images'.

(viii) *Deep Level Customization*—By default, Greenstone's collection icon area is a matrix grid (the N × 3 format). You can change the collection icon area by editing the '_content_macro' in 'home.dm'. You will need to remove the '_homeextra_macro' (this is the N × 3 table that the Greenstone C++ code automatically creates for you) and can then put whatever design customization you want into this area. You will need to put the icons and links to the collection yourself.

You can also achieve high end customization by replacing the 'home.dm' with 'yourhome.dm' in the \greenstone\etc folder.

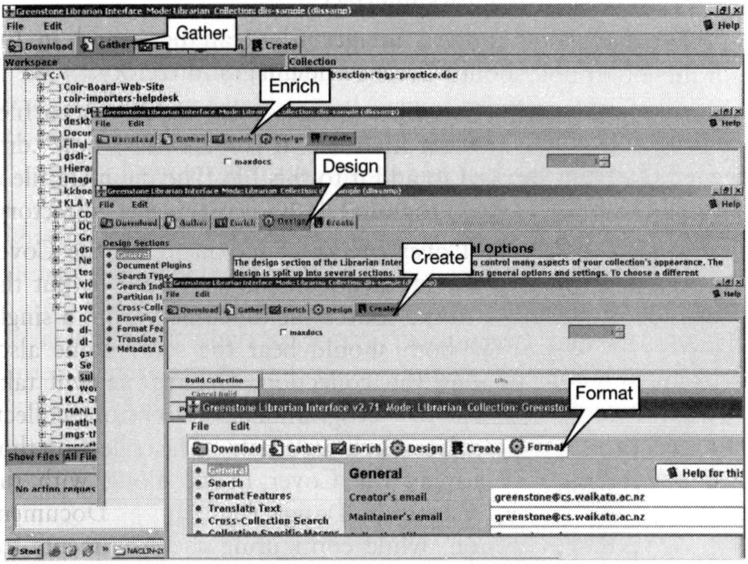

Fig. 1.2: GLI Panels for Gather, Enrich, Design, Create and Format

16. GSDL: Helpline, Archives

Greenstone's E-Mail list is a very useful and active listserv which shares and clarifies user experiences and stories dealing with real life situations. To subscribe or unsubscribe to the list via the World Wide Web, visit "https://list.scms.waikato.ac.nz/mailman/listinfo/greenstone-users" or, via e-mail, send a message with subject or body 'help' to "greenstone-users-request@list.scms.waikato.ac.nz". Greenstone has started one more List recently, for the Greenstone 3 Version (the latest Beta version) user group, and the details are available at "https://list.scms.waikato.ac.nz/mailman/listinfo/greenstone3".

UNESCO has initiated a Greenstone support organization for South Asia in 2006, supported by a group of experts in the region, and it is coordinated by IIM Kozhikode.[12] The site is rich with many of the Greenstone support materials. In addition, an E-list greenstonesupport@iimk.ac.in offers online support to professionals on Greenstone.

For those looking for quick solutions for their real-time or on-the-job trouble shooting while using the software, 'Greenstone Archives' is a treasure house. It is a database of the e-mail messages circulated in the List, and is searchable. The mails generated from the List and its threads are archived and made available for the user community. The archive is available at "http://www.sadl.uleth.ca/nz/cgi-bin/library?a=p&p=about&c=gsarch-e". This is the major list used worldwide for Greenstone and the content of the messages is usually global in nature. Developers and Greenstone users can avoid a great deal of unwanted labour by carefully going through the archive before they start working on problem solving, or before shooting a mail to the List.

17. Conclusion

The ever changing landscape of the information paradigm poses a host of new IT and information challenges not only to the library and information professionals, but to the users, patrons and scholars and the publishing community as well. Indeed the new environment throws up a host of unprecedented features and avenues, and interestingly enough, if we know how to tap them well, we find there is a plethora of opportunities, and most of them even for free. The 'free things', so belovedly called worldwide the 'Open Source Softwares', many of them could even be compared against their commercial counterparts in terms of their strength, efficiency, power and the ever increasing user base. Among the major challenges include the information professionals' emergent need to acquire the necessary skill sets and working knowledge on the cutting-edge information science and information technology areas and in leveraging them in a contextually relevant manner.

Working on a Digital Library project in general, especially working with the Greenstone Digital Library Software in particular, has been highly exhilarating, enriching as well as rewarding. The treasure of knowledge, skills, experience, expertise, and exposure we have achieved and accomplished during the past four years have been extremely enjoying and simply terrific. It is also important sharing the real life experience of a particular software as an application user, as there exist a great deal of difference in viewpoints when it comes from the software developers themselves. Frankly, we also have grown with the software from strength to strength. We have every appreciation to Greenstone as far as its usability, extensibility and flexibility are concerned. We are also indeed pleased with its consistent technology catch-up strategies and their untiring extension activities. One should appreciate the dynamic Greenstone team for their selfless open source philosophy, and their relentless work in this regard just for the cause of science. We have been closely watching the world scenario in the area of digital library research and we are quite convinced that Greenstone is a fast growing community coupled with deep commitments from the developers in taking this software to further heights and making this an outstanding open source model for digital library development. The Wiki and the OAI features of Greenstone and the ambitious 'Greenstone 3', released already and running in its version 3.03, which draws its strength from the open source family of 'Web Services' technologies facilitating configurable, extensible and dynamic digital libraries are all testimony to their commitment to excellence in digital library software development. In the meanwhile UNESCO came forward to support them unconditionally and it is a proud privilege to announce that we have the Greenstone Support for South Asia already launched with their support, to take care of the DL needs of this region.

NOTES

1. Van Orsdel, Lee and Born, Kathleen (2002). Doing the Digital Flip. *Library Journal,* 127 (7), 51-55.
2. http://www.oclc.org/reports/2003format.htm (Retrieved on 5th December, 2010).
3. Marchionini, G. (1998). Research and development in digital libraries. In Allen Kent (Ed.), *Encyclopedia of Library and Information Science*, 63, 259-79.
4. www.teriin.org/events/icdl/background.htm (Retrieved on 15th January, 2011).
5. Borgman, Christine L. (1996). Social aspects of digital libraries. In *Proceedings of the first ACM international conference on Digital Libraries* Bethesda, Maryland, 170.
6. Frumkin, Jeremy (Ed.) (2002). Open Source Software. *Information Technology and Libraries* 21(1).
7. http://www.opensource.org/docs/ definition_plain.html (Retrieved on 25th February, 2011).
8. http://www.oss-watch.ac.uk/talks/2003-09-24-csg/index.xml.ID=body.1_div.37 (Retrieved on 25th February, 2011).
9. Altman, M. (2001). Open source software for libraries: from Greenstone to the Virtual Data Center and beyond. *IASSIST Quarterly*. Winter, 1-7.
10. Witten, Ian H. et al. (2001). Greenstone : Open-source digital library software *D-Lib Magazine,* 7 (10), 1-16.
11. Witten, Ian H. (2003). Examples of practical digital libraries: Collections built internationally using greenstone. *D-Lib Magazine,* 9 (3), 1-15.
12. http://greenstonesupport.iimk.ac.in (Retrieved on 25th February, 2011).

Digital Archiving Using DSpace: An Experiment with Digitizing MLISc Dissertations of Calicut University

2

Rehana Ummer

1. Introduction

The growing impact of Information and Communication Technologies (ICT), web technologies and database technologies has compelled library and information centres to use these technologies effectively to render better services.[1] The very concept of digitization refers to the conversion of paper-based material into electronic format.[2] Digitization can be done for nearly every format and medium held by libraries, from maps to manuscripts, and moving images to musical recordings. The use of hardware and software for capturing an item and converting it into bits and bytes, matched by a quickly developing set of practices for describing and retrieving digital objects, is enabling the realization of the concept of "library without walls".[3]

Digitization is the process of conversion of any physical or analogue item into a digital representation or facsimile.[4] It can also be defined as the process of translating a piece of information such as a book, sound recording, picture or video, into bits which is the fundamental unit of information in a computer system.

According to Digital Library Federation[5] Digital libraries are organizations that provide the resources, including the specialized staff, to select, structure, offer intellectual access to, interpret, distribute, preserve the integrity of, and ensure the persistence over time of collections of digital works so that they are readily available for use by a defined community or set of communities. Digital Library is an assemble of digital computers, storage and communication machinery together with the context and software, needed to produce, emulate and extend those services provided by conventional libraries based on paper and other materials means of collecting, cataloguing, finding and disseminating information. A full service digital library must accomplish all essential services of traditional libraries and also exploit the well known advantages of digital storage, searching and communication.[6]

1.1 Methods of Digitization

Digital resources can be built by adopting the following methods[7]:

- Acquisition of Digital Media
- Buying Access
- Content Creation
- Conversion of Existing Print Media
- Portal Site
- Integrated Access Interface
- Digitization of Resources Produced/Published Internally

1.2 Digitization Process

The process of digitization involves the following[8]:

- Document Selection
- Metadata Creation
- Scanning (Image Capturing)
- Image Processing
- Batch Processing
- Optical Character Recognition
- Storage and Preservation

2. Digitization of MLISc Dissertations

Dissertations form one of the primary sources of information. They are very useful to get an idea about the development of knowledge in a particular field. The dissertations submitted to the Department of Library and Information Science belong to various subjects even though they can be classed under the broad subject Library and Information Science. As they amount to hundreds, it is very difficult for the users to find the specific information contained in them. Hence, digitization of MLISc dissertations was carried out with DSpace Digital Library Software.

3. The Work Flow

The step by step procedure followed in the digitization of MLISc dissertations in the Department of Library and Information Science, University of Calicut is described here.

3.1 Creation of Abstracts

Instead of scanning the whole document the investigator prepared abstract of the dissertations for uploading in the Digital Library.

Creating the standard abstracts of dissertations was a major task in this work. The abstract is informative and in ANSI Standard. All the important aspects of the study such as objectives, methodology and findings are included in the abstract.

3.2 Installation of DSpace

DSpace was installed on a system with Windows XP operating system and NTFS drive partition. The software required for the successful installation of DSpace were:

- Java SDK 1.4.2
- Apache 2.0.54
- Tomcat 5.0.28
- Apache Ant 1.6.5
- PostgreSQL 8.0.2
- Dspace-1.4.2-beta-source

The source files were:

- Java 2 SDK 1.4.2
  http://java.sun.com/j2se/1.4.2/download.html
- Apache 2.0.54
  http://httpd.apache.org/download.cgi
- Tomcat 5.0.28
  http://jakarta.apache.org/site/binindex.cgi

- mod_jk 2.0.4
  http://jakarta.apache.org/site/binindex.cgi
- Apache Ant 1.6.5
  http://ant.apache.org/bindownload.cgi
- PostgresSQL 8.0.2
  http://mirror.tomato.it/ftp/pub/PostgreSQL/binary/v8.0.2/win32/
- Dspace-1.4.2-beta-source
  http://prdownloads.sourceforge.net/dspace/dspace-1.4.2-beta-source.tar.gz

DSpace file configuration were:

J2SE SDK Path	:	C:\J2sdk1.4.2_09
Apache Path	:	C:\www\Apache2
Tomcat Path	:	C:\www\Tomcat5
Apache Ant Path	:	C:\Apache-ant-1.6.5
PostgreSQL Path	:	C:\Program Files\PostgreSQL
DSpace Path	:	C:\Dspace

The following softwares were installed in sequence.

Installing Java 2 SDK

- The investigator located and ran j2sdk-1_4_2_09-windows-i586-p.exe
- Installed in C:\forming C:\j2sdk1.4.2_09
- Finished the installation
- Added to PATH: C:\j2sdk1.4.2-09\bin
- An environmental variable JAVA-HOME=C:\j2sdk1.4.2-09 was added.

Installing Apache 2.0.54

- It was ensured that IIS was stopped
- Created a folder "www" on C:\
- Ran the file apache_2.0.54-win32-x86-no_ssl.msi on the CD\Software\Apache 2.0.54\

- Network Domain and server name were given as 'localdomain' and 'localhost' respectively.
- Apache HTTP Server 2.0 was installed to folder C:\www

Installing tomcat 5 and mod_jk2

- The investigator copied Tomcat5 folder on CD\Software\ to directory C:\www
- Copied file mod_jk2.so on CD\Software\Support-files\ and placed under the folder C:\www\Apache2\modules\
- Copied file tools.jar from C:\J2sdk1.4.2_09\lib\ to C:\www\Tomcat5\common\lib\
- Copied file workers2.properties on CD\Software\ Support-files\ and placed under the folder C:\www\Apache2\conf\
- Edited the file C:\www\Apache2\conf\httpd.conf and inserted the following code. LoadModule jk2_module modules/mod_jk2.so JkSet config.file "C:/www/ Apache2/conf/workers2.properties"
- Edited the file C:\www\Tomcat5\conf\jk2.properies and inserted the line 'channel Socket.port=8009'
- Apache was started at this point
- Opened the command-line prompt

  C:\www\Tomcat5\bin>service.bat install
- Apache Tomcat Service was started
- Tested the native Tomcat server

  http://localhost:8080/

Installing Apache Ant 1.6.5

- The investigator copied the folder apache-ant-1.6.5 to C:\
- Added to PATH : C:\apache-ant-1.6.5\bin
- Environmental variable ANT-HOME= C:\apache-ant-1.6.5 was set.

Installing PostgresSQL8.0.2

- The investigator located and ran postgresql-8.0.msi.

- Installed to C:\Program Files\PostgreSQL (Default location)
- Service configuration

  The investigator created a user 'postgre' for operating Postgre service.
- Initializing Database cluster
- The investigator created an internal database user dspace.
- Finished the installation
- Opened Start>Programs>PostgreSQL 8.0>Pg Admin III.
- Selected and right clicked on "PostgreSQL Database Server 8.0" and clicked 'Connect'.
- Opened "PostgreSQL Database Server 8.0" and selected Database.
- Right clicked and selected 'New Database'
- Created a database "dspace" owned by the user "dspace" with UNICODE encoding.

Installing Dspace-1.4.2-beta-source

- Copied the folder Dspace-1.4.2-beta-source to C:\
- Copied file postgresql-8.0-310.jdbc2.jar from C:\Program Files\PostgreSQL\8.0\jdbc\ to C:\Dspace-1.4.2-beta-source\lib
- Ensured that PostgreSQL Service was running
- Updated paths in C:\ Dspace-1.4.2-beta-source\config\dspace.cfg 'dspace.dir=C:/Dspace' and saved the file.
- Created a folder "Dspace" on C:\
- Opened the command-line prompt C:\Dspace-1.4.2-beta-source\ and gave the command ant fresh_install.
- Created an administrator account, C:\dspace\bin\dsrun org.dspace.administer. Create Administrator and entered the required information such as e-mail address-dlis@unical.ac.in, first name- DLIS Calicut, last name-University and password.

- Initialized the search and browse indices:

  C:\dspace\bin\dsrun org.dspace.browse.Initialize Browse

  C:\dspace\bin\dsrun org.dspace.search.DSIndexer
- Copied the .war Web application files from C:\Dspace-1.4.2-beta-source \build\ to C:\www\Tomcat 5.5\webapps
- Started the Tomcat service
- Browsed http://localhost:8080/dspace to view the Dspace home page.

Three services were required to run Dspace. They were:

- Apache Tomcat
- Apache 2
- Postgre SQL Database Server 8.0

The services were started by going to Start>>Run>> services.msc. The 'service' to be started was selected from the list and started by right clicking on it and selecting the start option.

3.3 Creation of Community

The top-level community 'MLISc Dissertations' was created by clicking on the 'Create Top-Level Community' option on the community/collection listing page. This provides provision to edit the community page. Figure 2.1 shows the details given in the community page.

Figure 2.1 shows that the required details can be given using the Community page. Name, Short Description, Introductory text, Copyright text, Side bar text are given.

3.4 Creation of Collections

There are 27 collections under the community 'MLISc Dissertations'. These collections are the subject-wise classification of the dissertations submitted to DLIS, University of Calicut. Figure 2.2 shows the list of collections created under the community 'MLISc Dissertations'.

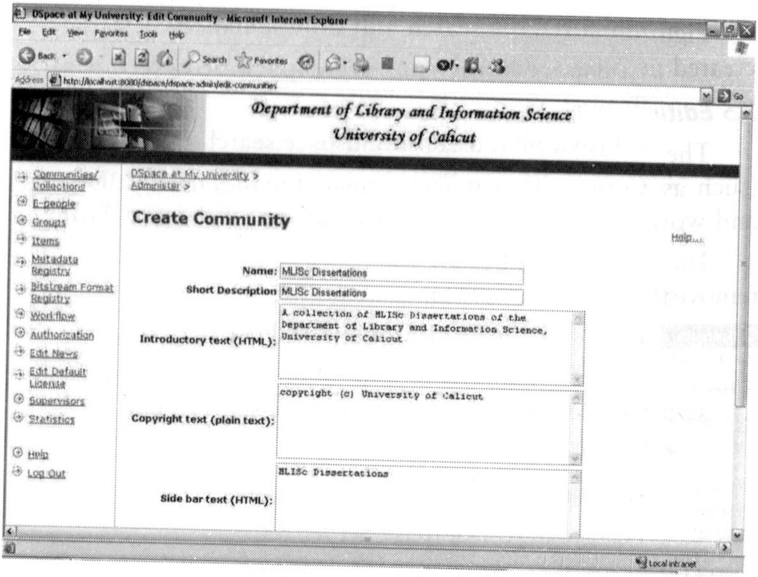

Fig. 2.1: Create Community

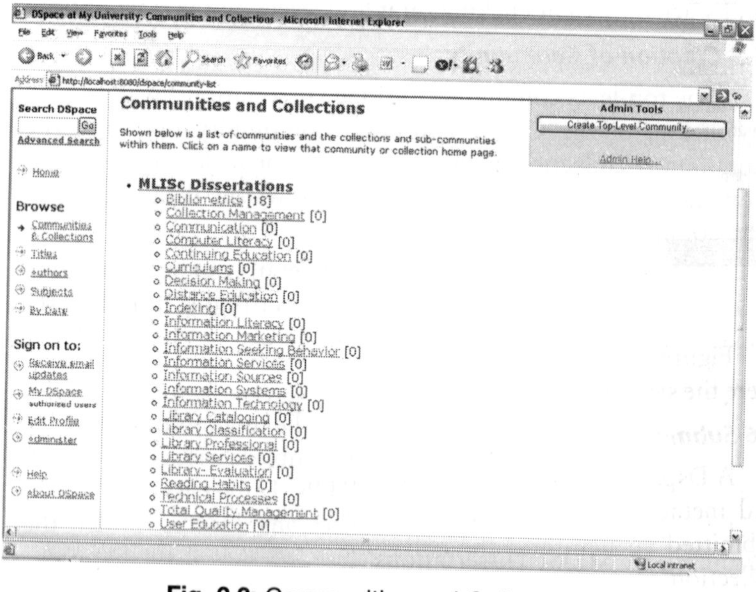

Fig. 2.2: Communities and Collection

Figure 2.2 shows that the names of subjects (collection) created in DSpace can be listed below the community name.

3.5 Editing Collection

The Edit Collection page can change collection metadata (such as name and introductory text), configure authorization and workflow, or delete the collection entirely.

The 'Delete' button (located at the top of the page) will remove the collection (including all its items) from the repository.

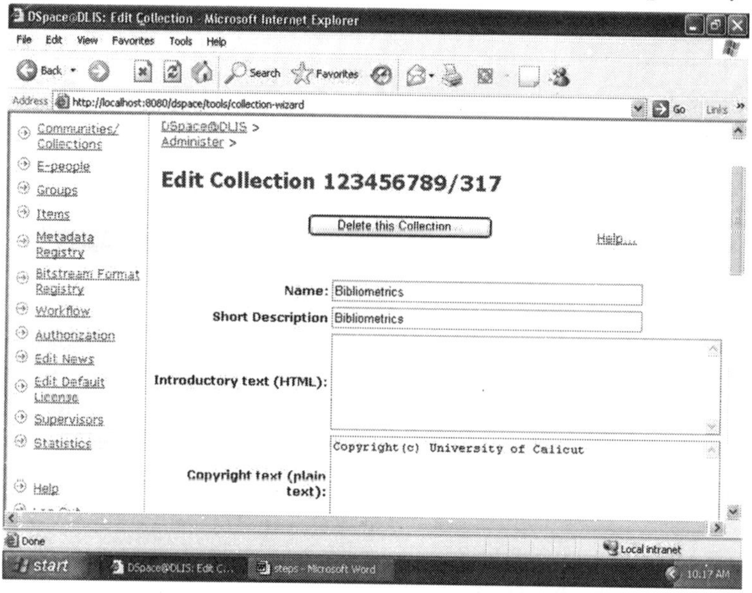

Fig. 2.3: Edit Collection

Figure 2.3 shows a sample of edit collection page of DSpace. Here the system administrator can change the details of collection.

3.6 Submission of Items

A Dspace item is a logical grouping of a useful set of content and metadata that are related in some way. The investigator submitted an item into the collection by selecting the specific collection, from the community home page as shown in Fig. 2.4.

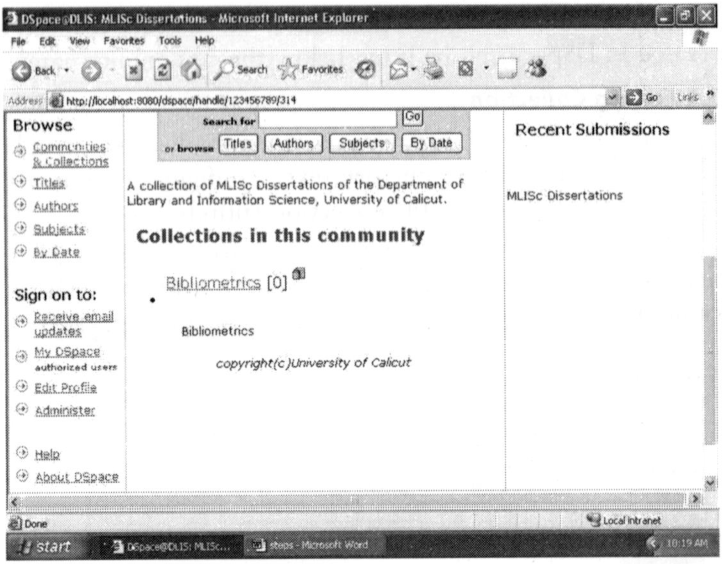

Fig. 2.4: Community Home Page

Figure 2.4 shows the community home page with collection name. When the collection name (Bibliometrics) is selected the new screen will appear for submitting item as shown in Fig. 2.5.

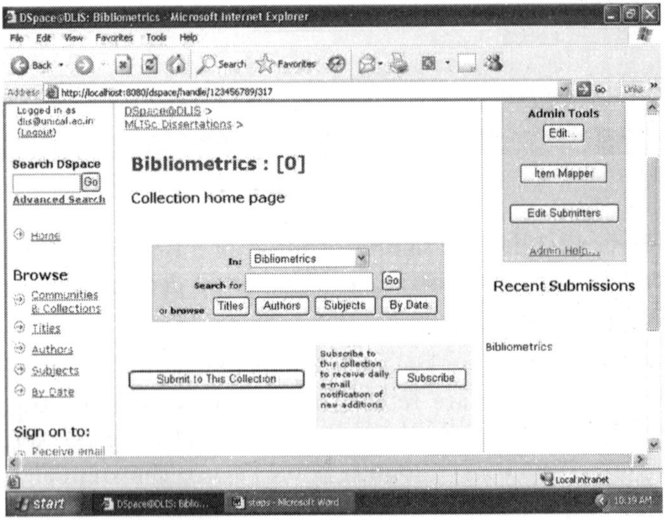

Fig. 2.5: Collection Home Page

To submit an item here, the investigator has to click on the 'Submit to this collection' button. This will activate the submission process as shown in Fig. 2.6.

Fig. 2.6: DSpace Workflow

Figure 6 shows that there are 7 oval buttons representing each step in the submission process. As the investigator moves through the process these ovals change colour. The investigator can use these buttons to move back and forth within the submission process by clicking on them. Data will not be lost by moving back and forth.

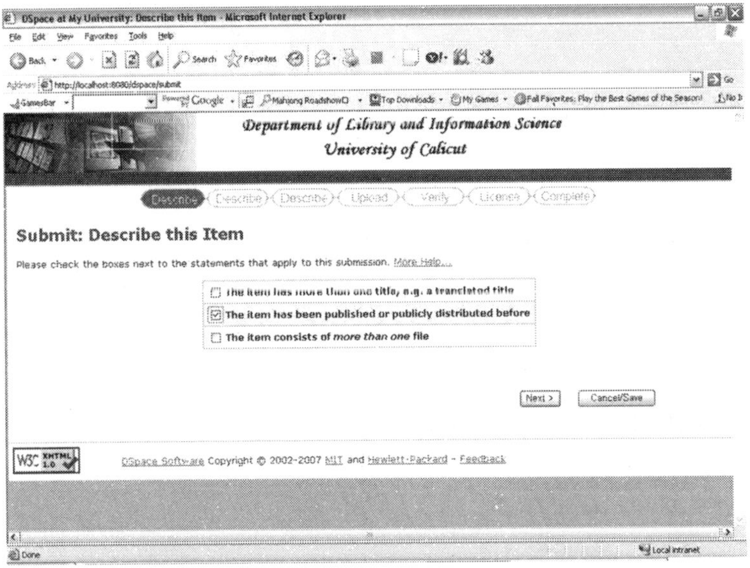

Fig. 2.7: Submit: Describing the Item - Page 1

Figure 2.7 shows the first page of the submit item page. Here the users can select the required items to get the required details according to the nature of the item as shown in Fig. 2.8.

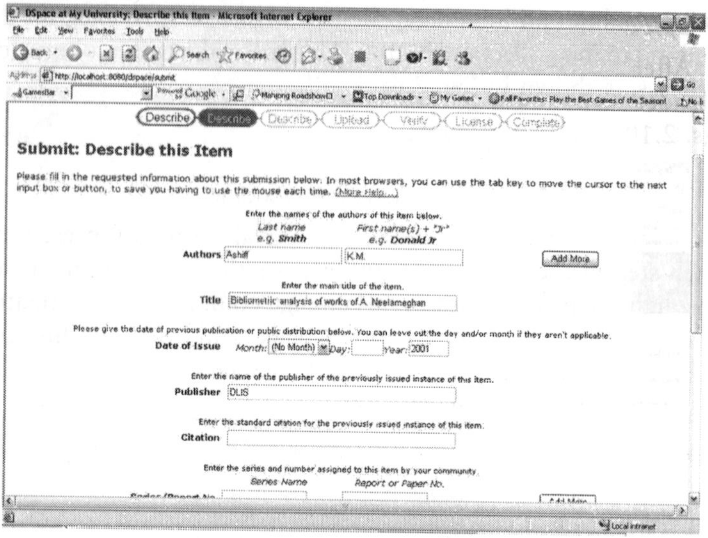

Fig. 2.8: Submit: Describing the Item - Page 2

Figure 2.8 shows how Dspace provides option to add the details such as author, title, etc. From this screen one can move to the next screen to give the key words, abstract and other details as shown in Fig. 2.9.

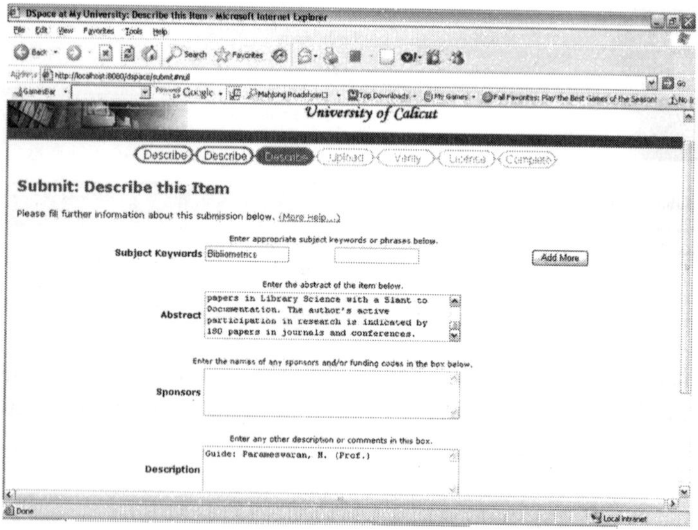

Fig. 2.9: Submit: Describing the Item - Page 3

3.7 Uploading File

After giving the necessary description, the file has to be uploaded for storing the file in Dspace database as shown in Figs. 2.10 and 2.11.

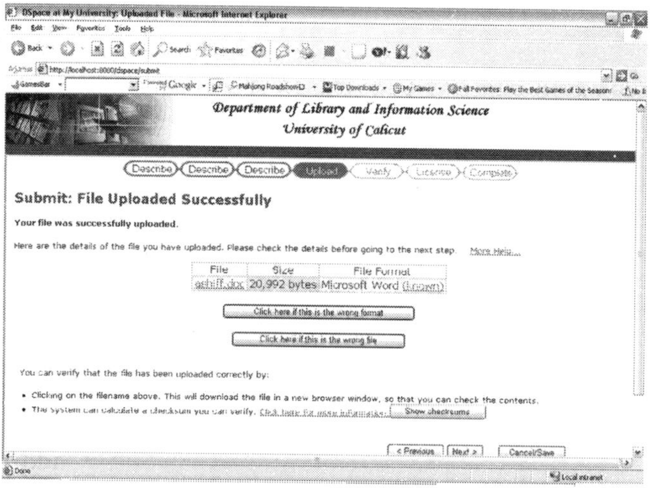

Fig. 2.10: Uploading File

Figure 2.10 shows the screen which allows uploading of a file.

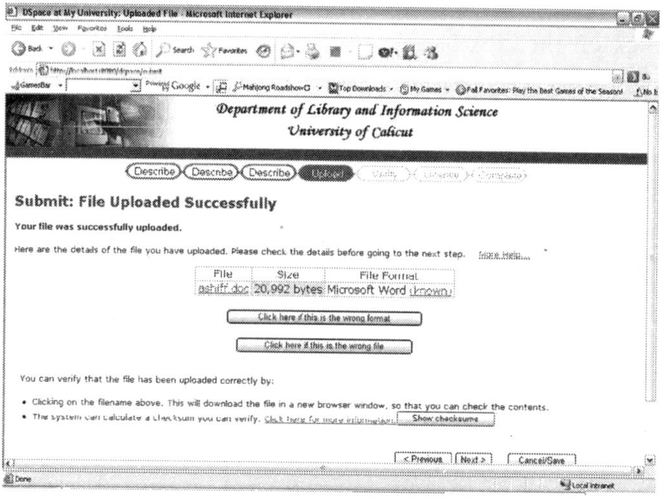

Fig. 2.11: Details of Uploaded File

Figure 2.11 displays the details of the file which is uploaded.

3.8 Verifying Submission

The details of the submitted files can be verified by clicking the Verify button.

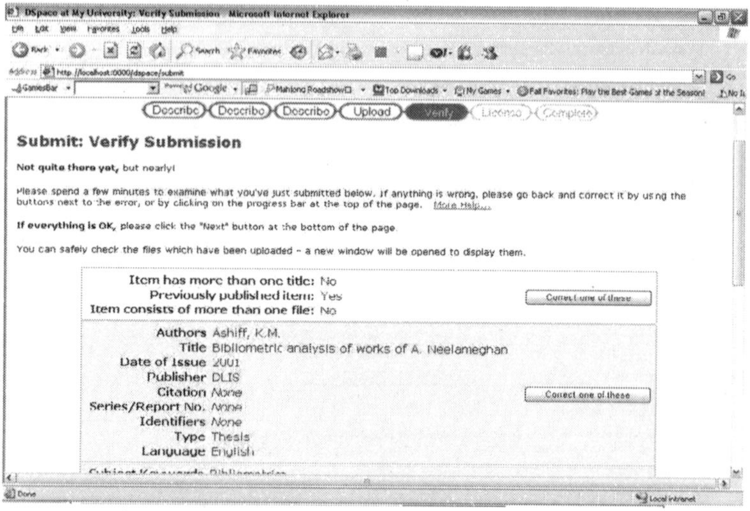

Fig. 2.12: Verifying Submission

Figure 2.12 shows the information that the investigator has entered to describe the item. To correct or edit information, one can click on the corresponding button on the right, or use the oval buttons in the progress bar at the top of the page to move around the submission pages.

3.9 Submit: License

DSpace requires agreement to the non-exclusive distribution license before the item could appear on DSpace as shown in Fig. 2.13.

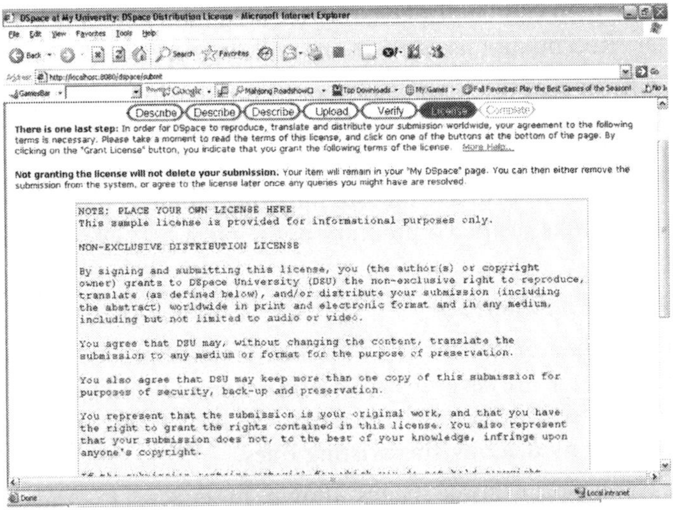

Fig. 2.13: License Agreement

Figure 2.13 shows the license agreement.

3.10 Completion of Submission

When the submission has been successfully entered into the DSpace system through the workflow process, the status of submission can be checked by going to the Communities and Collections page.

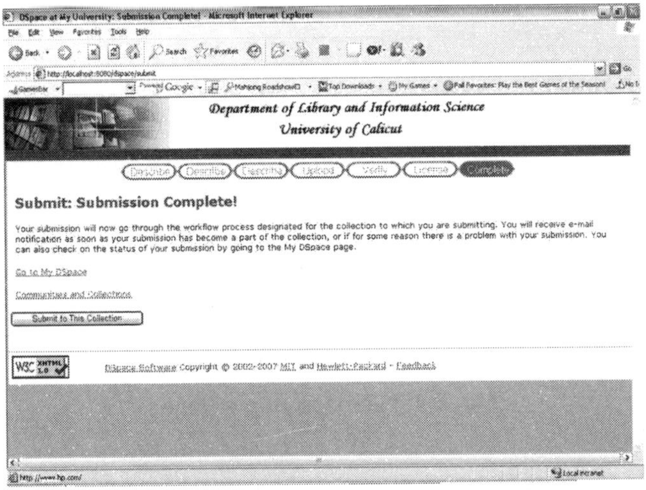

Fig. 2.14: Submit: Submission Complete

The item can be displayed by clicking on the item title given under 'Recent submissions' in the collection page.

Clicking on the 'Show full item record' button on the bottom of the item screen will display the Doublin Core metadata qualifier and element.

Figure 2.14 displays the 'submission complete' screen which provides links to the community home page and DSpace home page.

3.11 Creating Interface

Providing interface is of utmost importance in a digital library. There are several search options inbuilt in DSpace. The user can also customize the interface by providing more search options or by deleting the existing ones.

The DSpace home pages shown in Figs. 2.15 and 2.16 provide all browse options such as key words, communities and collections, title, author, subject and date.

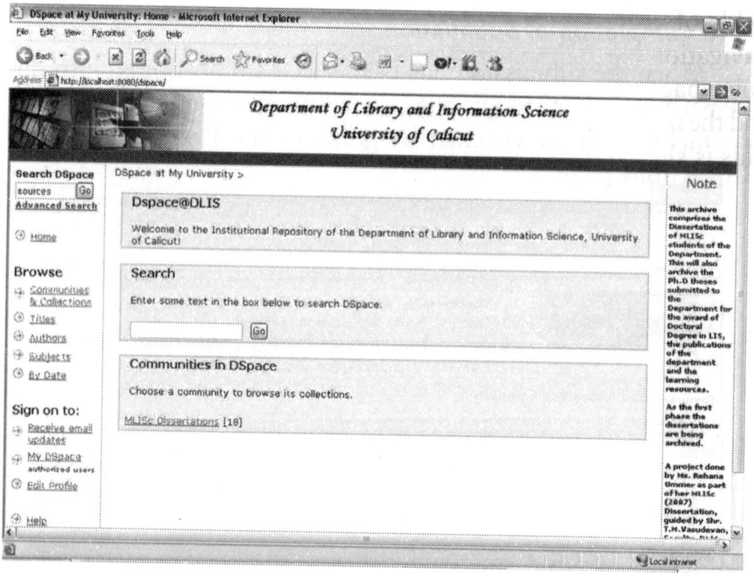

Fig. 2.15: DSpace Home Page

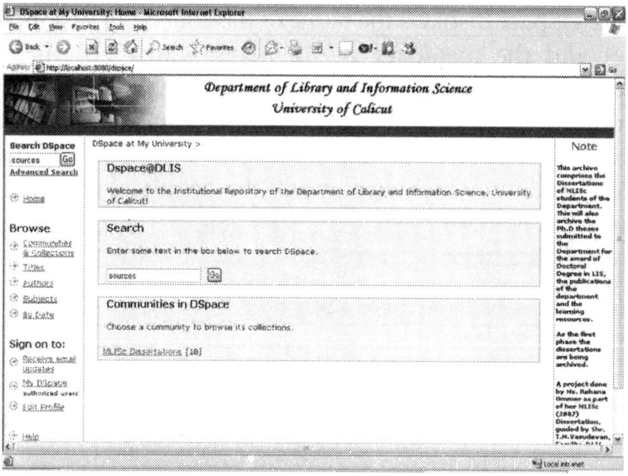

Fig. 2.16: DSpace Home Page

To search all of DSpace for the word "sources" against the title, author, subject, abstract, series, sponsor and identifier fields of each item's record, the search box at the top of the navigation bar on the left or the search box in the middle of the home page can be used. DSpace will display the collection name and the metadata of the items, which contain the word "sources". This is shown in Fig. 2.17.

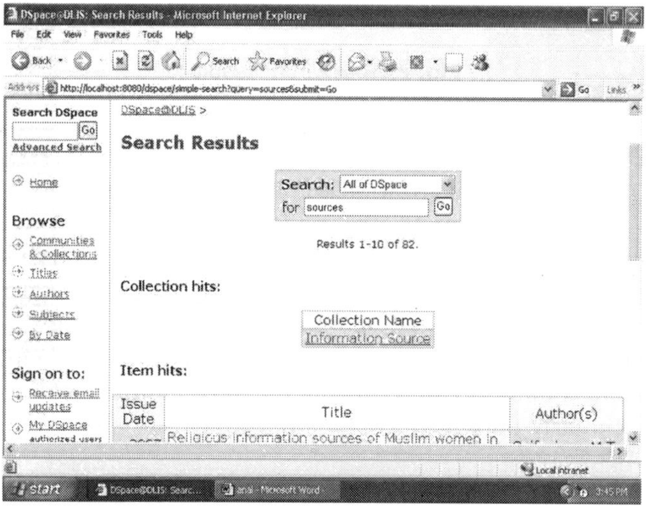

Fig. 2.17: Searching

Here DSpace displays the name of the collection (Information Source) and the metadata of 82 items which has the word "sources" in it. Clicking the collection name will display the collection home page from where the user can browse the items in the collection. Selecting and clicking the metadata will display the item window, which displays all the details of an item. This is shown in Fig. 2.18.

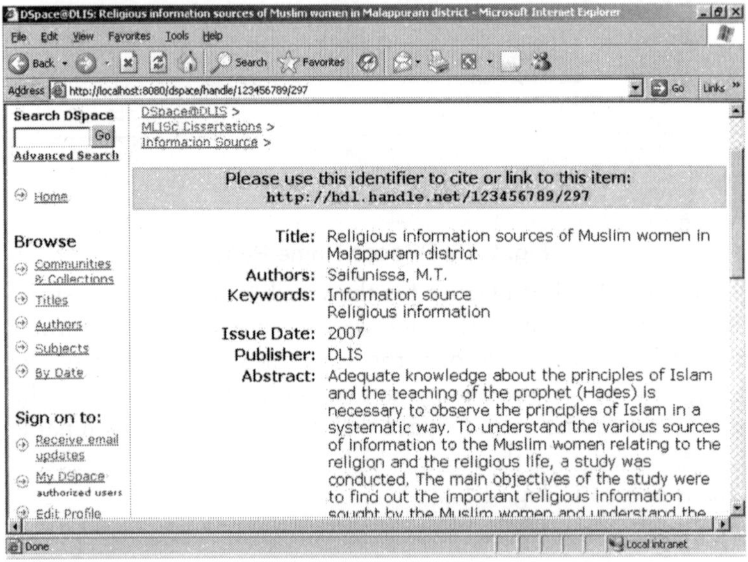

Fig. 2.18: Search Result

4. Conclusion

The experimental study of digitizing MLISc dissertation gives an insight that digitization is not a herculean task. However, care and commitment are necessary for its successful implementation. The Digital Library thus created is very useful to the students and research scholars in getting a background idea of the works already conducted. Digitization of all the dissertations and theses in all the departments will help the academic community in retrieving the information contained in such scholarly output.

NOTES

1. Sivaraman, V. (2006). Digital libraries in knowledge management: Opportunities for management libraries. In M.G. Sreekumar et al. (Eds.), *Digital libraries in knowledge management: proceedings of the 7th MANLIBNET annual national convention held at Indian Institute of Management, Kozhikode during May 5-7, 2005*. New Delhi: Ess Ess Publications, 367-81.
2. Rajgoli, lqbalahmad U. (2005). Digitization of selected collection in Indian libraries: Some practical tips. In Amitabha Chatterjee et al. (Eds.), *LIS profession in India: vision for 2010*. Kolkata: IASLIC, 89-94.
3. Anjana Bhatnagar (2006). Digitization in academic libraries. *Information Studies*, 12 (1), 35-54.
4. Deegan, Marilyn and Tanner, Simon (2002). *Digital futures: strategies for the information age*. London: Library Association.
5. Digital Library Federation (1998). A working definition of digital library (Retrieved November 11, 2007, from http://www.diglib.org/about/dldefinition.htm).
6. Fox, E.A. et al. (1995). Digital libraries. *Communications of the ACM*, 76-75.
7. Seshaiah, O. (2006). Building digital library resources. In C. Anandan and M. Gangatharan (Eds.), *Digital libraries: from technology to culture*. New Delhi: Kanishka Publishers, 54-58.
8. Rajgoli, lqbalahmad U. (2005). Digitization of selected collection in Indian libraries: some practical tips. In Amitabha Chatterjee et al. (Eds.), *LIS profession in India: vision for 2010*. Kolkata: IASLIC, 89-94.

CUSAT Digital Library Service: Issues and Strategies

3

Surendran Cherukodan and *G. Santhosh Kumar*

1. Introduction

Digital Libraries (DL) and Institutional Repositories (IR) are fast becoming popular among library and information professionals. Building DLs and IRs is a priority area of library work all over the world mainly as projects involving huge investment. The advent of Open Source Software (OSS) has accelerated the process of establishing DLs and IRs. Libraries use DLs and IRs for preserving and showcasing an institution's knowledge in various forms including theses, scholarly articles, research reports, presentations, images, teaching materials, and administrative documents. These items were remained the property of that institution most probably in print format inaccessible to those outside the institution. DLs and IRs brought a revolution in the visibility and use of information as large number of them provided open access to their collection. DLs and IRs are essential systems that support both users and librarians in numerous ways.

2. CUSAT Digital Library (CDL)

The CUSAT community of teachers, research scholars, students and staff produce large amount of knowledge in the form of journal articles, research reports, dissertations, theses, images, teaching materials and documents related to the university. Created both in digital and print formats, these are found scattered over the department libraries. Hence, organizing and managing these documents are important aspects of ensuring access to them. A digital library was essential for CUSAT for a systematic and continuous process of collection, organisation, preservation and dissemination of digital and digitized materials.

The CUSAT Digital Library (CDL) was started in 2003 with very less number of documents in it. It became popular and active in 2006 when a workshop was offered to CUSAT library staff on the installation and customization of DSpace software. Now it represents all departments in the University with more than 3000 documents. Figure 3.1 shows the CDL Home page.

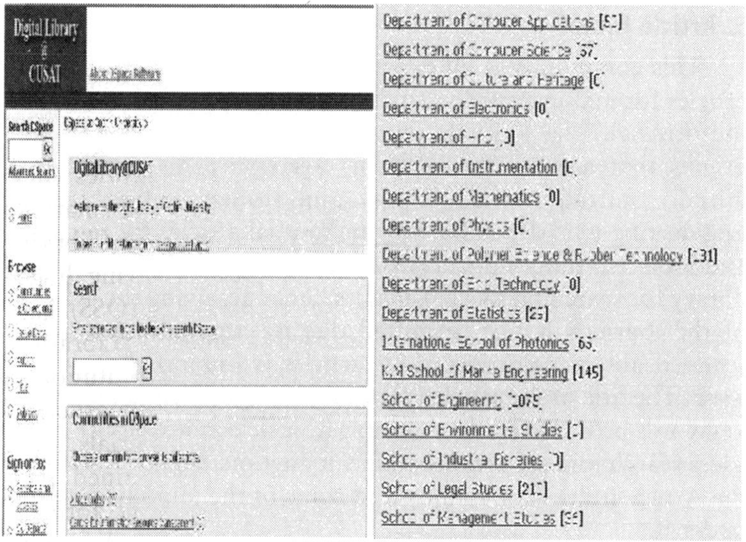

Fig. 3.1: CDL Home Page

3. Digital Library Software

There are many proprietary software packages for library automation. However, the presence of proprietary software for building DLs and IRs was limited. The Open Source Software (OSS) movement has made its impact on libraries all over the world. OSS for library automation and DLs and IRs are very popular among librarians. The OSS like DSpace[1], E-Prints[2], Fedora[3], Greenstone[4] are widely installed by libraries of all size and types for creating archives, data systems, DLs and IRs. CUSAT has used DSpace OSS for its DL. DSpace was developed by MIT Libraries and Hp Labs in 2002. Among the various OSS for DLs and IRs, DSpace is having more installations in the world.

4. Special Community Structure in CDL

The structure in any system that uses DSpace OSS is composed of communities, sub-communities, collection and item representing the departments, labs/library and individual documents in it. This paper tries to highlight some of the special communities in CDL.

5. Article Index

This community is an experiment of CDL to index journal articles for making article search easy and support the supply of the original. The journals selected for this service are Indian origins that are not having their e-version. This service was initially started for the faculty and students of School of Engineering who depend mainly on journal articles for seminars and projects. Many students from other institutions also visit the library for searching journal articles. Since archiving the full text of the journals is not permitted due to copyright issues, the scanned abstract portion of all articles is organized under an issue. The title of the article is given as such supplemented by the keywords provided by the author. The article index service helps users search journal articles online at anytime. Figure 3.2 shows the Article Index Community and some of the journals indexed under it.

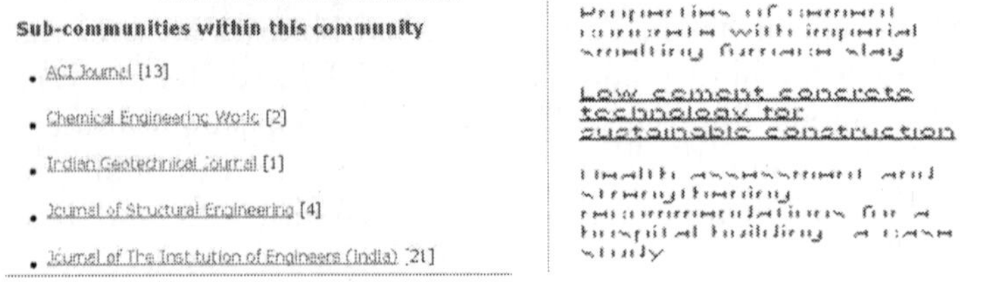

Fig. 3.2: CDL Article Index Sub-Community and List of new submissions

6. CUSAT Events

This community was started to capture documents generated in seminars and similar events. The proceedings of several conferences do not go beyond the participants and they are normally unavailable through commercial channels. Hence, making the knowledge open for all is very important for many reasons.

Fig. 3.3: CDL CUSAT Events Community

The service is done by scanning the print volumes of conferences and making it individual articles searchable by title, author, keyword or name of the conference. The work of scanning can be skipped if a soft copy of the proceedings is made available by the organizers. This community provides full text of articles as the copyright is owned by the university. Figure 3.3 shows the Events Community.

7. CUSAT News

Archiving news is another service provided in the CDL. The news items that anyway relate to CUSAT has been selected, scanned and archived for use. Though the importance of news items as a source of knowledge is well recognized by librarians, the strategies available are inadequate to capture media documents.[5] Though CUSAT CDL is focusing on documents related to the University, the model can be applied to archive important items of news, events, articles, reviews, interviews, etc. Figure 3.4 shows the list of news items archived in CDL and the downloaded form of a single item.

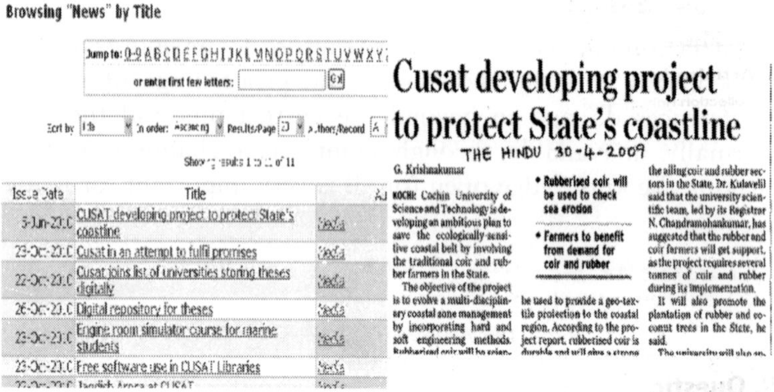

Fig. 3.4: CDL CUSAT News Titles and One scanned item

The items of news appeared in print media may not be seen and read by many as the coverage is region specific. The news items archived in DLs shall have more visibility. Moreover, it can be retrieved through search engines. Figure 3.5 shows the screenshot of Google results when searching "news at cusat".

Fig. 3.5: Google result for searching "news at cusat"

8. CUSAT Library Staff Articles

The intellectual output of library staff in a university can be properly organized and archived in DLs for wide access and visibility. CDL has arranged some of the articles of library staff under University Library Community. Providing full text of articles is not possible as journal articles have copyright restrictions. However some publishers permit authors to self archive. Figure 3.6 shows the sub-community of articles by Library staff.

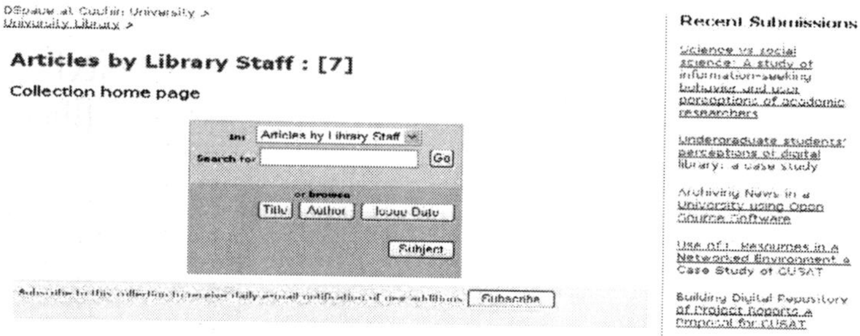

Fig. 3.6: Articles by Library Staff

9. Question Papers

Archiving research output in DLs is very common. However, the digitization and preserving of items like past question papers and syllabus are not considered important task by many librarians. But from the first author's experience, it was found that both students and library staff spend much time on locating question papers from the printed volumes. Hence, it was decided to digitize and put in DL all question papers available in the library. It takes around 3000 in number. The service has helped all students and faculty in and around CUSAT. Figures 3.7 and 3.8 show the DL's arrangement of the question paper for different branches of B.Tech and semester-wise arrangement under one particular branch.

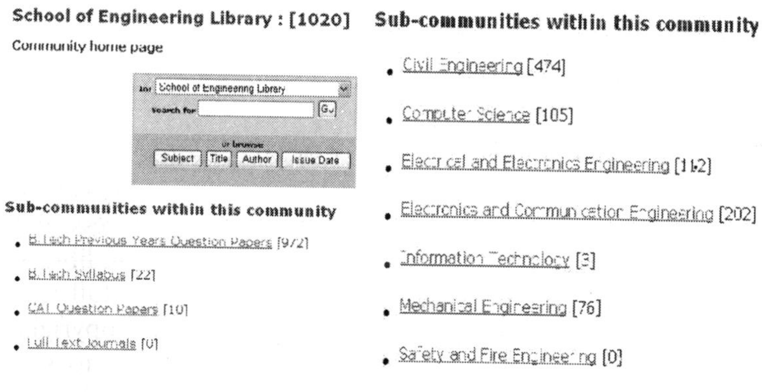

Fig. 3.7: SOE Library Sub-Community

Collections in this community

- Semester I [0]
- Semester II [0]
- Semester III [57]
- Semester IV [95]
- Semester V [103]
- Semester VI [132]
- Semester VII [60]
- Semester VIII [27]

Issue Date	Title	
22-Jul-2013	Analysis of Structures II Nov 2009 (99 Ad)	CUSAT
22-Jul-2013	Analysis of Structures I Nov 2009 (2006 Ad)	CUSAT
22-Jul-2013	Analysis of strucutres II Dec 2002 (99 Ad)	CUSAT
22-Jul-2013	Analysis of strucutres II July 2009 (02 Ad)	CUSAT
22-Jul-2013	Analysis of strucutres II July 2009 (99 Ad)	CUSAT
11-Nov-2013	Analysis of strucutres II July 2010 (02 Ad)	CUSAT
22-Jul-2013	Analysis of strucutres II June 2008 (99 Ad)	CUSAT
22-Jul-2013	Analysis of Strucutres II May 2006 (02 Ad)	CUSAT
22-Jul-2013	Analysis of Strucutres II Nov 2005 (02 Ad)	CUSAT
22-Jul-2013	Analysis of Strucutres II Nov 2006 (02 Ad)	CUSAT
22-Jul-2013	Analysis of strucutres II Nov 2008 (2006 Ad)	CUSAT
22-Jul-2013	Analysis of strucutres II Nov 2008 (99 Ad)	CUSAT
22-Jul-2013	Analysis of strucutres II Nov 2009 (02 Ad)	CUSAT
22-Jul-2013	Analysis of strucutres I July 2009 (2006 Ad)	CUSAT
22-Jul-2013	Civil Engineering Drawing Dec 2002 (99 Ad)	CUSAT
22-Jul-2013	Civil Engineering Drawing Dec 2004 (02 Ad)	CUSAT
22-Jul-2013	Civil Engineering Drawing July 2005 (02 Ad)	CUSAT
22-Jul-2013	Civil Engineering Drawing July 2009 (02 Ad)	CUSAT

Fig. 3.8: Semester-wise arrangement of Question paper

10. CDL Access Status

It is interesting to know whether people visit and use a system established for use. The CDL usage was taken using Google analytics service. The period selected is from January 2009 to September 2009. Figure 3.9 shows visitors overview. CDL got 23711 page views during the period, from 78 countries in the world. Major visit has recorded from India.

	Detail Level: Country/Territory	Visits
1.	India	14,135
2.	United States	142
3.	United Arab Emirates	79
4.	Saudi Arabia	36
5.	Qatar	36
6.	Brazil	18
7.	Singapore	15
8.	United Kingdom	15
9.	Spain	13
10.	Kuwait	12
11.	Malaysia	11
12.	Turkey	11
13.	Australia	10
14.	Hong Kong	10

Fig. 3.9: CDL Access Statistics

11. CDL Working Model

The CDL is contributing its service towards digitization, preservation and access to essential documents in the University. The CDL has not received any funding from outside agencies. The server is maintained by the CIRM Lab, CUSAT. It uses two scanners for digitization; Hp 5590 (Rs. 27000) and Hp N9120 (1.75 Lakhs). It is available online using the web service of the University. The second author acts as the administrator of CDL and the first author has uploaded the majority of the contents. Many library staff and faculty are associated with the CDL.

12. Conclusion

The CDL has been a successful system in supporting the teaching and learning activity of the University. It has not achieved its goal of covering all departments and all documents. However, it has been recognized as a service that saves the time of both staff and users. The service can be improved with the support of more library professionals and faculty who could help the growth of contents in the DL.

NOTES

1. http://www.dspace.org/ (Retrieved on 2nd February, 2011).
2. http://www.eprints.org (Retrieved on 2nd February, 2011).
3. http://www.fedora-commons.org (Retrieved on 2nd February, 2011).

4. http://www.greenstone.org (Retrieved on 2nd February, 2011).
5. Cherukodan, S. and Sheeja, N.K. (2010). Archiving news in a university using open source software (Retrieved March 15, 2010, from http://www.ignca.nic.in/ifla2010/IFLA_PDF IFLA_conf_papers.pdf).

PART II

WEB 2.0 AND INFORMATION PROFESSIONALS

Developments in Web 2.0: Challenges for LIS Professionals

4

K.G. Sudhier

1. Introduction

The profession of librarianship and the field of LIS have been in a constant state of flux. Today the buzz word or phrase in the technology is 'Web 2.0' which facilitates today's libraries to be more dynamic institutions. Web 2.0 or Web 2 is the popular term for advanced Internet technology and applications including blogs, Wikis, RSS and Social book marking. The two major components of Web 2.0 are the technological advances enabled by Ajax and other new applications such as RSS and Eclipse and the user empowerment that they support.[1]

Web 2.0 refers to a convergence of technologies, some new, some old, which are changing the way we experience what we have come to know as the Internet. With Web 2.0, the potential variety and richness of the user experience have grown substantially in library and information centres. The easiest way to get a grasp on Web 2.0 is to explore some of the applications and technologies with which it has been associated. There are three facets to this change: the particular information applications with which Web 2.0 is associated, such as wikis and blogs; new ways of managing information, such as social book marking and folksonomics, and new business models for providing information services.[2]

Web 2.0 is to make a reference to a group of technologies which have become deeply associated with the term: blogs, wikis, podcasts, RSS feeds, etc., which facilitate a more socially connected web where everyone is able to add to and edit the information space.[3]

As the Internet has become such an integral part of western culture, indeed our everyday lives, librarians, like any other professional group, must attempt to make sense of these changes within their domain of expertise and engage with the issues, opportunities and challenges raised.

2. What is Web 2.0

The term, 'web 2.0' was reportedly first conceptualized and made popular by Tim O'Reilly and Dale Dougherty of O'Reilly Media in 2004 to describe the trends and business models that survived the technology sector market crash of the 1990s. Most of the recent popularization of the term derives from a widely influential article by the information evangelist Tim O'Reilly. In a series of seminars, O'Reilly set out to define Web 2.0, exploring the characteristics of information systems and information services business models that appeared on face value to be changing the way in which users are interacting with information resources. O'Reilly[4] presented Web 2.0 as a second stage in the development of the web, superseding the predominantly publishing model of many web-based information applications and services. With it, information services are to become more dynamic, and more sensitive to user action.

Paul Miller[5] has also outlined the qualities intrinsic to the Web 2.0 programe. These include the freeing of data, to allow it to be manipulated in ways unconnected to the purpose for which it was gathered, the building of virtual applications that draw information and functionality from different sources, and growing importance of user participation. For Miller, Web 2.0 is about the development of modular information services, where developers and users are able to build applications from interoperable models.

The term Web 2.0 was officially coined in 2004 by Dale Dougherty, a vice president of O'Reilly Media Inc. (the company famous for its technology related conferences and high quality books) during a team discussion on a potential future conference about the Web. The team wanted to capture the feeling that despite the dot-com boom and subsequent bus, the web was 'more important than ever' with exciting new applications and sites popping up with surprising regularity.[6]

Web 2.0 is transforming the web into a space that allows users to create and share information online—a space for collaboration, conversation, and interaction—one that is highly dynamic, flexible and adaptable.[7]

3. Characteristics and Role of Web 2.0

The role of Web 2.0 in education and libraries are as per the following six key ideas:

- Individual production and user generated contents
- Harness the power of the crowd
- Data on an epic scale
- Architecture of participation
- Network effects
- Openness

The following are the important characteristics of web 2.0:

- Web 2.0 allows data to be exposed, discovered and manipulated in a variety of ways distinct from the purpose of the application originally used to gain access.
- It permits the building of virtual applications, drawing data and functionality from a number of different sources as appropriate.
- It is participative. The traditional web has tended to be somewhat one-sided, with a flow of content from provider to viewer.
- It allows the users to actively participate online by means of blogging, sharing files, or equivalent.
- Web 2.0 applications work for the user, and are able to locate and assemble content that meets our needs as users, rather than forcing us to conform to the paths laid out for us by content owners or their intermediaries.
- Its applications are modular, with developers and users able to pick and choose from a set of interoperating

components in order to build something that meets their needs.

- Web 2.0 is about sharing: code, content, ideas.
- It is about communication and facilitating community.
- It is smart. Applications will be able to capture user knowledge and deliver services to satisfy their needs.
- It is built upon Trust, whether that is trust placed on individuals, in assertions, or in the uses and reuses of data.[8]

Web 2.0 websites typically include some of the following features and techniques:

- Search
- Links
- Authoring
- Tags
- Extensions
- Signals
- Aggregation
- AJAX (Asynchronous Javascript and XML)
- API (Application Programming Interface)
- Embedding
- Virtual Architecture
- Widget[9]

4. Applications and Tools of Web 2.0

There are a number of web based services and applications that demonstrate the foundations of the Web 2.0 concept and they are already being used to a certain extent in education. These are not really technologies as such, but services (or user process) built using the building blocks of the technologies and open standards that underpin the Internet and the web. These include: Really Simple Syndication (RSS), wikis, weblogs, commentary and comments functionality, web personalization and 'my profile' features, photo sharing (Flicker, Picasa), social networking software, AJAX and API programming (Google maps), streaming media audio and video formats, personalized alerts, podcasting and MP3 files, folksonomics, tagging, social book marking (such as Delic.io.us), open source software, user driven ratings, and open access content.[10]

4.1 Weblogs

The blog, or weblog is the oldest of the applications of Web 2.0. The term blog was coined by Jorn Brger in 1997 and refers to a simple webpage consisting of brief paragraphs of opinion, information, personal diary entries or links, called posts, arranged chronologically with the most recent first. Blog first appeared as a simplified way of publishing to the web, obviating the need for dedicated web-publishing software, and replacing it with a combination of web-forms for inputting information and templates for displaying it.[11]

Two aspects of the blog are of particular interest. Firstly, the greater ease of web publishing that they have introduced. The second is the collection of tools that have grown up around the blog to make the blogging process easier.

Use of blogs in LIS applications are:

- Serve as a platform where the users can file their concerns, queries and suggestions regarding the services and activities of the library.
- As another form of publication.
- As collection development, where the users request the resources.
- Marketing of the information as well as the library.
- As discussion forum.

4.2 Wikis

Wikis, like the blog, are a simplified means of publishing to the web that again dispense with the need for dedicated web-publishing software. Unlike the blog, the wikis support the creation of full scale websites with its combination of templates, authoring tools and audit trails. It is a type of website that allows and encourages visitors to add, edit, change and hopefully improve on the existing content with the use of collaborative editing the wikis take the ethos of the open-source software movement with its realization of the benefits of collaboration resource management and development.

Their uses in libraries are:

- Social interaction and discussions among the librarians and users.
- It can also be used by the users to share information and enhance the content.
- Reference resources wiki can be built for frequently asked questions.
- For creating subject guides, subject gateways, etc.

4.3 Flickr

Flickr is a social network for sharing photos. It combines a social network with user generated content. Users can work together to collaborate on photo projects and use each others tags to find new photos. It enables users to contribute, organize, share and discuss photos.

4.4 RSS

RSS [Resource Description Framework (RDF) Site Summary, or Rich Site Summary, or Really Simple Syndication] is an easy-to-use XML format for distributing content on the web. It is a simple XML syntax for describing recent additions of content to a Website. These additions can include news items, blog updates, library acquisition, or any other information elements. A web site with one or more RSS feeds is said to be syndicated. Users subscribe to the feeds using an RSS aggregator or news reader that crawls the sites on a regular basis, usually several times per hour. An aggregator displays feeds and enables users to organize them and to access related web pages when these are available.

According to Barsky[12], RSS feeds even have the following applications:

- Blog updates
- Newspaper and journal articles
- Press releases and announcements
- News and database updates

RSS is becoming an essential communication tool that allows information professionals to provide the most up-to-date information to the clients.

4.5 Podcast

A podcast is simply the name given to a file that is a voice recording for playback on a computer, or saved onto an MP3 digital audio player and listened to at some future point. The name comes from the activity of broadcasting and listening to the file on an Apple iPod player, and was used in an article in *The Guardia* newspaper as a synonym for rather clumsy 'audioblogging'.[13]

Usage of Podcasts in library are:

- Recordings of book reviews for all ages
- Speeches by visiting authors
- Children's story times and book club promotions
- Audio training sessions and leased databases
- Podcast tour about the library services and about the usage of the library.

4.6 Mashups

Mashups are web applications that combine data from more than one source into a single integrated tool. They are aggregations of content from different online sources to create a new service. The methods of sourcing content for mashups include web feeds (RSS or Atoms), and screen scraping. Many people are experimenting with mashups using Amazon, eBay, Flickr, Google, Microsoft, Yahoo, and You Tube APIs, which has led to the creation of the mashup editor.

4.7 Tagging

Tagging is described as the process by which the resources in a collection are assigned tags in the form of words, phrases, codes or other strings of characters. The advantages of user tags are that it helps the data to be more easily searchable.

Tagging can be applied to the LIS for editing the subject headings from the user point of view and thereby enhancing the indexing and relevancy of the searches, making the collection more dynamic. It also greatly facilitates the lateral searching.

4.8 Peer-to-Peer Networking (P2P)

This is a technique for efficiently sharing files (audio, videos, or text) either over the Internet or within a closed set of users. Unlike the traditional method of storing a file on one machine, P2P distributes files across many machines, often those of the users themselves.

4.9 Collective Intelligence

This refers to any system that attempts to tap the expertise of a group rather than an individual to make decisions. Technologies that contribute to collective intelligence include collaborative publishing and common databases for sharing knowledge.

4.10 Instant Messaging (IM)

IM is a form of real-time communication between two or more people based on typed text. It has become increasingly popular due to its quick response time, its ease of use and possibility of multitasking.

The usage of IM in libraries are:

- Instant clarifications for the questions from users and *vice versa.*
- Providing virtual reference service.
- Integrating vendors answers with queries.
- Online meetings.
- Provides instant message about library related news.

4.11 Social Search

The social search is not a new phenomenon, its features of collaboration, conversion and interaction in a social space among users make it an imperative element of Web 2.0 technologies. The emerging popularity of folksonomies, with their users generating their own labeling system, has allowed social searching to distinguish itself from traditional search engines such as Google and Yahoo.[14]

Social search is frequently publicized as the next big thing after Google for improving information retrieval, relevance, and awareness. Sherman[15] defined social search as 'a collection of

Internet way finding tools informed by human judgment. That judgment takes place in the form of tags, click-through activity, search history, and other action.

4.12 Folksonomies

A folksonomy is a spontaneous, collaborative work to categories links by a community of users. Users take control of organize the content together.

4.13 YouTube

YouTube allows users to upload, tag, watch, rate, review, view, and blog, video footage and even create play lists. It can be used as a publishing tool for marketing of library and library products.

4.14 Social Networks

Social networks are relatively new kinds of virtual communities that are structured to delineate and build on relationships that members have with each other by virtue of their being part of that community. They are perhaps the most promising and embracing technology which enable messaging, blogging, streamlining media, tagging, etc. Informal social networking has existed since the inception of the web, but sites dedicated to social networking have been expanding exponentially since 2003.

- The social network sites offer a free and easy way to create personal web pages and fill them with content such as blogs, digital photographs, favourite music, short video clips and much more.
- Social networking could enable librarians and patrons not only to interact, but to share and change resources dynamically in an electronic medium.
- Libraries can create a page to approach to new users.
- For building network among the interested group in discussing the common interest.

Some of the more popular social network websites include MySpace (http://www.myspace.com), Facebook (http://facebook.com), LinkedIn (www.linkedin.com), Friendster (http://www.friendster.com), etc. LibraryThing (http://

www.librarything.com) is a library social network site and a place for members to register the books they have read, will read, or are in the process of reading. It promotes social interactions, book recommendations, self-classifications and monitoring of new books.[16]

5. Web 2.0 and the Library

Web 2.0 not only means new technologies, it also brings about a fundamental change in how libraries operate. The main characteristic of this new order is that information management and provision are no longer under the purview of the librarian. The best thing about social tagging is that everyone is allowed to categorize the information the way they want to.

Web 2.0 technologies offer diverse ways to add value to library services. Librarians and users recognize tools such as blogs, wikis and RSS feeds as facilitating communication. RSS is also a great way to encourage staff to keep up with professional reading. Librarians can subscribe to feeds from professionals blogs and journals and read them anywhere, anytime.[17]

The applications of Web 2.0 technologies in libraries and librarians are very well seen in the initiatives of Elsevier Inc. The Elsevier offers a number of services falling within the scope of Web 2.0 and they include[18]:

Podcasts

- ScienceDirect news: *www.info.sciencedirect.com/news/podcasts*
- The Lancet: *www.thelancet.com/audio*

RSS

Product alerts and feeds

- Engineering village: www.engineeringvillage.com
- ScienceDirect: www.info.sciencedirect.com/using/#
- Scopus: http://info.scopus.com/setup/promo/usertools

Alerts and newsletters for libraries

- Library Connect News: http://feeds.feedburner.com/libraryconnect
- Others: www.elsevier.com/librarians/alertingservices

Tagging

- Engineering Village: www.engineeringvillage.com

Elsevier's new tool that allows researchers to share bookmarks among a select group or the general public is 2collab (www.2collab.com). This tool acts as filtering mechanism for information.

6. Library 2.0

The term Library 2.0 was coined by Michael Casey on his blog *LibraryCrunch* as a direct spin-off the terms Business 2.0 and Web 2.0. Casey suggested that libraries, especially public libraries, are at a crossroad where many elements of Web 2.0 have applicable value within the library community. According to him, Library 2.0 is all about library users—keeping those we have while actively seeking those who do not currently use our services. It is about embracing those ideas and technologies that can assist libraries in delivering services to these groups, and it is about participation-involving users in service creation and evaluation.

It is the 'application of interactive, collaborative, and multi-media web-based technologies to web based library services and collections' and suggests this definition be adopted by the library science community.

Library 2.0 is a term that provides focus to a number of ongoing conversations around the changing ways that libraries should make themselves and their services visible to end users and to one another. It is a part of a whole new approach to information organization and dissemination. Tagging, blogs, wikis and RSS feeds are changing the traditional library functions of indexing, cataloguing and information dissemination. The greatest impact these tools are visible in the area of information access and delivery. Libraries today utilize wikis and RSS feeds to deliver library news and catalogue updates: they also solicit patron's feedback and participation in the form of blog comments and the ability to alter existing information.[19]

Amazon, Google, eBay, Skype and other initiatives of the Information Revolution do not threaten the progressive library. Rather, they create whole new opportunities for the professionals to engage with an empowered, interested and skilled set of audiences. Library 2.0 is a concept of a very different library service, geared towards the needs and expectations of today's library users. In this vision the library makes information available wherever and whenever the user requires it, and seeks to ensure that barriers to use and reuse are removed.[20]

A theory for Library 2.0 could be understood to have four essential elements:

(i) It is user-centered

(ii) It provides a multi-media experience

(iii) It is socially rich

(iv) It is communally innovative

Jadon and Rajput[21] listed the advantages of Library 2.0 as:

- Open access to information will be automatic
- Copyright will no longer exist because it will be replaced by clickable licenses among communities.
- No physical information required, trackable information events will take their place.
- Individual access convert to community access
- No research project will be initiated without an informatics associate on the team.

The challenges of Library 2.0 in Indian libraries are:

- Financial crunch
- Lack of ICT infrastructure
- Technical illiteracy in library personnel's and users
- Lack of training and orientation program

Thus Library 2.0 (interpolated from Web 2.0) as a buzzword used to describe all sorts of activities that constitute a major transition by modern libraries in their outlook, services, resources, etc., to reach out to non-users and potential users, then a pertinent question in librarianship, particularly in the context of less and least developed countries, would be. What have been major transitions in the theory or practice of librarianship in the recent past? Technologies might have changed the outlook of the libraries, but have Web 2.0 technologies in any way changed the way librarianship I commonly understood and practiced in these countries.[22]

7. The Dark side of Web 2.0

The emergence of Web 2.0 has brought with it collaboration on a global scale, which has been really great thing that has led to sites like Wikipedia, but it also has a dark side-copyright infringement. One issue with Web 2.0 copyright infringement is that most of the offenders do not even realize what they are doing or that it is wrong. The popularity of blogging and the ease at which articles and images can be passed around have made it very simple to inadvertently commit copyright infringement. Creative Commons is a popular alternative to the 'all rights reserved' copyright license. Clipmarks is also usually used since it provides a link back to the original article. For images, one should always check to see what sort of copyright restrictions or Creative Commons license is being used for the image.[23]

8. Future of Web 2.0

The large scale collection of user data and creation of user generated content, aggregated by web applications, will continue and deepen as people explore new ideas. The scale of this will grow through the network effect as more people come online and existing users increase their use of Web 2.0 services. The production process to generate online content will become more sophisticated with the advent of increasingly powerful and easy-to-use software and digital devices, and the use of mash-ups will grow.[24]

With so many different ways of accessing information (blogs, wikis, RSS feeds, etc.) there may also be a sense in which people worry that they do not understand or use all of these forms and a sense of anxiety may even develop as to whether they are as fully connected as they should be.[25]

The web, or the network, as platform and the idea of software above the level of a single device is becoming firmly entrenched as a concept and it is likely that over the next few years we will start to perceive personal computing more as a process of interacting with networked services rather than using particular computing device.

It is also beginning to see a change in the way in which we interact with other people: what Nigel Shadbolt refers to as "the fabric of people being connected", through the new technologies and the formation of new social communities in which we share information and carry out collective endeavour. The social aspects of the web's topological interconnectedness are becoming increasingly important and indeed this may be the most important long-term trend. In this context people are asking about, what will be Web 3.0 look like?

9. Web 3.0

Web 3.0 is a term used to describe the future of the World Wide Web. Following the introduction of the phrase Web 2.0 as a description of the recent evolution of the Web, many technologists, journalists, and industry leaders have used the term Web 3.0 to hypothesize about a future wave of Internet innovation.[26]

Views on the next stage of the World Wide Web's evolution vary greatly. Some believe that emerging technologies such as the Semantic Web will transform the way the Web is used, and lead to new possibilities in artificial intelligence. Other visionaries suggest that increases in Internet connection speeds, modular web applications, or advances in computer graphics will play the key role in the evolution of the World Wide Web.

Nova Spivack[27] defined Web 3.0 as the third decade of the web (2010-2020) during which he suggested several major complementary technology trends including:

- Transformation
- Ubiquitous connectivity
- Network computing
- Open technologies
- Open identity
- The intelligent web
- Distributed databases
- Intelligent applications

10. Conclusion

Web 2.0 has enormous potential to bring user-generated content to the Internet. The idea is to free data from corporative control and allow anyone to assemble and locate content to meet their own needs or the needs of clients. As a technology infrastructure of Web 2.0 is still complex and constantly evolving. Web 2.0 is ultimately a social phenomenon of user's experience of the web and is characterized by open communication, decentralization of authority, and freedom to share and re-use Web content.

Web 2.0 continues to stand out as a dominant theme in libraries today. Almost any conference that touches on libraries and technology gushes with presentations on blogs, RSS, social computing, wikis, user tagging, and other manifestations of the Web 2.0 brand.[28] Some of the most exciting new developments seen in library automation today involve some aspect of this new way of thinking about the Web-building, an environment that is more focused on the user, that embraces dynamic content over static pages, that not only delivers content to users but also seeks content from users, and that fosters engagement, participation, and collaboration.

We are living in one of the most exciting and challenging times for the information industry. As the information professionals, we take seriously our responsibility to deliver services including disseminating information, facilitating access to and sharing of scientific information, providing forums to create and share new knowledge, enabling collaboration, and connecting scientists and students. Web 2.0 technologies are enabling us to take such services to a new level and make them more interactive and participatory for our users.

NOTES

1. Ramesh Babu, B. Narendra Kumar, A.M. and Rao, P. Nageswara (2010). Recent Developments in Web 2.0: New avenues for LIS professionals. *Information Age*, 4, 3; 5-10.
2. Tredinnick, Luke. Web 2.0 and business. *Business Information Review*, 6, 23(4), 231.
3. Anderson, Paul (2007). What is web 2.0? Ideas, technologies and implications for education. *JISC: Technology and standards watch.*

4. O'Reilly, Tim (2005). Web 2.0: a compact definition. O'Reilly Radar blog (Retrieved December 25, 2010, from http://radar.oreilly.com/archives/2005/10/web 20 Compact definition. html).
5. Miller, Paul (2005). Library 2.0: The challenges of disruptive innovation. A Talis white paper (Retrieved December 28, 2010, from http://www.talis.com/resources/documents/447 library 2 prf1.pdf).
6. O'Reilly, Tim (2005). What is Web 2.0?: Design pattern and Business models for the next generation of software (Retrieved December 25, 2010, from http://www.oriellynet.com/pub/a/orielly /tim/news/2005/09/03/what is web 2.0.html).
7. Coombs, K.A. (2007). Building a library website on the pillars of Web 2.0. *Computers in Libraries*, 27(1), 16-19.
8. Sudhier, K.G. (2008). Web 2.0 and libraries. National conference on '*Library 2.0: the confluence of Web 2.0 and the library paradigm*'. 21-22 August, 2008. Dept. of Library & Information Science, University of Mysore.
9. Dash, Bedarata and Dash, Ranjith N. (2010). Library 2.0: An Information tools by application of Web 2.0 technologies. In *International Conference on Innovation Driven Librarianship* (ICIDL-2010), SRM University, Kancheepuram, Tamil Nadu, 17-19 June, 2010.
10. Barsky, Eugene (2006). Introducing Web 2.0: Weblogs and podcasting for health librarians. *Journal of Canadian Health Libraries Association*, 27(2), 33-34.
11. Tredinnick, Luke (200). Web 2.0 and business. *Business Information Review*, 6, 23(4), 231.
12. Barsky, Eugene (2006). Introducing Web 2.0: RSS trends for health librarians. *Journal of Canadian Health Libraries Association*, 27(1), 7-8.
13. Bradley, Phil (2007). *How to use Web 2.0 in your library*. London: Facet publishing, p. 38.
14. Barsky, Eugene and Cho, Allan (2007). Introducing Web 2.0: social search for health libraries. *Journal of Canadian Health Libraries Association*, 28(3), 59-61.
15. Sherman, C. (2006). What is the big deal with social search? Search Engine Watch, 2006 (Retrieved December 20, 2010, from http://searchenginewatch.com/showPage.html?page=3623153).
16. Barsky, Eugene and Purdon, Michelle (2006). Introducing Web 2.0: social networking and social book marking for health libraries. *Journal of Canadian Health Libraries Association*, 27 (3), 65-67.

17. Casey, Michael. Working towards a definition of Library 2.0. www.librarycrunch.com (Retrieved on 28th December, 2010).
18. Marques, David (2007). Elsevier strategically invests in Web 2.0 technologies. *Library Connect Newsletter*, 5(4), 4-5.
19. Pin, Wan Wee (2007). Library 2.0: The new e-world order. *Library Connect Newsletter*, 5(4), 2.
20. Miller, Paul (2005b). Web 2.0: building the new library. *Ariadne*, 45 (Retrieved December 28, 2010, from http://www.ariadne.ac.uk/issue45/miller/).
21. Jadon, N.S., Jadon, Gopal Singh and Rajput, Prabhat Singh (2007). Library 2.0 and Web 2.0 emerging technologies: its application in libraries. In *Developing Library and Information resources and services in the internet era*. 53rd All India Library Conference Proceedings, Hyderabad, December 13-16, 2007, pp. 266-72.
22. Kalra, H.P.S. (2010). 'Library One'—Forward from Library 2.0 and Further. In S. Humayoon Kabir and K.G. Sudhier (Eds). *Confetti of Thoughts on Library & Information Studies: Essays in honour of Prof. (Dr.) C.V. Rajan Pillai*. New Delhi: Authors Press, p. 380.
23. Hirwade, Mangala (2010). Editorial. *Information Age*, 4(3); 3-4.
24. Cerf, V. (2007). An Information avalanche. *IEEE Computer*, 40(1), 18-24.
25. Anderson, Paul (2007). All that glisters is not Gold: Web 2.0 and the Librarian. *Journal of Librarianship and Information Science*, 39(4), 195-98.
26. Wikipedia, the free encyclopedia. http://en.wikipedia.org/wiki/web_3.0/ (Retrieved on 25th December, 2010).
27. Spivack, Nova (2006). The third generation web is coming. www.kurzweilAl.net (Retrieved on 25th December, 2010).
28. Breeding, Marshall (2007). We need to go beyond Web 2.0. *Computers in Libraries*, 27, 22-26.

RSS Feeds as Web 2.0 Tool for Career Awareness Service in Libraries

5

Dineshan Koovakkai

1. Introduction

In the world of competition opportunities are to be grabbed by competing with people who may be better qualified and eligible. Getting a job may be easy for a person who has willingness to work. But getting the right job for the right person is important and it needs proper planning and selection. Career choice, like any choice and decision-making, needs proper planning and adequate information. Career decision is nothing but selecting one career from different alternatives. Only a person who is rich with up-to-date information can make proper selection.

There are innumerable career opportunities in the private, semi-government and government sectors. There are also innumerable career publications which publish the notifications of different establishments looking for the right human resource. With the proliferation of electronic information and web presence of organizations the job advertisements are now available on the web also. However, going through all the career publications and websites is a herculean task for a career seeker.

Here is the role of a librarian. To a modern librarian Current Awareness Service (CAS) is not a novel service. With the spread of Information Communication Technologies (ICTs), librarians are seriously involved in electronic Current Awareness Service as well. The same philosophy and methodology can be applied in the provision of Career Information Service also by applying modern tools and techniques. The electronic Career Information Service can very well be provided with the help of RSS Feeds.

2. RSS Feeds

RSS which stands for 'Really Simple Syndication' or 'Rich Site Summary' is a format for delivering regularly changing web content. Many news-related sites, weblogs and other online publishers syndicate their content as an RSS Feed to whoever wants it.[1]

Many of the websites of institutions, electronic journal publishers as well as newspaper publishers syndicate their content as an RSS feed which is indicated by the RSS logo against each item.[2] Figure 5.1 is a typical RSS logo which can be seen on many websites which syndicates their content.

Fig. 5.1: The RSS Logo

The RSS feed gives the user the opportunity of getting the latest content of the sites he is interested without browsing each and every site for getting the latest information. In order to get the contents, a feed reader (feed aggregator) is needed. A feed reader is a software which aggregates the syndicated web content. There are different types of feed readers as web based, desk top based or mobile device based. The first step in getting the alert from different website is to install a suitable feed reader. Downloading and installing a feed reader is very simple and it can be done without involving any cost as there are a number of free feed readers available online.

3. An Experiment with FeedReader

"FeedReader" is a free RSS news aggregation solution that provides robust, state-of-the-art features in an intuitive, user friendly environment. It provides the users with a seamless and convenient experience—without the need for advanced technical knowledge—by delivering the broadest range of features through a simple, easy-to-use interface.[3]

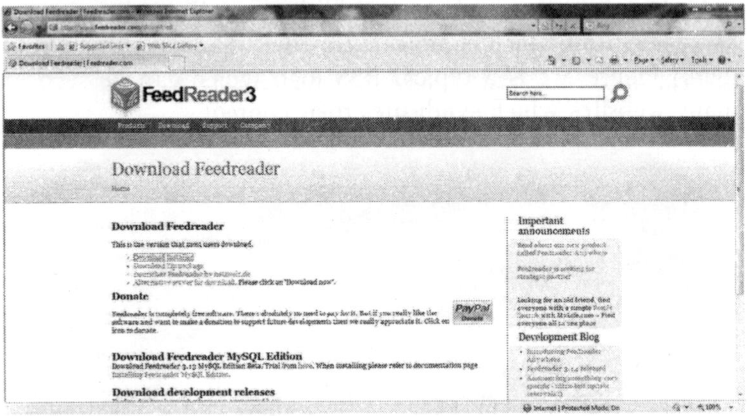

Fig. 5.2: The Home Page of FeedReader

3.1 Installing FeedReader

Downloading and installing FeedReader is some clicks ahead. No technical expertise is needed to install the FeedReader as it is

Fig. 5.3: The FeedReader Icon

just a matter of following the instructions and clicking at appropriate buttons. When the installation is complete your computer desktop will show the icon similar to the Fig. 5.3 if you have clicked the option to create short cut.

3.2 Adding New Feeds

New feeds can be added to the feed reader by opening the websites with RSS logo and copying and pasting the feed address by clicking "New" and pasting the address in the address bar. For this, the job sites which provide RSS feeds are to be found out. The web address of institutions which offer jobs and syndicate their content also can be added.

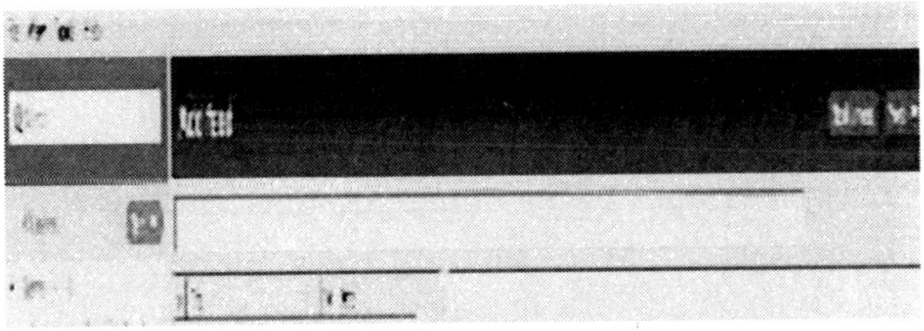

Fig. 5.4: The FeedReader Address Bar to add new Feeds

The reader will instantly grab the contents and will display the details on the screen. This is shown in Fig. 5.5.

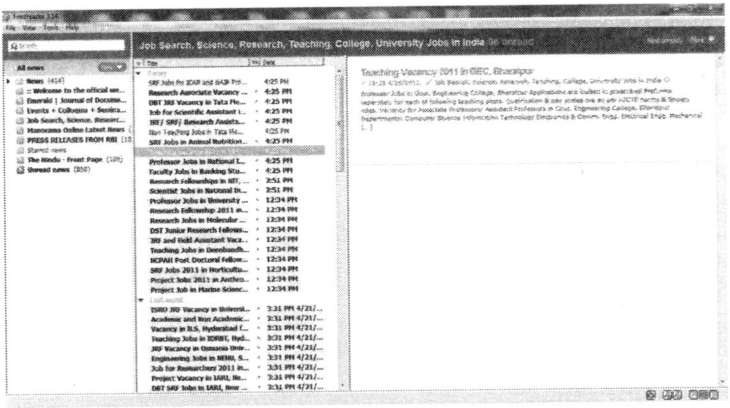

Fig. 5.5: The Information Displayed by FeedReader

4. Providing Career Awareness Service Electronically

The job information received through the RSS feeds can instantly be disseminated to the career seekers identified by the library. For providing the career information electronically, libraries can create a group mail of the career seekers. Creating group mail is easy and the messages can be sent to every career seeker at the same time through such group mail.

4.1 Creating Mail Group

The groups can be created without any cost using the service providers such as Google or Yahoo. The group can be created in a few steps as[4]:

4.1.1. Creating an account

4.1.2. Setting up of group

4.1.3. Inviting people

4.2 Posting Messages to the Career Seekers

The messages collected from the feeds can be posted to the group mail so that every members of the group will get the information instantly. This can be done at periodic intervals as is done in the case of general Current Awareness Service. Figure 5.6 shows the screen shot of a typical posting.[5] This message will be delivered to the mail box of all in the group instantly making the career seekers aware of the opportunities.

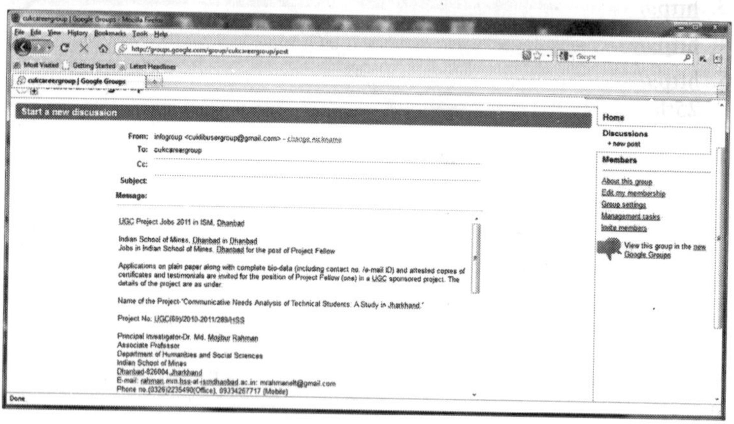

Fig. 5.6: Group Mail Posting

5. Conclusion

Career and job information is of great importance for those who search for the job seekers and career changers. Getting the right information at the right time is inevitable for applying for the post and for making preparations for the competitive examinations and interview. Right information also helps to select the right career. With the development in computer and communication technologies and new tools and techniques of imparting information in libraries, providing career information is becoming more easy and effortless. Being a social institution libraries have the responsibility of helping the youth by providing job and career information. Librarians who have adequate knowledge in providing Current Awareness Service can very well provide Career Awareness Service also electronically using the new techniques and adopting new technologies.

NOTES

1. http://www.whatisrss.com/ (Retrieved on 5th April, 2011).
2. Dineshan Koovakkai (2010). Library outreach through RSS feeds. In Khaisar Muneebulla Khan, V. Gopakumar and B.K. Vishala (Eds.), *Empowering library professionals in managing digital resources: UGC sponsored national level conference proceedings*. Mangalore: Library and Information Centre, St. Agnes College, 407-13.
3. http://www.feedreader.com (Retrieved on 15th April, 2011).
4. http://groups.google.com/ (Retrieved on 25th April, 2011).
5. http://groups.google.com/group/cukcareergroup/post (Retrieved on 25th April, 2011).

Managing Scholarly Communication in the Web 2.0 Environment: The Role of University Libraries

6

C. Beena, S.N. Archana and *V. Jayasree*

1. Introduction

Scholarly communication over the past 10 to 15 years has gained a tremendous momentum with the advent of Internet and the World Wide Web. The web has transformed the ways by which people search, find, use and communicate information. Innovations in web technology since 2005 have brought out an array of new services and facilities and an enhanced version of the web named Web 2.0. Web 2.0 facilitates a collaborative environment in which the information users can interact with the information. Web 2.0 enables its users to create, annotate, review, share re-use and represent the information in new ways thereby optimizing the information dissemination.

2. Web 2.0 Basics

Web 2.0 refers to or is associated with the web applications that facilitate participatory information sharing, interoperability, user-centered design, and collaboration on the World Wide Web. According to Wikipedia[1], "Web 2.0" is a term coined in January 1999 by Darcy DiNucci, a consultant on electronic information design (information architecture) in her article, "Fragmented Future". She used the term mainly to refer to the Web design, aesthetics, and the interconnection of everyday objects with the Internet. Her usage of the term does not directly relate to, the current uses of the term. The term and concept Web 2.0 that we use today owes for its popularity to Dale Dougherty and Tim O'Reilly of the O'Reilly media.

There is no agreed-upon definition for Web 2.0. JISC in a 2007 report defined it as:

> "Web 2.0 encompasses a variety of different meanings that include an increased emphasis on user-generated content, data and content sharing and collaborative effort, together with the use of various kinds of social software, new ways of interacting with web-based applications, and the use of the web as a platform for generating, re-purposing and consuming content."[2]

According to Theimer[3], the term Web 2.0 describes a confluence of changes in Web design and functionality that resulted in fundamental differences in the ways developers and users approach the Web. He enumerates the most significant features of Web 2.0 as follows:

"Network as platform" or "cloud computing", "live on the Web, not on your local computer."

- Open standards, open source, openness in general
- Creation of syndicated content—use of (Really Simple Syndication) RSS.
- Customized web experiences for users
- Broad use of interactivity
- Prevalence of user-created content
- Integration of user-to-user connection

The website of the online book retailer amazon is a best example to experience this effect. Once you sign-up with this site it presents you with a customized homepage. Based on the products you look at or buy on the site, amazon.com makes recommendations for other products that it thinks you may have interest. Amazon also facilitates customer interaction with its product by way of ratings, writing reviews, comments, etc.

2.1 Web 2.0 Tools

2.1.1 RSS

RSS (Really Simple Syndication) is a method for delivering regularly changing or updated Web content. Many blogs and Internet publishers syndicate their content as an RSS Feed to allow people to subscribe to it easily. The RSS feed includes full or summarized text along with metadata related to authorship, publishing date, etc.

2.1.2 Tagging

A tag is a descriptive word or a phrase assigned to a digital document such as web page, blog post, digital image, etc. either by its creator or its user. Tags most probably describes the general content or special qualities of the digital object.

2.1.3 Social Bookmarking

In the web environment, bookmark refers to a locally stored Uniform Resource Identifier (URI). Almost all web browsers provide bookmarking facility. Social bookmarking is a method for Internet users to organize, store, manage, share and search for bookmarks of resources online. Instead of saving the bookmarks in the local browsers, they are saved in the web. Social bookmarking sites provide facilities to access a consolidated set of bookmarks from various computers, organize large numbers of bookmarks, and share bookmarks with contacts.

2.1.4 Social Networking

Social networking facilitates a meeting place for people of likelihood to share content, experience, ideas, etc. Websites like Facebook, Orkut, Linkedin, Twitter, Myspace, etc. are the popular social networking sites used by Indians. There are specialised social networking sites for academics (such as ResearcherId, Scispace, etc.) that enable discussion of research findings, identifiying research partners, etc.

2.1.5 Podcasting

A podcast is a series of digital media files (either audio or video) that are released episodically. They can be downloaded through web syndication. Podcast can be viewed via a computer or a portable device. Within academic publishing, podcasts are becoming increasingly common adjunct to online journals.

2.1.6 Blogging

Blogs/weblogs are personal websites usually maintained by individuals or institutions. Blog consists of a series of entries or posts that can be viewed by others. Most blogs are interactive, allowing visitors to leave comments. Blog posts can be text, images, video or audio content, etc.

2.1.7 Wikis

Wiki is a website that allows many people to contribute to the content by adding and editing. Academic community use wiki for sharing and dissemination of information across institutional and international boundaries.

2.1.8 Multimedia Sharing

Multimedia sharing is another web 2.0 application. Sites like Flickr, YouTube, etc. provide facilities to post and share images and video respectively.

3. Changing Scenario of Scholarly Communication

Scholarly communication is a constitutive of researcher's everyday activities. It is primarily concerned with the publication of peer-reviewed research. In a broader sense, scholarly communication involves both formal and non-formal means of communication for the purpose of conducting research, developing ideas, preparing the formal research output and communicating the scholarly ideas to broader communities.

Association of College and Research Libraries[4] defines scholarly communication as "the system through which research and other scholarly writings are created, evaluated for quality, disseminates to the scholarly community and preserved for future use. The system includes both formal means of communication such as publication in peer reviewed journals and informal channel such as list serves."

Print journals remained as the prime medium of scholarly communication till the emergence of the World Wide Web. Growth of the cyber infrastructure resulted in the transition from print to electronic publishing. Now web based e-journals dominate the role, as scholarly communities increasingly publish their research findings in subject-specific and web-based archives for wider and faster dissemination.

Innovations in digital library technology led to the development of digital/institutional repositories that help to store, manage and reuse digital materials. Academics are the prime harnessers of this technology. By way of adding, or self-archiving, items that they have authored into the repository, instant access to their work is being provided to wider communities. As its name implies institutional repositories (IR) manage the content developed within the institution. The main purpose of IR is to preserve and disseminate scholarly communication, rather than publication. A full-blown institutional repository will contain the intellectual works of faculty and students—both research and teaching materials—and also documentation of the activities of the institution itself in the form of records of events and performances and of the ongoing intellectual life of the institution. It will also house experimental and observational data captured by the members of the institution that support their scholarly activities.

The emergence of open access movement and the Open Archive Initiative (OAI) further enhanced the speed of scholarly communication. Problem of costs and license restrictions in subscribing e-journals have overcome by open access movement. Open access facilitated free availability of literature on public domain permitting any user to read, download, copy, distribute print, search or link to full text of these articles. Most of the IR are now in the public domain. The availability of high quality peer-reviewed research and other scholarly documents in the public domain have accelerated the speed of research and development activities all around the world.

With the popularity of web 2.0 tools, schoarly communications have attained greater speed and dissemination and sharing of scholarly literature has become much easier. Personal blogs are now a richer source of scholarly literature. Many of the commerical journal publishing sites are now using web 2.0 tools to enable its users to share many of its content. Many studies have revealed that conducting research in comprehensive digital environments that are interactive and that have high levels of computational, storage and data transfer, resulted in better scholarly communication which in turn positively influence and enhance the quality of scholarly productivity.

4. Role of University Libraries

Universities being the prime centers of research activities and robust generators of scholarly communication, an organized procedure is required in these institutions to identify, store and preserve their research output. University libraries are vested with this responsibility of managing the scholarly content. Librarians over the time have employed, evaluated and researched better means of preserving and managing the scholarly communication and scholarly content. Library professionals always try to be in tune with the technological developments and are ready to harness them in order to provide better and faster services to its clientele.

In the changed scenario of web technology and scholarly communications, university libraries manage the research output, organizational knowledge and information resources that support R&D activities by way of the following means.

4.1 Library Websites/Homepages

Website is the public face of an institution through which it communicates. Like-wise, homepages of the library websites are the junctions through which university libraries impart a good percentage of its services to its users. Incorporating web 2.0 tools in its homepage, a university library can enhance the speed of access and usability of its products and services. RSS feeds are the most widely used web 2.0 tool in the library websites by which the subscribers are notified of the latest additions to the websites. Many university libraries syndicate their users about the new additions, new services and products, etc.

4.2 Library Blogs

Library blogs provide space for interaction by the users. Many academic libraries maintain library blogs (The Duke University Libraries maintain library blogs for different categories like 'Data & GIS', 'Scholarly communications @ Duke', etc.[5]). Library blogs act as an effective means of collecting user suggestions and feedbacks. It helps the libraries to self-evaluate its services and products. Libraries can maintain multiple blogs for different purposes. Developing and maintaining a separate blog for scholarly communication may receive a warm acceptance from the academics. Other web 2.0 tools like Facebook, Twitter, Flickr, Youtube, etc. can be incorporated in the blog.

4.3 Institutional Repositories

Institutional repositories are an important source of scholarly literature. Open access initiative and institutional repositories have changed the way academics get access to scholarly literature. Institutional repositories play a greater role in resource mobilization within and outside the universities.[6] Many IRs of universities and other research centers around the globe incorporate web 2.0 tools in their homepages to further enhance this process. IRs promote self-archiving of scholarly literature and web 2.0 environment facilitates the users to add comment and review the content thereby the scholars can evaluate their work and understand what others think about it. This is beneficial in the sense that the scholars will become more conscious about the quality of their work.

5. Conclusion

Many studies revealed that web 2.0 has beneficially changed the practice of scholarly communication. University libraries being the channels and managers of scholarly literature, cannot keep its face away from such changes in the web environment. Incorporating web 2.0 tools with its various online services, the university academia can receive better, timely and interactive environment for scholarly communication. Web 2.0 also promotes collaborative research, which in turn is an unavoidable academic activity in universities. To make this effectively and efficiently, policies with vision are to be framed by the universities.

NOTES

1. http://en.wikipedia.org/wiki/Web2.0 (Retrieved on March 16, 2011).
2. Anderson, P. (2007). What is Web 2.0? Ideas, technologies and implications for education (Retrieved March 16, 2011 from http://www.jisc.ac.uk/media/documents/techwatch/tsw0701b.pdf).
3. Theimer, Kate (2010). Web 2.0 tools and strategies for archives and local history collections. London: Facet Publishing.
4. Association of College and Research Libraries (2004). Principles and strategies for the reform of scholarly communication (Retrieved

March 18, 2011 from http://www.ala.org/ala/mgrps/divs/acrl/publications/whitepapers/principlesstrategies.cfm).

5. http://blogs.library.duke.edu/scholcomm/ (Retrieved on March 24, 2011).
6. Beena, C. and Padmakumar, P.K. (2010). Role of IR in information resource mobilization and management in the current scenario of higher education: A case study of Cochin University of Science & Technology (CUSAT) (Retrieved 20 March, 2011 http://shodhganga.inflibnet.ac.in/dxml/bitstream/handle/1944/988/48.pdf).

Trends in Social Networking Services

7

Rekha Rani Varghese

1. Introduction

Internet has become the most significant technological development of the 20th century. Web 2.0 has enabled a read/write web for the masses, and the smarter connective technologies accelerated the velocity of ideas. It has allowed people to easily make connections and provided a self-service web. Social networking services (SNSs) are one successful example of web 2.0 applications. Social networking sites are growing fast in the Internet. SNSs provide an on-line private space for individuals and tools for interacting with other people in the Internet. SNSs help people to find others of a common interest, establish a forum for discussion, exchange photos and personal news, and many more.[1] Web 3.0, the evolving development of the World Wide Web has reformed the social networking services. The semantic Web in which the meaning (semantics) of information and services on the web is defined, making it possible for the web to understand and satisfy the requests of people and machines to use the web content. Web 3.0 and mobile 2.0 technologies enabled the users to design and create a digital community quickly and cheaply.

2. Social Networking

Social networking is the grouping of individuals into specific groups, like small rural communities or a neighbourhood subdivision. Although social networking is possible in person, especially in the workplace, universities, and high schools, it is most popular online. This is because unlike most high schools, colleges, or workplaces, the Internet is filled with millions of individuals who are looking to meet other people, to gather and share first-hand information and experiences about cooking, golfing, gardening, developing friendships or professional alliances, finding employment, and business-to-business marketing.[2] The topics and interests are as varied and rich as the story of the world. When it comes to online social networking, websites are commonly used. These websites are known as social sites. Social networking websites function like an online community of Internet users.

"On the Internet, social networking is the process and practice of individuals, businesses and other types of organizations to interact with each other through common websites and specialized areas within those websites for the purpose of sharing, gaining, propagating and discussing all manner of information."[3] The first significant Social Network online was AOL which offered countless chat rooms, discussion groups, news groups etc. whereby individuals shared common space and common interests to share or promote ideas, experiences, insights as well as simply to talk and connect with others, if for no other reason to make a new friend or just have someone to talk with.

2.1 Social Networking Sites

Social networking is a quite new Internet invention that brings every kind of social group together in one place and lets them interact with each other. It is all about communication. People with common interests are able to share information with each other via a huge variety of social networking sites, sites created specifically to make sharing, communicating, and creating information as simple and efficient as possible. As per the surveys available on the Internet, Facebook is the most used social networking site with more than 500 million users.The top ten social networking sites are given in the Table 7.1.[4] Rank list of social networking sites shows that most of the top sites are from USA.

Table 7.1: Top Ten Social Networking Sites

Rank	Website	URL	Country	Starting Year
1.	Facebook	www.facebook.com	USA	2004
2.	Twitter	www.twitter.com	USA	2006
3.	LinkedIn	www.linkedin.com	USA	2003
4.	MySpace	www.myspace.com	USA	2003
5.	Digg	www.digg.com	USA	2004
6.	Orkut	www.orkut.com	USA	2004
7.	hi5	www.hi5.com	USA	2003
8.	Badoo	www.badoo.com	London	2006
9.	Stumbleupon	www.stumbleupon.com	Canada	2001
10.	Netlog	www.netlog.com	Belgium	2003

Social networking is no longer a notion on the web, it has found its big share and consign in our day today lives too. A huge number of social networking sites are available now for shopping, chatting, books, etc. The social networking sites related to books are given in Table 7.2.[5]

Table 7.2: Books Related Social Networking Sites

Social Networking Site	Type	URL
Book Rabbit	Sharing and discovering new books	http://www.bookrabbit.com
Booktribes	Discover great new books	http://www.booktribes.com
LibraryThing	Devoted to books	http://www.librarything.com
Reader2	To tag books with a keyword and categorize them any way you want.	http://reader2.com
Shelfari	Global community of book lovers	http://www.shelfari.com
Ravish	Book reviewing social network	http://www.revish.com
Goodreads	Library cataloging, book lovers	www.goodreads.com
Wattpad	For readers and authors to interact & e-book sharing	http://www.wattpad.com
weRead	Books	http://weRead.com

2.2 Benefits of Social Networking

Social networking is a recent invention and "communication with others" is one of the main goals of social networking.

Social networking is a way for one person to meet up with other people on the Net. It offers numerous benefits that could help to grow, personally as well as professionally. The main advantages of social networking include talking to others, building relationships and finding people who are similar to us. The benefits of social networking are as follows[6]:

- Keeping in Touch: Provides a great way for you to stay in touch with people who may have moved away.
- Meet new people: Social networking sites are the perfect spot to meet new people online.
- Get Feedback: A great way to get feedback on ideas immediately, or to ask questions and get answers quickly.
- Share Multiple Points of View: Helps to learn about diversity and get exposure to multiple points of view.
- Business Promotion: Social networks like Facebook and MySpace are being increasingly used for promoting every type of business from a small one-person business to mega corporations.
- Job seeking: Useful for those who are seeking legitimate work at home jobs.
- Increases Visibility: Social profiles and contents will increase visibility.
- Refined Search: Social networking sites offer Internet users with a search directory that can be used to locate particular individuals or groups.
- Low costs: It is free to use social networking sites for personal and business use.

2.3 Social Networking Software

Social networking websites have drawn the interest of people from all over the world—the current trend is to start a social networking site for gaining popularity and not just for earning money. A number of open source Social Networking Software are available now. Some of the free downloadable Open Source Social Networking Software are:

(a) Socialengine

(b) BOONEX
(c) AROUNDME
(d) PHPsocial
(e) SocialCMS
(f) Appleseed
(g) Box Social
(h) myMates

Commercial social networking software like Kootali, iFdate, iSocial, scritter, etc. are also available nowadays.

3. Future

One form of social networking that is growing in popularity is mobile social networking. Web 3.0, the new generation of the World Wide Web has introduced the semantic social networking. All these new technologies provide a great way to stay in touch with people who may have moved away.

3.1 Mobile Social Networking

The popularity of smart phones and powerful mobile applications open the era of the Mobile 2.0. Mobile social networking is a small part of the way people use their cell phones, but industry officials expect that use will grow, and not just for teenagers who want to text their friends or send short video clips. Mobile social networking makes sense because mobile devices are personal and they are taken everywhere, offering the potential for transmission of quick ideas or images. Mobile social networks will (and some already do) put video, GPS, text, voice and collaboration into the palm of a user's hand.

3.1.1 MoSoSo (Mobile Social Software)

MoSoSo is software designed for mobile devices that facilitates mobile social networking among interconnected mobile users. The basic idea of a MoSoSo is to overlay a location and time element to the idea of digital networking. It enables users to find one another, in a particular vicinity and time, for social or business networking.[7] Dan Malinger of Socialight defined MoSoSo as "social software designed for use while mobile. This includes software that augments human social or collaborative abilities by supporting group communication." MoSoSo helps users to find old friends or potential new ones. There are three types of MoSoSo. They are[8]:

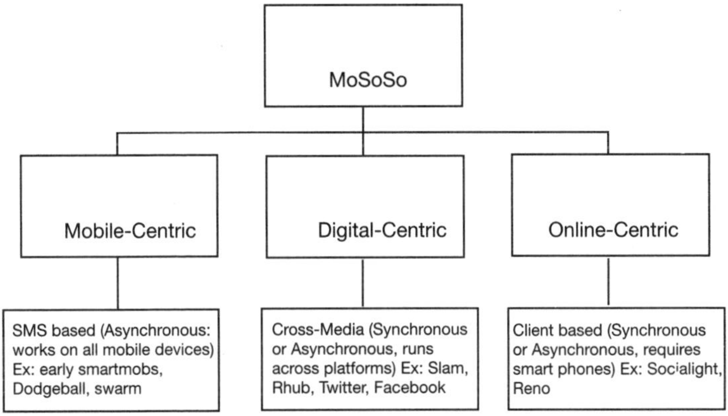

Fig. 7.1: Mobile Social Software

Mobile Social Software are used to find friends (eg: dodgeball, nokia sensor); to access online social networks (eg: facebook) and to access multiple social networks at once (eg: Funnelry). MoSoSo is connected to the wider trend of digital convergence, which encompasses technological, economic, cultural and social meanings.

3.2 Semantic Social Networking

Web 3.0 is the new generation of the World Wide Web, through which Web 2.0 technology joins hands with the Semantic Web, making it possible for humans as well as machines to access and use the information stored in the Web. Basically web 2.0 is a social change. The technical part of the web has not changed very much. But web 3.0 will be driven by technological changes. Web 3.0, the semantic web is about the meaning of the data. Semantics is the branch of linguistics that deals with the study of meaning, changes in meaning, and the principles that govern the relationship between sentences or words and their meanings or the study of the relationships between signs and symbols and what they represent. Semantic web frameworks provide a graph model (RDF), a query language (SPARQL) and schema definition frameworks (RDFS and OWL) to represent and exchange knowledge online.[9] These frameworks provide a whole new way of capturing social networks in much richer structures than raw graphs.

3.2.1 FOAF (Friend of a Friend)

A popular application of the semantic web is Friend of a Friend (FoaF), which uses RDF (Resource Description Framework) to describe the relationships people have to other people and the things around them. FOAF permits intelligent agents to make sense of the thousands of connections people have with each other, their jobs and the items important to their lives; connections that may or may not be enumerated in searches using traditional web search engines. Because the connections are so vast in number, human interpretation of the information may not be the best way of analyzing them.[10] FOAF is an example of how the Semantic Web attempts to make use of the relationships within a social context.

4. Conclusion

Web 2.0 has been about creation, sharing and use of user generated content mostly for information and entertainment purposes. The recent trend is about co-creation, provision and consumption of community generated services (CGS) satisfying basic needs in a cost efficient, transparent and environment friendly way. The main purpose of all recent technologies in social networking is to support interaction among interconnected individuals.

NOTES

1. Ahn, Yong-Yeol et al. (2007). Analysis of topological characteristics of huge online social networking services. WWW '07: Proceedings of the 16th international conference on World Wide Web. New York, USA. pp. 835-44.
2. Boyd, D.M., and Ellison, N.B. (2007). Social network sites: Definition, history, and scholarship. *Journal of Computer-Mediated Communication*, 13(1) (Retrieved January 6, 2011, from http://jcmc.indiana.edu/vol13/issue1/boyd.ellison.html).
3. http://www.whatissocialnetworking.com (Retrieved on 5th January, 2011).

4. http://orangecopper.com/blog/list-of-the-best-social-networking-websites-2011 (Retrieved on 5th January, 2011).
5. http://en.wikipedia.org/wiki/List_of_social_networking_websites. (Retrieved on 5th January, 2011).
6. What Are the Advantages of Social Networking? http://www.life123.com/parenting/tweens-teens/social-networking/advantages-of-social-networking.shtml (Retrieved on 5th January, 2011).
7. http://en.wikipedia.org/wiki/MoSoSo (Retrieved on 5th January, 2011).
8. Lugano, Giuseppe (2010). Mobile Social Software. (Retrieved January 6, 2011, from http://www.slideshare.net/gilugano/mobile-social-software-historical-roots-state-of-the-art-and-future-prospects).
9. http://www.articlesbase.com/internet-articles/an-introduction-to-web-30-629715.html (Retrieved on 6th January, 2011).
10. http://www.psfk.com/2008/04/10-social-networking-trends.html (Retrieved on 7th January, 2011).

Research 2.0: Prognosis of Web as a Research Platform

8

Sabitri Majhi and *Bulu Maharana*

1. Introduction

Social software tools were built on principles of participation, collaboration, and sharing. In recent times, with the advent of the Web 2.0, researchers have access to user-friendly tools that can create virtual spaces to interact, collaborate, and disseminate research findings in a most effective and efficient manner. Web 2.0 is regarded as a movement from a passive information dissemination platform (Web 1.0) to a web that is more interactive, customizable, social, and media-intensive. The basic philosophy of the new Web environment is to provide a platform in which content is created, shared, remixed, repurposed, and transmitted. It has been built upon the concept of "the wisdom of crowds", "the long tail theory" and allows people to connect with each other to boost their knowledge and their ability to learn. In the research arena, it allows researchers to connect with each other around common research ideas and collaborate using a host of new tools such as, wiki, blogs, social networking sites, survey tools, etc. Web 2.0 tools have a wider research application in almost all the areas of research including, identification of the research problem, discussion with the peers, collection of data, review of research literature, dissemination of the research results, etc. The interactive nature of Web 2.0 allows subjects to have a more active role in research.

2. Web 2.0 and Research 2.0

The development of the term 'Web 2.0' in 2004 is usually credited to O'Reilly Media Inc., the American media company.

The term has come to be associated with 'social software' and user generated content, which share some of the features identified by O'Reilly, such as participation, the user as contributor, harnessing the power of the crowd, and rich user experiences.[1]

As a research tool, the new technology has a great potential which is yet to be fully explored. Research 2.0 is a concept that embraces research practices and methodologies that are able to complement, support and, even, enhance traditional research activities and methodologies that have arisen from the creative and increasing use and access to current and emergent tools, applications and services that are utilising the so-called "Web 2.0" technologies.

Furthermore, Research 2.0 looks to explore and exploit these technologies to facilitate all phases of the research process. It is concerned with technologies that are able to support all of the processes involved in research including (but not limited to) creating and sustaining research collaborations and discovering, analysing, processing, publishing, storing and sharing research data and information.

3. The Beliefs of Research 2.0

Pareto's 80/20 Rule alternatively known as the theory of *Vital few and trivial many*, has now been replaced by the Long tail theory which focuses on each individuals who are insignificant but when aggregated as a significant contributor to the integrated whole. The research process is collaborative and participative in nature. Needham[2] explored the potential of web 2.0 for market research as, "the opportunity is that now we have a large amount of natural information about consumers' habits, tastes, opinions, lifestyles and attitudes available online and for free". The social data gathered through the social computing tools is used to identify (who you are), contacts (who you know) and activities (what you do). Personal profiles on sites such as MySpace, Bebo, Facebook allow marketers access to preferences, allegiances, recommendations and conversations they could not have dreamt of without these tools. The basic tasks of the Web 2.0 tools for which they are thought to be important by the researchers include[3]:

- Collaboration: finding colleagues and peers to work with.
- Advertising or Promoting: a way of showing what a researcher can do.
- Dissemination: either of information or 'products', where products could be 'papers' or 'software'.
- Networking/Community Building: all online communities require you to have an online 'persona'.
- Contact: a way of people finding you, perhaps after seeing a presentation or reading a paper–often they will 'Google you'.
- Saving time: having an online presence is something you can send people to if they want to know more about your work, etc., rather than you writing individual e-mails.
- The Web is an established medium: "if you're not on the web, you don't exist".

4. Traditional (Research 1.0) vs. Research 2.0

The emergence of Research 2.0 has brought about substantial changes in the way the research is carried out. Research in the new web environment is more interactive, dynamic, participative, and collaborative than ever before. The advantages of Research 2.0 over the traditional research can be summarized Rathi and Given[4] as follows:

4.1 User-generated Live Data (Data 2.0)

In any research, there is nothing more vital than the data itself. Traditionally, passive data were collected from designated information sources and thus has a lot of limitations as regards to their validity. However, in Research 2.0 environment, this concept might best be referred to as 'Data 2.0', where a specialized database that stores Web 2.0 data (e.g., blog data, temporal data of wikis, social tagging data, etc.) would be primary data sources, created especially for research purposes, only in a web environment. This data could be used by researchers at anytime; and, the data would continually regenerate as the website, itself, is used by individuals visiting the sites.

4.2 Free from Spatial and Social Barriers

Research 2.0 has been able to remove the spatial and societal barriers in research. Researchers are now able to involve participants who are not only geographically dispersed but also socially separated from each other. Although some researchers travel great distances in traditional projects, to conduct research in other countries or to gather data from multiple jurisdictions, the Web 2.0 environment can facilitate a broader international reach at much less cost. The archived data from sources such as blogs and YouTube could support the examination and analysis of the emergence of new social practices and cultures over time.

4.3 Perpetual Data

Research 2.0 involves the notion of Perpetual Data, a never-ending stream of data gathered throughout the research cycle. In any research, data collection is quite discrete in nature, beginning and ending with the posting of a questionnaire or responses to the interview participants. However, in a Research 2.0 environment, where individuals are involved in the design and execution of the project, data gathering is continuous in nature. For example, it is estimated that every minute, ten hours of video clips are uploaded on YouTube[5] and thus would be a valuable resource for data gathering and analysis of video data. Further, RSS tools could also be widely used to monitor the real-time updates of the content added by users.

5. Useful Applications for Research

Web 2.0 has myriad resources to discover, search, store, and collaborate on the Internet. But it is vital to find out how many of these new-technology applications are truly useful. Undoubtedly, the social networking technologies are personally rewarding. However, the usefulness of any of the social bookmarks, wikis, mashups, and other Web tools to conduct and organize research is a worthy question. Furthermore, it is important to examine whether any of the new applications contribute to better research results. Fortunately, there are many Web 2.0 tools currently available that are useful in many ways. Research 2.0 could, for instance, manifest itself in the following ways as shown in the Table 8.1.

Table 8.1: Research Manifestations of Web 2.0

Research Manifestations	Web 2.0 Tools
Disseminating and encouraging peer review of research project	blog or podcasts
Collaborating in the production and/or collation of research articles and papers	Wiki
Sharing and commenting upon photographic artefacts	Flickr
Sharing and commenting upon video artefacts	YouTube
Distribution and retrieval of web-based surveys	SurveyMonkey, Google Doc
Open ended or structured text-based interviews conducted via e-mail or computer-mediated conferencing.	Google, Yahoo!
Net-based telephone interviews	Skype
Sharing bibliographical references	Connotea
Managing and sharing research project activities	BaseCamp
Gathering up-to-the-minute information about research interests	RSS feeds
Socially network with colleagues, students and research partners	Ning
Analysis of web-logs and other tracking tools for measurement and synthesis of online activities	Sawmill
Analysis of social behaviour in virtual reality environments	SecondLife
Managing references	Endnote
Literature review	CiteULike

6. Popular Web 2.0 Tools for Research

There are millions of Web 2.0 tools found on the Internet with varieties of applications especially for social networking, bookmarking, tagging, sharing of content online, etc. A good number of such tools with high degrees of research implications as reported in relevant literature are as follows:

6.1 Blogs

Blog refers to a simple webpage consisting of brief paragraphs of opinion, information, personal diary entries, or links, called posts, arranged chronologically with the most recent first, in the style of an online journal.[6] Blogs now provide one of the most important sources of up-to-date information on the Internet as without technical barriers or editorial processes information is made instantly available as bloggers post new entries to their blogs. It is having a large range of potential use in research. The implication of blog in research can be enumerated as follows:

- Creation of research projects
- Using user-created web content as sources of data
- Inviting researchers to discuss issues
- The crowdsourcing experience
- Using syndication technologies to easily keep track of new posts.
- Using FAQ comments

6.2 Wiki

Wiki is a collection of web pages designed to enable anyone who accesses it to contribute or modify content, using a simplified markup language. Wikis are often used to create collaborative websites and to power community websites."[7] A great example of a large Wiki is the Wikipedia, a free encyclopedia in many languages that anyone can edit. Wiki could be used as an interesting tool for research in the following way:

- Fostering appropriate engagement between researchers and participants.
- Creating a FAQ about the research plan and methodology.
- Allowing community members (i.e., researchers and participants) to edit and add new content.

6.3 Social Bookmarking

Bookmarking enables web users to store interesting web pages, offline, on their computer, so they can easily retrieve these pages at a later stage. But social bookmarking is the practice of saving bookmarks to a public website and tagging them with keywords, thereby making them accessible from anywhere, to anyone. The key implications of social bookmarking tools for research can be summarized as follows:

- Sharing personally classified bookmarks and collaborative filtering of digital content.

- Accessing the pre-selected and tagged list of resource in the same area of interest.
- Finding out the popularity of websites by counting the number of tags for a particular resource.
- Finding out the people, doing research in the same area by visiting their tagged resources in the Web.

Citeulike (http://www.citeulike.org)

Citeulike is a Web-based tool to help scientists, researchers and academics store, organise, share and discover links to academic research papers. It has been available as a free Web service since November 2004 and like many successful software tools, it was written to solve a problem the authors were experiencing themselves. It is highly helpful for academic activities due to its following features:

- Easily store references found online
- Discover new articles and resources
- Automated article recommendations
- Share references with peers
- Find out who's reading

Connotea (http://www.connotea.org/)

Connotea is a free online reference management service for scientists, researchers, and clinicians, created in December 2004 by Nature Publishing Group. It is one of a new breed of social bookmarking tools, similar to CiteULike and delicious, where users can save links to their favourite websites. It recognizes a number of scientific websites and automatically collect metadata for the article or page being bookmarked. It also quickly retrieves the reference for a print article that has an electronic counterpart with a DOI.[8]

2collab (http://www.2collab.com/)

2collab is an Elsevier online collaborative research tool that enables researchers to share bookmarks, references or any linked materials with their peers and colleagues. Users can share, collaborate and discuss resources either in private groups or openly with the wider scientific community. Through the integration of 2collab into other scientific platforms such as Science Direct and Scopus a lot of researchers are enabled to transport not only the bookmark but also the bibliographic data of research papers into their accounts.

6.4 RSS Feeds

RSS (Really Simple Syndication) is a technology which has brought about a significant advance in the fundamental architecture of the web.[9] RSS is an XML format which allows users to know about the content of RSS-enabled websites, blogs, or podcasts without necessarily visiting its actual site.[10] The information from the site is collected within a feed (which has RSS format) and "piped" to the user in a process known as syndication. Among the considerable number of service available on the Web, google reader is a popular example of this RSS feeds.

- RSS is a better solution than an e-mail list subscription.
- RSS feeds have also made it possible to keep a tab on the site for updated contents.

6.5 Research Mashup

A mashup is a Web page or application that uses and combines data, presentation or functionality from two or more sources to create new services (Wikipedia). The data collected from various sources such as blogs, wikis or forums can be mixed with other content to conduct research. In a Research 2.0 project, a researcher might 'mash' the following types of data: (a) using participants' location information with Google maps and analyzing their posted comments to look for the emergence of any regional phenomena; (b) using mobile location-based data and mixing with a map application programming interface to analyze participants' buying location and behaviour; (c) using RSS feeds to extract data from different sources (e.g., blogs of different social shopping websites) and mixing the contents (using, say, discourse analysis) to provide in-depth understanding of consumers' mindset and their behaviour on social shopping websites.

7. Conclusion

The review of the facts both in the literature and the practical implications of the online tools have proved the suitability of

Web 2.0 for research purposes. The modern educational and research practices are technology-centric which believes in increased levels of interaction, collaboration and participation. However, there is a common feeling that the application of Web 2.0 technology has not reached a breakthrough yet, owing to lack of awareness of these technologies and absence of competence in handling them. The velocity of Internet innovations makes its difficult to keep up to speed as a research community with developments in this field. There was also a feeling that there was a generation gap between 'native' users of Web 2.0 and the researchers. As younger people, the so-called Y generation, enter the research community, the problem may be combated in future.

NOTES

1. Anderson, P. (2007). 'What is Web 2.0? Ideas, technologies and implications for education', JISC Technology and Standards Watch, Feb 2007 (Retrieved February 15, 2011, from http://www.jisc.org.uk/publications/publications/twweb2.aspx).
2. Needham, Andrew (2009). Web 2.0 and social media create new opportunities for research. Admap. Sep 2009 (Retrieved March 10, 2011, from http://ldn.co-creationhub.com/wp-content/uploads/2010/03/AdMap-Research-3.0-Sep-09.pdf).
3. JISC (2009). Research 2.0? risks and rewards of using emergent technologies (Retrieved March 10, 2011, from http://www.slideshare.net/Lawrie/research-20-398979).
4. Rathi, Dinesh and Given, Lisa M. (2010). Research 2.0: a framework for qualitative and quantitative research in Web 2.0 environments (Retrieved March 19, 2011, from http://www.computer.org/portal/web/csdl/doi/10.1109/HICSS.2010.317).
5. www.youtube.com/t/fact_sheet (Retrieved on 19th March, 2011).
6. Doctorow, C. et al. (2002). Essential Blogging. USA: O'Reilly.
7. http://www.wikipedia.org (Retrieved on 19th March, 2011).
8. http://en.wikipedia.org/wiki/Connotea (Retrieved on 19th March, 2011).
9. O'Reilly, Tim (2005). What Is Web 2.0: Design Patterns and Business Models for the Next Generation of Software. (Retrieved March 13, 2011, from http://oreilly.com/web2/archive/what-is-web-20.html).
10. Anderson, P. (2007). 'What is Web 2.0? ideas, technologies and implications for education', JISC Technology and Standards Watch, Feb. 2007 (Retrieved February 15 2011, from http://www.jisc.org.uk/publications/publications/twweb2.aspx).

PART III

LIBRARY PROFESSIONALS AND PROFESSIONAL ASSOCIATIONS

E-Publishing in Academia: Opportunities and Challenges for Library Professionals

9

K. Mohamed Musthafa and *P.M. Naushad Ali*

1. Introduction

The developments of computers and communication technologies, especially in 1990s popularized the new modes and methods of scholarly publishing. The high capacity digital storage devices like compact discs and other movable devices along with Internet and WWW opened the doors to a new era of electronic publishing. Publication really took off, however, following the WWW software by Tim-Berners Lee in 1991 and the invention of the Mosaic Web-browser in 1993. The impact of these developments was immediate; traffic on the Internet expanded at an annual growth rate of 341,634 per cent. Thus the fast growing media has become a reality and provided many opportunities to the Library and Information Science professionals in collection and dissemination of information.

2. E-Publishing: What and Why

Lancaster[1] defines Electronic publishing as a "publication process where the manuscripts are submitted in electronic format, edited, printed, and even distributed to readers (users) in electronic form by employing computer and telecommunication technology".

According to *Encarta Online Dictionary*[2] it is the 'publishing on computer network or disk: the production of documents in computer-readable form for distribution over a computer network or in other formats such as CD-ROMs.

Unsworth[3] opined that 'electronic publishing refers to the dissemination of information, whether text-only or multimedia, via the internet or through some hybrid or local media and networked archives. Networked electronic publishing can be the basis for producing these other media, and indeed for producing print.'

One of the important problems faced by any library in the contemporary world is the 'serial crises'. A study conducted by Okerson[4] reveals that America's 3,500 academic libraries spend more than $1.25 billion a year on acquisitions out of which 58 per cent spent on serials. Contrary to this, they found, about 70 per cent of scientific journal articles are from universities. But universities are increasingly unable to 'buy back' their own work. It is not surprising that a vision of university based publishing captures the imagination of parts of academe. A marketing survey in 1990 determined that universities publish at most 15 per cent of their scholars' output. It is a stretchy 15 per cent including not only work of university presses, but also publications of individual academic departments, working papers and periodicals. About 90 per cent is produced by scholarly and scientific societies as opposed to the commercial sector but soft evidence suggests that since World War II, half or more of what used to be not for profit output is now commercially published. Universities could compete and influence price by retrieving control of a proportion of the academic literature and strengthen the arm of university publishing without through lack of interest, support, glamour or profitability. In the US in 1991, university based publishing is receiving significant attention as well as tremendous re-vitalization from the university linked networks.

A recent report issued by the Association of Research Libraries (ARL) concluded that 'publishing services are rapidly becoming a norm for research libraries, and that the question no longer whether libraries would offer publishing services, but what kinds of services libraries will offer'. In a survey of ARL libraries, 44 per cent of 80 responding libraries reported they were delivering publishing services, and another 21 per cent were planning to do so in the future.[5]

Now-a-days e-publishing has become an essential part and parcel of any academic libraries in some way or other. In India almost all major academic libraries have started publishing of their intellectual contribution through institutional repositories or open archives.

3. E-Publishing Models

Different types of models and methods are followed for electronic publishing. Some of them which are suitable and applicable in academic environments are discussed below:

3.1 E-Books

An e-Book is a written work readable on a computer screen, downloaded to a PC or digital assistant or placed on a reader designed for that purpose, i.e., professionally produced and edited text available in an e-format.[6]

3.2 E-Journals

The e-Journal is a version of the traditional print or paper-based journal which is disseminated electronically in some form or the other directly to the end-user. Although electronic journals have been in existence since 1976, full-fledged E-journals came into limelight only in the 1990s.[7]

3.3 Institutional Repositories

An institutional repository is an online locus for collecting and preserving in digital form the intellectual output of an institution, particularly a research institution. For a university this would include materials such as research journals articles, preprints and post-prints undergoing peer review, and digital versions of theses and dissertations.[8]

3.4 Blogs/Weblogs

The blog or weblog is web application that contains periodic, reverse chronologically ordered posts on common web pages. Scott[9] defines a blog as 'a page containing brief, chronologically arranged item of information. A blog can take the form of a diary, journal, what's new page or links to other websites.' Typically, Weblogs are published by individuals and their style is personal and informal. Weblogs first appeared in the mid-1990s, becoming popular as simple and free publishing tools became available towards the turn of the century.

3.5 E-Zins

E-zine means electronic magazine and it is also called web-zins. E-zines are the electronic version of print magazines which are published at a regular interval. The articles that are stored on a file server may be distributed or accessed via computer networks.

3.6 E-Newspaper

An eNewspaper is a self-contained, reusable, and refreshable version of a traditional newspaper that acquires and holds all information in the newspaper electronically.

3.7 Electronic Thesis and Dissertations (ETD)

An ETD is an electronic document that explains the intellectual works or research of a researcher. It is expressed in a form simultaneously suitable for machine archives and worldwide retrieval as well as similar to its paper predecessor, at the same time it provide a technologically advanced medium for expressing ideas with less expensive, small space, easy handling, high longevity and never collect dust.

3.8 Print-on-Demand (POD)

Print-on-Demand allows books to be, printed one at a time, or on demand. This method helps free publishers from the process of printing several thousand books at a time. The technology involves complex laser printing systems and electronically formatted text, which the printers can read.

3.9 Digital Content

Digital content generally refers to the electronic delivery of fiction, which is shorter than book-length, nonfiction, documents and other written works of shorter length. Publishers of the digital content deliver shorter sized works to the consumer via download to handheld and other wireless devices. Technology used for delivering digital content includes Adobe PDF, XML, HDML (Handheld Device Markup Language), WAP (Wireless Application Protocol) and other technologies.

3.10 Electronic Ink

Electronic Ink could be used to create a newspaper or book that updates itself. The technology could also be used on billboards, clothing, walls and homes to allow content to appear and this content could be programmed to change at any time.

3.11 E-Mail Publishing

E-Mail publishing or newsletter publishing, is a popular choice among readers who enjoy the ease of receiving news items, articles and short newsletters in their e-mail box. The ease of delivery and production of e-mail newsletters has led to the development of a massive number of available e-mail newsletters, mailing lists and discussion lists on a large variety of topics.

3.12 Web Publishing

Web publishing is one of the medium practices of information dissemination. Almost all the institutions, companies, business groups, organizations, NGOs, government agencies, departments have their own websites in one kind or other. HTML and XML are still the most widely used web programming languages. XML is valuable because it allows publishers to create content and data that is portable to other devices.

3.13 Wikis

Ward Cunningham, an Oregon-based software engineer, developed the first wiki software in 1995 to enable Portland Pattern Repository programmers to work together of software code and publish it quickly. The Wikis are websites where visitors can not only read content but also add their own content or edit the content added by others through a web browser. Interact with existing content and how the two spaces organize and present added information. While blog sites consist of chronologically ordered dialogues of written exchanges or 'posts' between the blog author and its visitors, Wiki sites are a collection of interlinked topical pages that any (if a restricted wiki, any authorized) visitor can quickly and easily create, expand, revise and link together.

3.14 Podcasts and Vodcasts

The term podcasts is coined by former MTV video jockey Adam Curry by taking the most popular portable audio device and melding it with broadcast. The Podcasts are simply audio files that are created usually on a schedule, and when a new podcast is created it is sent to your aggregator, just like a new issue of a magazine is sent to your home. You can listen to the podcast on your computer or take it with you on your portable audio device. Podcasts come in three flavors: audio, video and enhanced. Each has its own unique creation methodology. With the debut of the video iPod in 2005, vidcasts or VODcasts (video on demand) have become popular. Along with vidcasts, screencasts and enhanced podcasts provide visual information as well as aural. Vidcasts are created using a video camera (digital camera preferred). The screencasts differ from vidcasts in that they are partly or wholly a computer screen with audio commentary to describe the action on the computer screen with audio commentary to describe the action on the computer screen enhanced podcasts incorporate slides, PDFs, websites and images with audio. They use the AAC (Advanced Audio Coding) format with extra scripting to bring up the visual image or website.

4. E-Publishing in Academia: Opportunities

E-publishing promises many benefits and solutions for the problems faced by the p-publishing in academia. The examples of academic electronic publishing go back to 1970's.[10] However electronic journals did not proliferate until the 1990's when the widespread use of the World Wide Web made electronic publications relatively simple.[11] The academic journals are a unique genre in the world of publishing by their nature. The Internet and electronic publishing systems supported the academicians and researchers to communicate with others directly without much delay in publication and peer review processes. Due to the advantages of electronic publishing many journals from India started producing electronic versions. By 1999, *Current Science* from Indian Academy of Sciences, *Neurology India* from Neurological Society of India, *Indian Journal of Critical Care Medicine* form Indian Society of Critical Care Medicine and

Indian Pediatrics from Indian Academy of Pediatrics were online. The electronic versions provided full text of the articles in HTML and PDF format. The Calicut Medical College, one of the premier institutes leads medical researches in Kerala, India started scholarly e-publishing in 2001.[12]

- The Open Source Software available free of cost and downloadable from the Internet is an opportunity for the small and less budget libraries to depend upon for the e-publishing solutions. Many reputed journals are publishing online using open sources software like OJS (Open Journal System). The *DESIDOC Journal of Library & Information Technology* (DJLIT) and the *Journal of Tropical Agriculture* are using Open Journal System. Some of the open sources e-journal publishing tools are DPubs, GNU Eprint, Hyper Journal, and Open Journal System.
- As the library plays a central role in the academic system in information collection and dissemination, it is the most suitable place for working as publishing house of an institute where the information professionals can play as the publishers. The librarian can coordinate the entire process of electronic publishing of the scholarly contribution of the faculty and researchers of the academia through a networked environment.
- The Internet tools and services can be used for all the publishing activities from collecting the manuscripts of authors to peer review process to final publishing of a paper. It is easy in case of any of the e-publishing models like e-journals, e-book, ETDs, web publishing, e-mail publishing, institutional repositories or podcasting.
- The search engines make it possible to retrieve the appropriate article. The publishers can provide keyword and author search so that the librarian do not want to waste their time in additional indexing and abstracting. Electronic publications also provide hyperlink to cited related articles and other useful sources.

- In electronic publishing, the data can be maintained up-to-date and this enables 'on-demand publishing' and allows retrospective searching and SDI. The electronic version also provides Boolean search of the full text.
- The most important advantage of electronic publishing over print publishing is the turn-around time, i.e. the time lag in submission, processing and dissemination of information. Electronic publishing ensures timely publication, which is of utmost importance to the research community.
- The electronic publications can be disseminated worldwide without the need for separate rights negotiation for different countries and without the cost of distribution or reprinting where an electronic publication is charged for, the producer does not incur the costs associated with retail bookselling, that is there are no 'middleman' costs.
- As the role of librarians as the gatekeepers of externally-published information resources begins to shrink, their role as the guardians of internally-produced information resources has the potential to expand. Librarians are used to providing robust institution-wide services to a range of users. They have experience of working with people from different subject areas in order to support their activities and to deliver services to them. Librarians have a culture of customer service. They also have professional skills associated with the management and curation of information. Institutional repositories represent an opportunity to extend these skills into a new area on behalf of the institutions.[13]

5. Challenges for Library Professionals

- One of the biggest challenges is that the scholarly communication environment is still evolving. These services are still new and standard services models do not yet exist. Publishing services within academic libraries are even more embryonic. Not only are there no established service models, and widely differing administrative and organizational models, but most library-based publishing activity is taking place in 'a vacuum of community discussion'.

- While libraries are well suited to provide the hosting and dissemination aspects of publishing there are other areas of traditional publishing where they do not have real expertise or capacity, including peer-review, marketing, business models, printing and distribution. While there is clearly a role for libraries in scholarly publishing, the nature of the role is still not clearly defined.
- Understanding and articulating the implications of scholarly communication change is difficult when the system is still in flux and the full long-term implications are not clear. Not everyone needs to be a specialist and known all the nuances, but even staying up-to-date on general trends is challenging for staff who are already busy trying to simply keep up with their own daily responsibilities.[14]
- The electronic publishing not only represents an opportunity but also a challenge to the library profession. As well as seeing the electronic publishing as opportunities for exercising information management skills and vehicles for achieving contend dissemination, it is essential that e-publishers set up services that further the strategic objectives of their institution.
- The electronic publishing can be used to generate management intelligence for the institution and help to inform the development of research strategy. They can also be a vehicle for knowledge transfer and commercial liaison. The library has to ensure that its professionals are equipped to engage in the wide-ranging discussion associated with the general processes of the electronic publishing as well as in the specific area of electronic information management.

- One of the specific functions of electronic information management that will continue to be important is preservation. Apart from the technical challenges, no clear organizational workflow or funding models for digital preservation have yet emerged. The whole question of digital preservation needs to move from a largely theoretical or proof-of concept stage to a practical production level stage. The library professionals should be capable to address all the issues related to preservation.
- Particular areas of expertise, such as knowledge of intellectual property rights, will be essential here. Advising users on IPR in relation to their own content or that of others is required. This is especially important in complex areas where content can be easily made up of different components form different rights holders where different permissions are applicable; something which is becoming increasingly common.

6. Conclusion

The emergence of electronic publishing must change our fundamental approach to information. To change and broaden our professions gives clear and definite advantages. The first of these is that we can exercise much greater influence over development than we can from our present limited position. In the past the approach of most Librarians and information scientists to electronic products has been far too passive but recently there is a hopeful change. If broadening our profession will help us influence development, it should also help improve the status and rewards of our professions. It is long overdue that we recognized that both librarianship and information science are appallingly low-paid professions. The role of librarian as publisher is a need of the day and the modern technology positively support them to undertake the responsibility of this emerging task.

NOTES

1. Lancaster, F.W. (1995). The evolution of electronic publishing. *Library Trends,* 43 (4), 518-27.
2. http://uk.encarta.msn.com/encnet/features/dictionary/dictionaryResults.aspx?lextype=3&search=electronic%20publishing (Accessed on 13th November, 2009).
3. Unsworth, J. (1995). An electronic publishing FAQ (Retrieved, November 17, 2008, from http://knowledgeway.org/living/publishing/unsworth.html).
4. Okerson, A. (1991). Back to academia? The case for American universities to publish their own research. *LOGOS, 2* (2), 106-12.
5. Hahn, Karla L. (2010). Research library publishing services: New options for university publishing (Retrieved December 10, 2010, from http://www.arl.org/bm~doc/research-library-publishing-services.pdf).
6. Sahoo, K.C. (2004). *Information management with IT application.* Ludhiana, Medallian Press.
7. Hitchcock, S., Carr, Les ad H.W. (1996). A survey of STM online journals—1990-95: The calm before the storm. In D. Mogge (Ed), *Directory of Electronic Journals, Newsletters and Academic Discussion Lists*. Washington DC: Association of Research Libraries, 7-32.
8. Nazim, Mohammed and Maya Devi (2008). Open access journals and institutional repositories: Practical need and present trends in India. *Annals of Library and Information Studies, 55*(1), 27-34.
9. Scott, Peter. *Blogging and Libraries.* www.hiis/liblog wa.html (Accessed on 13th November, 2009).
10. Turoff M. and Hiltz, R. (1982). The electronic journal: A progress report. *Journal of the American Society for Information Science,* 33, 195-202.
11. Hovav, Anat. (2001). Managing academic electronic publishing: Six case studies. *Proceedings of the 9th European Conference of Information systems. Bled, Slovenia.* June 27-29, 2009.
12. Musthafa, M. and Ali, N. (2011). Electronic publishing at Calicut Medical College, Kerala: A case study of three open access journals. In K.K. Faruqi and M. Pathak (Eds.), *Managing libraries in new information environment.* New Delhi: Book Age, 280-91.
13. Pinfied, S. (1998). Libraries and open-access: The implications of open-access publishing and dissemination of libraries in higher

education institutions. In Rae Earnshaw and John Vince (Eds.), *Digital Convergence: Libraries of the future*. New York: Springer, 119-33.

14. Rosenblum, B. (2008). Developing new skills and expertise to support digital scholarship and scholarly communication. *Proceedings of the 74th IFLA General Conference and Council: World Library and Information Congress*, Quebec, Canada, August 2008 (Retrieved, March 23, 2010, from http://www.ifla.org/IV/ifla74/Programme2008.htm).

Use of Online Communication Tools by Librarians

10

L.S. Suguna and *A. Gopikuttan*

1. Introduction

With the advent of Internet, individual's expectations for access to information have increased significantly. It is no longer considered practical or acceptable to travel to a specific location during certain hours to locate needed information.[1] The growing impact of ICT (Information and Communication Technology) and Web Technology has compelled libraries to use the technologies effectively to provide service to users. It has become imperative for Library and Information Professionals to properly play their roles in disseminating information to their users. The Internet has made tremendous impact on the academic activities of the faculty, researchers and the students. A significant transition can be seen in the approach and the way the librarian seek information and the methods they employ for research and learning activities. This has become possible as the Internet provides a wealth of new course materials and acts as a powerful supplement to the traditional ways of teaching and learning.

The Internet is now facilitating online communication and exchange of ideas and collaboration in research globally. The Internet can be accessed for the latest developments in any area of research at an amazing speed.[2] Internet has also provided a number of services like e-mail, chat, blogs, RSS, wikis, social networking, etc. which can be effectively used for academic purposes. The academic community is more familiar with the above mentioned online communication technologies. Online communication services and web 2.0 technologies are increasingly becoming embedded in many areas of life as more people, from teenagers to national governments, recognise and harness these powerful communication tools.[3] Similarly, libraries and librarians all over the world are using online communication technologies to promote services, share information, engage with users and network with colleagues, on a global scale.

Because the nature of work has changed and people are working more remotely, the use of online communication tools is growing. Programs like Skype allow free online video conferencing, which many young people already use to communicate. Brief, synchronous online communication through instant messaging and Twitter, a micro blog application, allow real time conversations not bound by physical space or time limits. The value of these technologies goes well beyond social interaction. Online communication tools provide students with invaluable experience in remote collaboration that prepares them for future careers. Desktop video conferencing knocks down walls and brings subject experts and co-learners from all over the world into the room. And when a chat feature is inserted into library blog or website, suddenly the learning hours is extended beyond those of the traditional day.[4] There are a variety of tools that are used in an online setting to communicate and collaborate. Because many of these tools are used in real-time settings, rely on different media (visual, auditory, etc.) and can have complex interfaces.[5]

What are online communication tools and how the library professionals use them to enhance services to users? This study concentrates on the present level of knowledge about online communication technologies and their use by librarians.

2. Objectives

1. To study the use/dependency/impact of different types of online communication technologies by librarians.
2. To identify the different purposes for which online communication technologies are being used by the librarians.
3. To suggest some ways and means for improving their knowledge of online communication technology applications.

3. Methodology

This study attempts to examine the awareness and use of online communication technologies among the librarians. It is primarily a fact-finding venture. The survey method has been employed and in that questionnaire was used, supplemented with interview as well, to elicit data. A set of questions were formulated keeping in view, the need and objectives of the study. A total of 150 questionnaires were distributed among users and 121 duly filled in questionnaires were received, thus resulting into a response rate of 80.66 per cent.

4. Sampling

A sample of 150 members from various libraries is randomly selected for the study. While selecting samples a stratification method is applied with a view to give relative weightage to all categories. Thus, the sampling comes under stratified random sampling.

5. Data Analysis

The data collected has been subjected to analysis and interpretation. The collected data are tabulated according to the objectives stated. The sample of the respondents includes certificate holders, graduates, postgraduates, M.Phil. holders and Ph.D. holders in Library and Information Science. The analysed data was given under the following heads:

5.1 Rate of Response

The total sample is categorized into five groups on the basis of their professional qualifications. Out of the 121 respondents there are 10 Certificate holders, 20 B.L.I.Sc. holders, 54 M.L.I.Sc. holders, 25 M.Phil. holders and 12 Ph.D. holders (Fig. 10.1). This clearly shows that the majority of the librarians have Post Graduation in Library and Information Science.

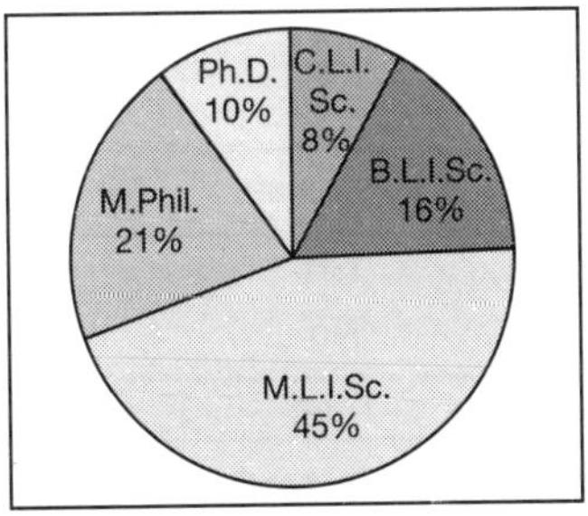

Fig. 10.1: Rate of Response

5.2 Awareness about Online Communication Technologies

Many of these tools are common today. Library profession gains momentum through these technologies. An examination of Table 10.1 reveals that, out of the total 121 respondents, 92.561 per cent of the librarians are aware of online communication technologies and 7.438 per cent of the librarians are not aware of online communication technologies. This shows that a majority of the librarians are aware of these technologies. Only a small number is not aware of these interacting facilities.

Table 10.1: Awareness about Online Communication Technologies

Response	No. of responses received	Percentage (%)
Yes	112	92.561%
No	9	7.438%
Total	121	100%

5.3 Use of Online Communication Technologies in Enhancing Interpersonal Cooperation in Research and Learning

As these tools are extremely easy, online communication technologies can be used for developing interpersonal cooperation among librarians. This is also helpful in research and learning. Table 10.2 shows librarians opinion about this. 90.082 per cent of the librarians are of the opinion that these technologies can enhance interpersonal cooperation in research and learning. It is a good sign that many professionals are making use of it. 9.917 per cent negatively responded to it. This result is presented in Table 10.2.

Table 10.2: Online Communication Technologies in Enhancing Interpersonal Cooperation in Research and Learning

Response	No. of responses received	Percentage (%)
Yes	109	90.082%
No	12	9.917%
Total	121	100%

5.4 Attitude towards Online Communication Technologies

A study of data in Table 10.3 indicates the interest of librarians in knowing online communication technologies. It is noted that out of the total 121 respondents 57.024 per cent of the librarians are interested in orientation or training programme in online communication technologies. 31.404 per cent librarians said that they like to hear more about online communication technologies. And 11.57 per cent are interested in online communication technologies. This shows that almost all the librarians like to get more information regarding online communication tools and how they could make of its services in the field of library and its activities. Orientation and training programmes will help in this regard.

Table 10.3: Attitude towards Online Communication Technologies

Statement	No.	Percentage
I'm interested in online communication technologies	14	11.57%
I would like to hear more about online communication technologies	38	31.404%
I am interested to attend an orientation program on online communication technologies	69	57.024%
Total	121	100%

5.5 Online Communication Technology Users

It is observed that out of the total 121 respondents; 86.78 per cent librarians tried at least one online communication tool. 10.743 per cent did not try any one. 2.479 per cent librarians did not respond to the question. This is represented in Table 10.4. Though most of the librarians are aware that online communication tools are useful in interpersonal cooperation, research and learning, some of them have not tried any of the tools yet.

Table 10.4: Online Communication Technology Users

Response	No. of responses received	Percentage (%)
Yes	105	86.78%
No	13	10.743%
No response	3	2.479%
Total	121	100%

5.6. Librarians' Initiation to Use Online Communication Technologies

The Internet services frequently used by librarians include E-mail, Chat, Conduct search, create own website, editing of pictures/videos, posting of comments, Maps, online registration, etc. One question was asked to know librarians use of different category of online communication technologies. Fig. 10.2 introduces a few of the most popular technologies used by librarians to communicate over the web. Out of the 121 respondents, 105 librarians tried e-mail. This reveals that e-mail has an important impact on the level of online communication. About 12.94 per cent tried social networking. 12.47 per cent tried wikis. 11.76 per cent used Internet forums, LIS-Forum, Knowledge Management Forum, bulletin boards, discussion groups, etc. Social viewing sites consisting of online videos, video conferences, video and audio sharing sites, Media sharing were used by 11.06 per cent. Instant Messaging and Chat service of Yahoo! Messenger, Face book, Google Talk, Windows Live Messenger, etc. were tried by 8.71 per cent librarians.

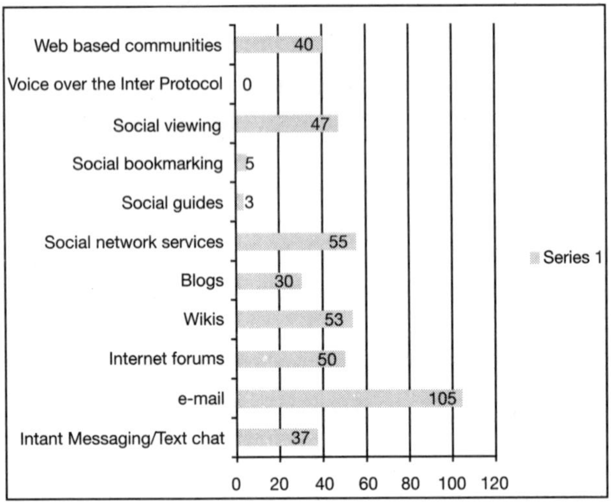

Fig. 10.2: Most Popular Online Communication Tools Used by Librarians

Social guides which contain information about places in the real world and social bookmarking are the least tried one. Voice over the Internet Protocol (VoIP) which is one of the newest communication tools that allows make telephone talk to others using the computer at low cost is found to be not used. Thus there is a significant level of difference exist between the use of various online communication tools.

5.7 Facilities of Online Communication Tools

Online communication technologies facilitate interactive information sharing, inter-operability, user centred design, collaboration, rich user experience, dynamic content, openness and user participation. Communication is for various purposes and by using various methods and media. 17.78 per cent of the librarians are of the opinion that online communication technologies facilitate real time communication. The summary of the result in Table 10.5 shows how the librarians make use of online communication technologies.

Table 10.5: Facilities of Online Communication Technologies

Category	*No.*	*Percentage*
Interactive Information Sharing	71	15.78%
Inter Operability	16	3.55%
User centred design	27	6.00%
Collaboration	30	6.67%
Rich user experience	40	8.89%
user-generated content	77	17.11%
Openness	26	5.78%
User participation	34	7.55%
Real time communication	80	17.78%
Enrich discussions	49	10.89%

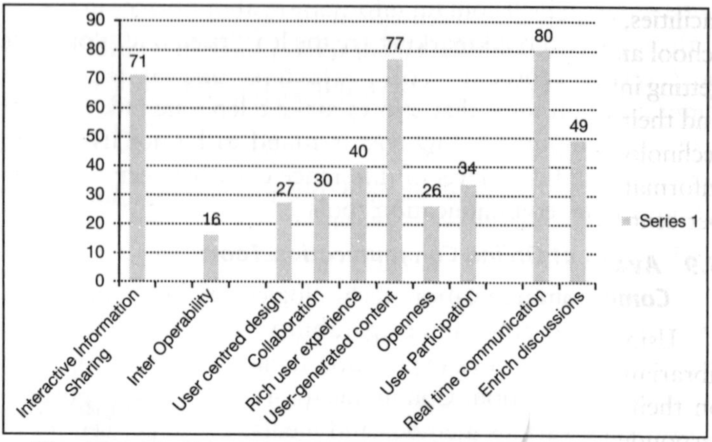

Fig. 10.3: Facilities of Online Communication Technologies

5.8 Purpose of Using Online Communication Tools

It is important to know how well these tools are made use of by LIS professionals to better serve the community. It is found that librarians mainly use online communication tools to collect information on various fields ranging from book selection to providing online services to users. Integrating the use of these technologies into libraries has become a subject of interest among library professionals and policy-makers. Out of the 121 respondents 99 librarians use online communication technologies to collect general information. The General area includes library

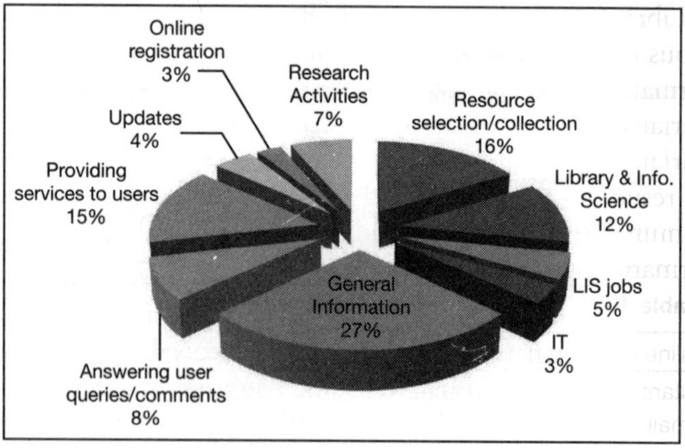

Fig. 10.4: Purpose of Using Online Communication Technologies

facilities, conferences, discussion with experts, seminars, projects; school and college syllabus in all subjects, etc. Next they prefer in getting information related to various types of Information sources and their procurement details. 14.86 per cent librarians use these technologies to serve their users. 11.62 per cent is interested in information related to Library and Information Science. And 3.51 per cent like to get information on IT and related areas.

5.9 Availability of Latest Information Using Online Communication Tools

Using online communication technologies majority of the librarians (81.81per cent) are able to gather latest information on their subject of interest. Only 18.18 per cent of librarians responded that they could not gather latest information using online communication technologies (Table 10.6). Thus it is clear that online communication technologies can be used to get new information on any subject area.

Table 10.6: Availability of Latest Information Using Online Communication Technologies

Response	No. of responses received	Percentage (%)
Yes	99	81.81%
No	22	18.18%
Total	121	100%

5.10 The Services Best Used by Librarians to get Information

Librarians collect information from various sources. By using various online communication technologies also librarians collect information. The online communication services best used by librarians to get information are wikis (19.642%). 16.37 per cent librarians use social networking to collect interested information. The result of the comparison in Table 10.7 shows the online communication services used by librarians to get adequate information.

Table 10.7: The Services Best Used by Librarians to get Information

Online communication tools	No.	Percentage
Instant Messaging/Text chat	11	3.274%
e-mail	20	5.952%
Internet forums	50	14.88%

(Contd.)

Wikis	66	19.642%
Blogs	45	13.392%
Social network services	55	16.37%
Social guides	3	0.89%
Social bookmarking	5	1.49%
Social viewing	48	14.285%
Voice over the Internet Protocol	0	0.0%
Web based communities	33	9.82%

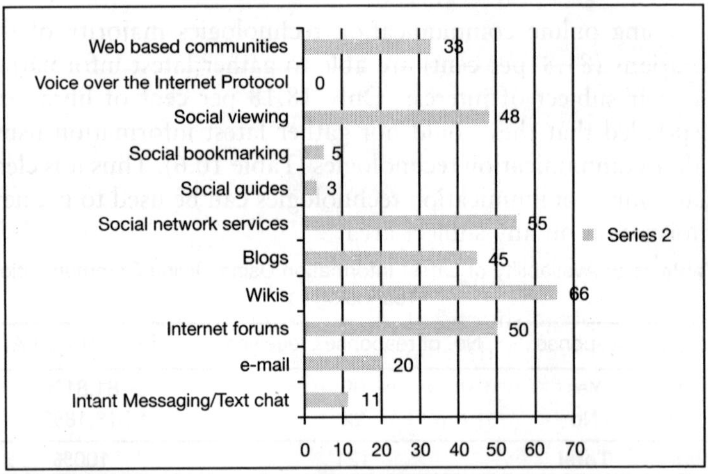

Fig. 10.5: The Services Best Used by Librarians to get Information

6. Suggestions

Based on the opinion given by the respondents and findings of the study, the following suggestions have been made to improve the use of Internet and online communication technologies.

1. The responsibility of the library professional is increasing day-by-day in a changed environment. But the present study/survey revealed that the majority of the library staff do not have much idea about social guides, social bookmarking, voice over IP, etc. These issues should be addressed by providing adequate training to the library staff about the use of online communication tools and first make them confident

users. This will certainly bring about remarkable changes in the information communication process.

2. Orientation/training programme for the librarians should be conducted at regular intervals for effective improvement. This empowers librarians with high specialised knowledge and skills.
3. To facilitate the use of online communication tools, the directory of such websites in Library and Information Science should be prepared and updated frequently.

7. Conclusion

The analysis reveals the awareness and use of various online communication tools among the librarians. Many librarians now use Twitter, for example, to get information about activities and initiatives going on elsewhere; and to share ideas or ask colleagues for support. This rapidly expanding network draws on the experience of colleagues at an international level, allowing for the widespread sharing of information and expertise, which then feeds into service developments at a local level. Participation in this online community can significantly improve staff development, skills and motivation, leading to direct benefit for library services.

The analysis shows that librarians are aware of online communication tools and they are also active users of them in interactive information sharing. Most of the librarians tried e-mail, social networking, etc. And wikis are the most used online communication service used by librarians to get information. Librarians use these technologies to get general information. Most of the librarians agree that these technologies will help in interpersonal cooperation, research and learning.

The global nature of web based services means that libraries can reach a vast audience, serving more people in the virtual sphere than would be possible at a physical location. For example, by establishing a presence on social media websites, libraries can reach beyond the 'walled garden' to interact with users in online spaces that they are already visiting, rather than passively waiting for users to seek us out. This presents opportunities to appeal to difficult to reach user groups, such as teenagers or young males, who are traditionally less likely to visit the physical library building. A strong web presence, including representation on social media sites, improves awareness of library services and contributes to a progressive and modern image, which may in turn lead to increased physical visits.

Online communication technologies have to be integrated into library services. Social media websites have great potential to enhance the delivery of library services and to contribute to the professional development of library staff. As service users increasingly come to expect interactive online services in all spheres of life, libraries must keep pace with developments elsewhere in order ensuring a responsive service for the future.

NOTES

1. Marlon, E. (2009). Using Web 2.0 for scientific applications and scientific communities. *Concurrency and Computation: Practice and Experience*, 21 (5), 583-603.
2. Felicia, W.S. (2010). Theorizing Web 2.0. *Information, Communication & Society*, 13 (2), 249-75.
3. Dirk, S. (2009). Web 2.0 and the empowerment of the knowledge worker. *Journal of Knowledge Management*, 13 (6), 509-20.
4. http://horizon.nmc.org/k12/Communication_Tools (Retrieved on 6th December, 2010).
5. http://www.ncdae.org/tools/factsheets/communication.cfm (Retrieved on 16th December, 2010).

Professional Associations and Academic Librarianship in Kerala

11

K. Susan Mathew

1. Introduction

The library professional in an academic institution has to anticipate the changing expectations of the users, and be flexible in adopting new skills and levels of awareness. Technology has drastically changed the way librarians define themselves and the way they think about their profession and the institutions they serve. In addition to the technical and professional skills, commitment to user centred services and skills for effective oral and written communication; they must have other skills, including business and management, teaching, leadership, etc. Eventually, library and information professionals in academic libraries need to update their knowledge and skills in Information and Communication Technology (ICT) as they play the role of key success factor in enabling the library to perform its role as an information support system for the society.

2. Significance of Professional Associations

Professional associations have a major role in supporting and raising awareness in professional development at the national level and within the profession and providing opportunities to gain practical skill through active participation in professional activities. An effective national association is expected to influence the development of professional manpower in a variety of ways by enforcing standards for library and information education programmes, provision of better salary and service structure and developing a positive image about the profession and professionals in the society.[1] Library Associations provide a common forum to bring together all persons engaged in library activities or interested in library development.[2] Just as a library professional is concerned with a user's quest for knowledge, the professional association must provide a support network for its members. The professional associations have an important role in developing and marketing distance education courses to library staff.[3] A librarian's network of contacts can be cultivated and refined at the conferences sponsored by professional associations. Participating actively in professional associations exposes one to a variety of perspectives and viewpoints. Librarians who are active in professional associations have realistic opportunities to improve or enhance their leadership skills. Participating in professional associations also provides opportunities to become familiar with the processes of research and publication. These important processes contribute to the librarian's professional development.[4]

3. Professional Associations: An Overview

Some of the important Professional associations and organizations in India are Indian Library Association (ILA), Indian Association of Special Libraries and Information Centres (IASLIC), Indian Association of Teachers of Library and Information Science (IATLIS), Society for Information Science (SIS), Indian Academic Library Association (IALA), Society for the Advancement of Library and Information Science (SALIS) and at the state level: Kerala Library Association (KLA) and Kerala Library Professionals Organisation (KELPRO). Most of these Library Associations organize yearly conferences, which encourage the professionals to participate in conferences and to publish their research output. Most of the Professional Associations in India also conduct workshops once a year in conjunction with the annual conference. Professional associations and organizations such as ILA, IASLIC, IATLIS, and SIS are also helping to revise curricula to meet current demands. ILA organized the 22nd All India conference, Library and Information Science curriculum for 3rd World Countries, in 1987. IASLIC organized a conference on LIS Profession in India: Vision 2010. IATLIS organized a national seminar in 2000, Infrastructure Facility for LIS Education and Research in India. SIS also organized a conference in 2000, Accepting the Challenges of IT Re-inventing the LIS Profession in the New Millennium.[5]

3.1 Professional Associations: National Level

Indian Library Association (ILA) was formed in 1933 with the aim of developing library movement and library science education in India. Its publications include ILA Bulletin, ILA Newsletter and proceedings of the seminars and conferences conducted at different parts of the country. Its membership is open to individuals and institutions that fulfill the prescribed conditions.[6]

Another important national level association is Indian Association of Special Libraries and Information Centres (IASLIC) which has also contributed a lot to promote the professional development of Academic Librarians by conducting regular conferences and workshops throughout the country. IASLIC was established in 1955 as a non-profit professional body to coordinate the activities among the special libraries, scientific, technological and research institutions, and other information centres.[7] IASLIC Bulletin is published quarterly and other publications include IASLIC newsletter, conference proceedings, etc. Different categories of membership are open to library professionals and institutions across the country.

Indian Association of Teachers of Library and Information Science (IATLIS) was formed in 1969 to further the cause of library education in India. Its membership is open to teachers of library and information science, staff of libraries, researchers, students and others interested in library and information science education and research. As part of the continuing education programme the association holds periodic seminars on various aspects in LIS teaching. Its publications include IATLIS communications and conference proceedings.

Society for Information Science (SIS) is an all India professional body devoted to encouraging interaction among information professionals, and users, established in 1975. One of the important aims of the society is to encourage the professionals to maintain their professional competence. Society for the Advancement of Library and Information Science (SALIS) is another library association catering to the needs of library professionals and was established as a professional association in 2002. The primary focus was to provide need-based service to the profession and to work for the advancement of Library and Information Science. Its membership is open to library professionals and institutions all over India. Its publications include quarterly newsletter and free e-journal called SALIS *Journal of Library and Information Science*. Its activities include periodical lectures on emerging trends and special programs to impart soft skills essential for library professionals. Indian Academic Library Association (IALA) is another active library association established to serve the university and college librarians of the country.

Majority of the states in India have their own library associations supporting continuing education programmes in their respective states. In addition to library science education, short-term training programmes are offered by professional associations of librarians in different states. The professional associations such as Delhi Library Association (DLA) and Kerala Granthasala Sanghom are also imparting LIS education at lower level such as Certificate/Diploma in Library and Information Science.

3.2 Professional Associations: State Level

In Kerala, professional associations were late to materialize due to the shortage of qualified librarians. The Kerala Library Association (KLA) was formed in 1972 to strive for the development of libraries in the state, to represent the interests of the qualified librarians working in different libraries and provide proper library services. KLA has played a major role in developing proper library and information system in the state. Membership of the association is open to all library professionals who satisfy the required minimum qualifications.[8] The publications include KLA Newsletter published quarterly and distributed freely to its members, various books and souvenirs. The association organizes through its study circles at regional levels, various workshops and seminars to keep the professionals abreast of the latest developments in the field of library and information science. Kerala Library Professionals' Organization, popularly known as

KELPRO, is another active library association in Kerala started in 1992 with the joint effort of a group of young, energetic and enthusiastic practicing librarians and information scientists. Publication programme is one of the important objectives of KELPRO. It has been publishing its official journal KELPRO BULLETIN (half-yearly) from 1997 onwards encouraging research publications from the professionals, teachers and students in LIS.

3.3 Professional Associations: International

At the international level IFLA, ALA, SLA and CILIP are some of the associations actively involved in the training and continuing education of library professionals. The International Federation of Library Associations and Institutions (IFLA) is the leading international body representing the interests of library and information services and their users. Founded in 1927 it serves the library professionals all around the world. IFLA provides institutional membership and personal membership to individuals. A range of professional meetings, seminars and workshops are held around the world by IFLA professional groups and Core Activities. The website of IFLA[9] and IFLA journal provide all the required details regarding its activities and professional development programmes.

The American Library Association (ALA), the oldest library association in the world was founded in 1876. Its aim is to provide leadership for the development, promotion, and improvement of library and information services and the profession of librarianship in order to enhance learning and ensure access to information for all. ALA through its membership and various conferences, training, workshops, online learning modules, etc. promote library education and continuous learning for LIS professionals.[10]

Membership in Special Libraries Association (SLA) also provides opportunity to numerous professional development activities to its members in the form of webinars, and online portals to world of learning opportunities to information professionals. Information outlook published eight times a year is the authoritative source for information on the profession and its online version is available exclusively to its members.

Chartered Institute of Library and Information Professionals (CILIP) was formed in 2002 following the unification of the Institute of Information Scientists and the Library Association, London.[11] Membership in CILIP helps to keep the skills and knowledge up-to-date through member-only content on the CILIP website, CILIP Update magazine, the latest titles from Facet Publishing and CILIP Training and Development courses. All these international associations provide a wide range of online courses which, if properly utilized, will help in self-education and thereby improve the professional development of information professionals. The professional associations are thus accessible by library professionals within the country and across international boundaries.

4. Membership in Professional Associations

As part of a survey of library professionals employed in the major universities of Kerala viz. University of Kerala (UOK), Mahatma Gandhi University (MGU), Cochin University of Science and Technology (CUSAT), University of Calicut (UOC), Kannur University (KAN), Sree Sankaracharya University of Sanskrit (SSU), and Kerala Agricultural University (KAU), to evaluate their Professional activities, their membership in regional, national and international associations was also studied. The study found that library professionals in the universities in Kerala are aware of the importance of library associations in the development of the profession.

Of the total 185 library professionals surveyed, 128 (69.2%) of the library professionals have membership in one or two library associations. None has membership in library associations at the International level during the period of study. National level associations like IASLIC (3.1%) and ILA (7.3%) have very few members from the Universities of Kerala as evident from the Fig. 11.1 and SALIS has 1.7% members. Majority of the professionals of Kerala Agricultural University, Sree Sankaracharya University and Kannur University who have membership in library associations, have membership in KLA, and in general, 63.8 per cent of the library professionals have membership in the state library associations as KLA and 19.5 per cent in KELPRO. The library professionals are to be made aware of the importance of professional associations in career development and encourage them to enroll in more library associations at national as well as international levels.

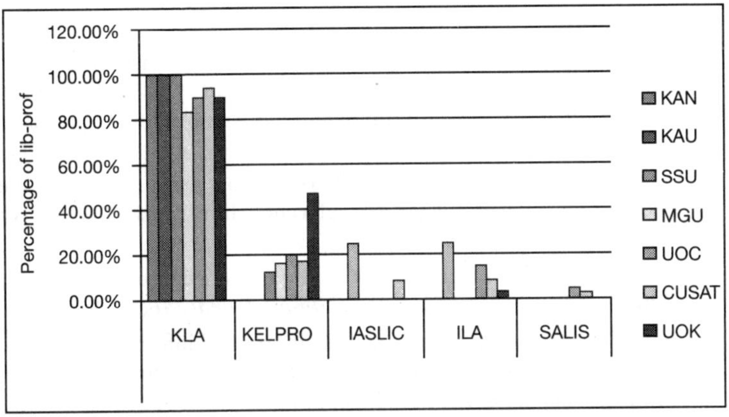

Fig. 11.1: Membership In Professional Associations

5. Conclusion

Though University Grants Commission (UGC) conducts refresher courses regularly, it benefits only a very small percentage of qualified senior library professionals. DRTC, NISCAIR, DELNET and INFLIBNET conduct workshops and training programmes in ICT applications relevant to library profession. But India lacks an institution to provide regular training programmes for the continuing professional development of academic librarians. Associations can play an active part in improving the standards of library profession and thereby improve the standards of library service. The conferences and meetings sponsored by professional associations provide a forum not only for learning, but also for professional exchange, keeping them abreast of current trends, problems, and solutions. Professional Associations have to take more initiatives to conduct regular continuing education programmes for library professionals at all levels of the profession. Lack of active participation by the members and inadequate funds are some of the problems faced by the Professional Associations in conducting various programmes.

NOTES

1. Rehman, S., Abu Baker, A.B. and Majid, S. (1998). Needed capabilities and development strategies for future information professionals: A Malaysian perspective. *International Information and Library Review, 30*, 123-41.
2. Mohankumar, T. (1989). Role of professional associations in continuing education. In M.N. Ramakrishnan et al. (Ed), *Library and information science education in India*. Trivandrum: Department of Library and Information Science, University of Kerala, 216-27.
3. Chan, D.C., and Auster, E. (2003). Factors contributing to the professional development of reference librarians. *Library & Information Science Research*, 25, 265–86.
4. Frank, D.G. (1997). Activity in professional associations: The positive difference in a librarian's career. *Library Trends, 46*(2), 307-19.
5. Singh, J. (2010). Changing needs of library and information science curricula in India (Retrieved June 13, 2010, from http://www.webpages.uidaho.edu/~mbolin/ lpp.htm).
6. http://www.ilaindia.net/ (Retrieved on 5th December, 2010).
7. http://www.iaslic1955.org.in (Retrieved on 15th January, 2010).
8. http://www.keralalibraryassociation.org (Retrieved on 24th February, 2010).
9. http://www.ifla.org (Retrieved on 25th February, 2010).
10. http://www.ala.org (Retrieved on 25th February, 2010).
11. www.cilip.org.uk (Retrieved on 25th February, 2010).

PART IV
PUBLIC LIBRARIES

Lessons from the British Council Library Experience: Pointers to University and Public Libraries

12

M. Lalitha

1. Introduction

A study was conducted in 2005[1] on the British Council Libraries in India and the major objective was to delve deep into the role played by the British Council Libraries (BCLs) in promoting higher education in India and in fulfilling the education and informational needs of the higher education sector in India. The hypothesis was proved right that

1. Though the British Council Libraries are public libraries by virtue of their collection and services, they act as academic libraries by providing the best in the education field; and that
2. The British Council Libraries supplement the work done by university libraries by providing timely information with the help of information technology.

Many changes have taken place since then. This paper takes a look at the findings of the above study that compared the British Council Library with the State Central Library and the University Library, all at Thiruvananthapuram and analyses the present scenario after the closing down of the British Council Library in 2008.

2. Background

Having worked at the British Council Library for some years and having used the library since school days, the researcher had always assumed that the British Council Library had everything to satisfy one's educational needs. Being a public library, it has a good collection of materials suitable for recreational and general purpose. At the same time, thanks to the book selection policy and also the customer-oriented approach, it seems to have all the latest, especially in Science and Technology.

Still one can never undermine the role played by the university libraries in promoting higher education. There are seven universities in Kerala catering to the needs of nearly four lakh students. The libraries attached to these universities and the colleges/departments affiliated to them provide books and other materials to support their academic needs. Compared to this, what can a single library do? For the whole state of Kerala, there is only one British Council Library which is not even centrally located. How can one expect this library to play an important role equal to that of a University Library?

Similarly when we talk about role, the question that comes to our mind is: What is a British Council Library? If it is a Public Library, according to British Council's own definition, then why is it concentrating so much on education and academics? On the other hand, if it is to be treated as an academic library, how is it to be justified?

A comparison between the University Library, the Public Library and the British Council Library seemed inevitable if an answer were to be found for this.

3. Methodology

For the purpose of the survey, teachers and students in the colleges and university departments in the Thiruvananthapuram City who also held valid membership in the British Council Library, Thiruvananthapuram, were contacted. In all, 500 questionnaires were distributed and 351 responded (70.2%).

4. Scope and Limitations of the Study

There are more than one lakh members in the British Council Library network in India and the work done in British Council Libraries and British Libraries is more or less the same. Thus questionnaires were administered only in the British Library in Thiruvananthapuram and that too only to a sample. The above library had about eight thousand members out of which four thousand odd members accounted for family membership, that is, children below the age of fifteen and their parents. So the sample was taken from the rest of the four thousand members and five hundred questionnaires were administered on a selective basis. The questionnaires were administered on those students, teachers and researchers who had membership in the British Library and it was ensured that only the professional, post-graduate and research students, teachers in colleges/departments and those in the higher education sector participated.

Since the study was about the users in the higher education sector, the junior students of degree courses were excluded but those in their final year of degree courses were brought under the study. This was because it was felt this group would have a better understanding of their chosen subjects and would exercise better judgment and a keener sense of direction while using the library. Since the British Council Library has members ranging from the primary class, this kind of cutting off has been necessary to get a correlation between study and library use. But the majority of the population was from professional courses, postgraduate courses and those doing research in the various departments. Those doing correspondence courses were also excluded.

5. The Question

The hypotheses one started out with was that though the British Council Libraries are public libraries by virtue of their collection and services, they act as academic libraries by providing the best to those in the academic field. In all the five sections there were some questions relating to this aspect of the British Council Library. In the first section on membership and personal details, there was a question on membership in other libraries. The second section, Library use, tried to correlate so many things: the libraries consulted, why they were consulted, what needs they served and what needs the British Council Library served. Collection and Services, the next two sections, had naturally questions that tried to find out the importance of these in a student's/teacher's life and the way the British Council

Library provided these things to them. The last and final section asked the users to assess the library by themselves and here again, the emphasis was on collection, services and other aspects like physical facilities and the efficiency of staff.

Analysis of the first five sections had proved that the collection of the British Council Library was best suited to satisfy the educational needs of students, especially postgraduates. The services being provided with the help of the latest technology were also beneficial to them.

Accordingly the users were asked to compare six library aspects of the British Council Library with any other library of which he/she is a member. The assumption was that this question would automatically generate a comparative study between the British Council Library and the Public Library and again between the British Council Library and the University Library since to a previous question on membership in other libraries, 197 had responded they were members of the University Library and 112 were members of the Public Library. Out of the total responses received in connection with this question, only these two libraries were selected for the purpose of analysis. This was because British Council Library is basically a public library and by virtue of its policy, it is essentially an academic library as well. The six criteria given were physical environment, collection, services, staff, support facility and IT support.[2]

5.1 The Scenario in 2005: Analysis I

Table 12.1 was prepared after collecting data from the Kerala University Library, the State Central Library (Public Library) and the British Council Library, all located at Trivandrum and all invariably catering to the needs of the local population. University Library may be slightly different in that it has a vast special population to cover.

Table 12.1: University Library, Public Library & British Council Library in 2005: A Comparison

Particulars	Public Library	University Library	British Council Library, Trivandrum
Year of Establishment	1829	1942	1964
Parent Body/Dept.	Dept. of Higher Education	University of Kerala	British High Commission and ICCR
Branch libraries/ other centres	–	Kollam, Alappuzha, Pandalam and Kariavattam	Part of the British Council Library Network of 11 libraries located at New Delhi, Chennai, Kolkata, Mumbai, Bangalore, Bhopal, Pune, Chandigarh, Hyderabad and Ahmedabad.
Categories of membership	Individual but there are 5 categories (A-D)	Students, Teachers, Research Scholars, Graduates	Individual, Institutional, Honorary R/F and Family
Subscription or free	Only refundable deposit	Only refundable deposit, valid for course period	Subscription to be renewed annually
Total no. of Members	30,670	42,304	8,804
Language of the collection	English, Malayalam, Tamil, Hindi, Telugu and Sanskrit	English, Malayalam, Hindi, Tamil, German, Russian, French, Sanskrit and Urdu	English
Total no. of books in collection	2,97,967	2,86,520	27,173
Journals	139 (Subscription) 304 (Gift)	240 (Indian), 49 (Foreign), 11 (Foreign Abstracts), 6 (Indian Abstracts), 20 (gift); 43 (Popular magazines)	43
Issues: Average book loans per day	640	750-615	750-850
Visitors per Day	400	300-400	500-550
Newspapers	27	17	5 (British only)
Working hours	8.30 am–11.30 am; 2-7 pm from Mon – Sat.; 8 am–2 pm on Sundays	8 am – 8 pm on Mon – Sat.; 2–8 pm on Sundays	11 am – 7 pm Sunday Holiday

(***Sources***: University of Kerala Annual Report; Statistics from the Circulation Section. State Central Library Statistics 2005, Country Summary: India 2004/2005 brought out by Library and Information Services Management Information System, British Council.)

Of the three libraries, the British Council Library was the 'youngest', only 42 years old then, compared to the older University Library and the very old Public Library. The difference starts from this point. While University Library is part of the University of Kerala, the Public Library is under the Department of Higher Education, Government of Kerala. In other words, it has the status of a department. British Council Library is jointly administered by the British High Commission and Indian Council for Cultural Relations. The Public Library is only one of its kind in the state; the same can be said about the British Council Library but in a broader sense, it is one of the 11 libraries in the British Council Library Network in India. University Library, on the other hand, has a campus library in Kariavattom, Trivandrum and three other centres in Kollam, Alappuzha and Pandalam, thus gaining a better geographical coverage than the other two.

All the three libraries are subscription libraries and the similarity ends there. University Library, as the name itself implies has all those studying, teaching and even those who had studied or taught in the University, as its members. There are students, teachers, research scholars and graduate members. The British Council Library[3], by virtue of its policy, has students and teachers as its target members. Keeping with its tradition as a Public Library the British Council Library's membership is open to anyone above the age of 16 and there are various other categories like institutional, family, etc. But among the individual members, students are the target groups, otherwise known in the Council circles as T3. The Public Library remains just that—open to the public, with no 'specialism', such as the one exhibited by the British Council Library. The services of the libraries are also designed accordingly. The British Council Library offers the latest developments in technology for the benefit of the students. University Library has also an Internet lab where students and researchers can browse and search specially chosen databases. The British Council Library offers online services, Internet facility and there is the facility for searching specially selected online databases like Infotrac and EBSCO. The Public Library, being more a government department than a library, is slow to catch up with the modern technology. But things seem to be changing for the better if the current budget allocation of Rs. 1 crore is any indication.[4]

The differences seem to widen from this point onwards. The membership figures point to a Grand Canyon-type gap between University Library and Public Library on one side and the British Council Library on the other. University Library has 42,304 members, the Public Library, a total of 30,670 and the British Council Library has just 8,804, which is not even 30 per cent of the other two libraries' memberships. The total book collection is also along similar lines. The University Library boasts of a whopping collection of 2,86,520 and the Public Library, a still higher number of 2,97,967. British Council Library's paltry 27,173—this includes the reference collection as well—appear to be an apology of collection beside the other two figures. In the number of available journals also, the huge disparity is visible. The British Council Library has just 43 British journals including subject and popular magazines. The other two libraries cross the 350-mark very easily. They provide both Indian and foreign journals and those in Malayalam and Tamil also. Their collection also has books in various Indian languages unlike that of the British Council Library, which has only English books, and most of these are UK publications, since their objective is to promote Britain, British ideas, culture and their language.

There are thus so many restrictions or barriers for the British Council Library, when compared to the University Library or the Public Library. The scope, the language, the collection, all these definitely put the British Council Library at a disadvantage. But figures speak differently. The other two libraries may have more members, more books, and more journals. The final outcome is dependent on what the users make of the resources. This way, the number of people who visit the library per day or on an annual basis, the number of books issued per day or in a year—these are the fine and the most important indicators of a library's effectiveness and efficiency. And this is where the British Council Library scores over the other two. The annual report of the University Library for the year puts down the issue figure at 1,11,615 out of which 35,582 are science books, 47,063 from humanities and 28,970 belong to social sciences. On an average,

750-850 books are loaned out per day. In the Public Library, this is estimated as 640 books per day. As for people coming to the library, the University Library has, on an average, 300-400 visitors per day whereas about 400 visit the Public Library. Both the libraries work for 6 days a week and half-day on Sundays also.

On the other hand, with a collection of 27,173 English books, 43 British journals and just 8,804 members, the British Council Library, Trivandrum, had a total of 2,19,901 book loans which is 1,08,286 more than the University Library's transaction for the same period. The British Council Library shows an equal number of issues per day i.e., 750-850, whereas the Public Library's is less. As for visitors, 1,63,342 visited the British Council Library during a year which comes to 550-600 visitors per day. The University Library and the Public Library show this as 300-400 and 400 respectively.

These figures speak volumes. They show that British Council Library has been able to achieve much with very little, when compared to the other two libraries. The number of issues speaks of the care and quality check and above all, a finger on the user's pulse that the British Council Library has. Compared to the University Library and the Public Library, with just one tenth of the stock, the library seems to be satisfying the needs of a less number of people, with double the number of book loans of University Library and Public Library. This means that members have been coming back again and again to borrow books. They will not do it unless they have something to gain from it. This, in turn, is an acknowledgment of the aptness, relevance and usefulness of books selected and made available to the users. It also indicates the strength and quality of the book selection policy adopted by the British Council Library. It also reveals the immense use the materials put to by the users.

5.2 The Scenario in 2005: Analysis II

5.2.1 Comparison Between British Council Library and University Library (2005)

The 197 British Council Library members, who were also members of the University Library, evaluated the two libraries on the basis of their physical environment, collection, services, staff, support facility and IT support.

Table 12.2: Comparison: British Council Library and University Library in 2005

Attribute	Excellent		Good		Adequate		Poor	
	British Council Library	University Library	British Council Library	University Library	British Council Library	University Library	British Council Library	University Library
Physical Environment	121 (61.43)	10 (5.08)	49 (24.87)	98 (49.75)	24 (12.18)	56 (28.42)	3 (1.52)	33 (16.75)
Collection	40 (20.30)	116 (58.88)	95 (48.22)	69 (35.03)	49 (24.87)	9 (4.57)	13 (6.60)	3 (1.52)
Services	98 (49.75)	20 (10.15)	71 (36.04)	95 (48.22)	24 (12.18)	69 (35.03)	4 (2.03)	13 (6.60)
Staff	75 (38.07)	19 (9.64)	79 (40.10)	102 (51.78)	39 (19.80)	65 (32.99)	4 (2.03)	11 (5.58)
Support Facility	66 (33.50)	14 (7.11)	83 (42.13)	75 (38.07)	47 (23.86)	79 (40.10)	–	29 (14.72)
IT Support	101 (51.27)	49 (24.87)	73 (37.06)	89 (45.18)	23 (11.68)	49 (24.87)	–	10 (5.08)

Table 12.2 shows that the British Council Library scores high on the excellent side except in the case of collection and it does not have many branding it as poor in any of the attributes given. Taken together, only 24 in all have said that physical environment/collection/services/staff are poor. No one has rated the support facility or the IT support provided by the British Council as poor. As for the University Library, it scores very high on the collection: 58.88 per cent consider it to be excellent, 35.03 per cent say it is good and only 1.52 per cent have a poor opinion about the collection of the University Library. In all other aspects, the University Library has more on the good and adequate side. It scores poorly in physical environment and support facility: 16.75 per cent and 14.72 per cent think these two are poor when compared to the British Council Library.

One positive thing about this comparative evaluation is that the University Library does not come out as inferior to the British Council Library. Looking at the University Library scenario in the country as a whole, it has been observed that many problems plague them. Paucity of funds is the greatest problem; attitude of people is another one. However good one's intentions are, nothing can be done without proper administrative support. This has been confirmed by this evaluation also. What have been rated poor in the case of the University Library are its physical environment and support facility, which shows lack of infrastructural support.

It is here that British Council's professionalism and the organizational ability score over the University Library. The Council has always placed great importance on service standards and this includes physical environment as well. It emphasizes on proper seating arrangement, lighting, ventilation and even on toilet facilities. Refurbishment of libraries has always been one of its priorities since the Council is of the opinion that the physical environment has to change keeping in with the changed IT environment. It is not surprising then that physical environment of British Council Library is rated excellent by as much as 61.43 per cent as against a low 5.08 per cent for the same aspect of the University Library.

Going by the natural reaction of people, one would have expected the University Library to come nowhere nearer to the British Council Library in matters like services and staff. That this has not happened goes on to prove the maturity and sensitivity of the evaluators. It is clear that they have not been bowled over by the exquisite interior of the British Council Library or the British-like briskness of its staff. When interviewed, many of the respondents said they were aware of the differences between the two libraries. In their opinion, the British Council Library is what it is because it is the library and only that matters. Everything is focused on the library and its users. There is a management which has a vision and which is always bringing about the latest changes. Nothing is spared in its efforts to satisfy the customers. This is because the British Council Library is managed like a multinational company.

The same users are aware that such a thing is never possible in a university library. For one thing, its scope and coverage is very wide. There are about 103 colleges that come under the University of Kerala. The total number of students, including those studying in the newly started engineering and medical colleges and those doing self-financing courses, come to more than 60,000 and there are about 8000 teachers.[5] The University Library is supposed to support to all these categories of users.

The enormity of this situation makes the users more sympathetic towards the staff. This is evident in the way they respond to the same situation in both the libraries. They know that the University Library is lacking in certain departments. Still, they seem to have no serious complaints against it. But in the case of the British Council Library, nothing seems to satisfy them fully. This is due to the expectation they have of the same.

5.2.2 Comparison Between British Council Library and Public Library (2005)

A similar attitude is there towards the Public Library also. There were 112 respondents who were members of the latter. They were also asked to evaluate the two libraries on the basis of the same six attributes.

Table 12.3: Comparison: British Council Library and Public Library in 2005

Attribute	Excellent		Good		Adequate		Poor	
	British Council Library	University Library	British Council Library	University Library	British Council Library	University Library	British Council Library	University Library
Physical Environment	99 (88.39%)	4 (3.57%)	9 (8.04%)	36 (32.14%)	4 (3.57%)	54 (48.21%)	–	18 (16.07%)
Collection	31 (27.68%)	59 (52.68%)	50 (44.64%)	40 (35.71%)	27 (24.11%)	–	4 (3.57%)	13 (11.61%)
Services	55 (49.11%)	–	40 (35.71%)	40 (35.71%)	13 (11.61%)	50 (44.64%)	4 (3.57%)	22 (19.64%)
Staff	50 (44.64%)	5 (4.46%)	45 (40.18%)	40 (35.71%)	13 (11.61%)	45 (40.18%)	4 (3.57%)	22 (19.64%)
Support Facility	59 (52.68%)	4 (3.57%)	45 (40.18%)	18 (16.07%)	4 (3.57%)	40 (35.71%)	4 (3.57%)	49 (43.75%)
IT Support	72 (64.29%)	–	36 (32.14%)	4 (3.57%)	4 (3.57%)	45 (40.18%)	–	63 (56.25%)

In this case, the judgment is more pronounced. Compared to the Public Library, the physical environment of the British Council Library is adjudged excellent (88.39 against 3.57) and it can even be said that there is no comparison between the two. The British Council Library scores in services, staff, supporting facility and IT support.

When it comes to collection, as in the previous case, the British Council Library seems to suffer. Though not by a huge margin, the Public Library definitely has the upper hand here (it is 52.68 against British Council Library's 27.68). Except for this, in all others, what the British Council Library has or provides is excellent, good or adequate.

The Public Library seems to fare very badly in support facility and IT support, the latter more so. The Public Library is only now being initiated into IT-enabled services and Internet browsing has also been introduced recently. But experience shows that quality consciousness is not much in evidence. If something goes wrong, it takes a long time to set it right. This ultimately affects the quality of service and it comes as no surprise that no one considers the services offered by the Public Library as excellent. Table 12.3 shows that very few people have found anything excellent about the Public Library except its collection, whereas very few people have found anything poor about the British Council Library. Only 16 out of 112 (14.29%) have found something poor about the British Council Library's collection, services, staff and supporting facility while the reverse is the case with the Public Library.

6. Findings of the Study (2005)

It cannot be said that all that the Public Library does or offers is below the required standard. Except for supporting facility and IT support, the rest are evaluated as either good or adequate. The overall judgment, however, seems to be in favour of the British Council Library.

There seems to be only one aspect where the British Council Library suffers in comparison with the other two libraries, i.e., the collection. In the case of the University Library, it had 116 out of 197 (58.88%) saying that the University Library's collection was excellent whereas there were only 40 who thought so about the British Council Library's collection. This accounted for 20.30 per cent. In the case of the Public Library, the rating was slightly better for the British Council Library: 52.68 per cent. The Public Library's collection was excellent and 27.68 per cent considered that of the British Council Library to be excellent. The differences in the respective percentages apart, this points to the psyche of the academic community in India. Students prefer standard textbooks, study guides and such materials that are more text bookish and are easy to assimilate. With such materials they do not have to think or critically evaluate anything. Everything is readily available and all they need do is just copy it down or learn by rote. On the other hand, the books that are available at the British Council Library are mostly written by the British. Their style of presentation has a distinctive flavour which makes it difficult for an ordinary student to understand what is being said. Moreover, both the University Library and the Public Library have books written in vernacular languages. This makes it more popular, especially with the undergraduates, many of whom may have studied in Malayalam medium schools.

When we look at the assessments on British Council Library's collections and services in isolation, what strikes us most is the fact that the users are very level-headed. They exhibit a keen sense of judgment. There seems to be a judicious mixture of appreciation and clear-headedness. They do not accept everything that is meted out to them as excellent. Only those that meet and satisfy their requirements are recognized as excellent, very good or good. Even then, the first two are not that easy to come by. In spite of being provided with the very latest in various fields, as students or teachers, they feel there is still a lacuna. To a previous question on library use, they had shown that British Council Library did lack in theses, dissertations, etc. that are very much required by researchers. In such cases, they exhibit a reservation and the evaluation of collection is one such example. This vouchsafes their clarity of purpose and clarity about their needs.

The University Library and the Public Library score over the British Council Library in the case of collection. The physical environment, services, staff, support facility and IT support provided by the British Council Library are superior to that by the other two. Compared to University Library and Public Library, British Council Library is 'younger' and has a small membership base. But except for collection, in all other departments, the British Council Library is considered better by students and teachers.

British Council Library, like the Public Library, provides books and other materials for recreational and general reading.

But it differs from the Public Library in that its members are not general public. It is a special library in the sense of having a special group—students—as its target group. Thus it resembles a university library. But collection-wise, it is less than a university library. There are subject books, and other materials that the academic and students communities need. At the same time, materials supporting research students like theses, reports are not available at the British Council Library.

All these make the British Council Library more than a Public Library but less than a University library. It plays a supportive role and supports and augments what the university library does.

7. Present Scenario in 2011

7.1 British Council Library, Thiruvananthapuram

As mentioned at the outset, the above study was conducted in 2005. Many changes have taken place since then. The BCL Network has no longer a library in Thiruvananthapuram. It was closed down in 2008 and the BCL collection was added to the Public Library stock in 2010. It is being kept as a separate section and steps are being initiated to update the collection. This has been the result of the realization that updating and the currency of the collection have been the USP of the BCL.

The BCL Network itself has undergone changes. It has a presence only in 9 cities in India—Ahmedabad, Bangalore, Chandigarh, Chennai, Hyderabad, Kolkata, Mumbai, New Delhi and Pune. Still it is the Council's largest operation in the world. It is still helpful to the student community with much of its extension work aimed at them. BCL offers free online preparation for IELTS; there is an Exam Newsletter; under e-library, it has 38,000 books that form the academic collection, covering topics like education, business and economics, psychology, sociology, medicine and engineering. Though only confined to 9 cities, it still has the power to reach out to millions of people across India, through scholarships, courses (especially in ELT for teachers), workshops, seminars, projects and lectures. A BCL is not a traditional library. Still they claim that their libraries are "the gateway to a world of opportunity".[6]

7.2 Present Scenario (2011): State Central (Public) Library and University Library

Both these libraries seem to have moved with the changing times. Both have become more user-friendly and technology-driven.

7.2.1 State Central Library, Thiruvananthapuram in 2011

The major innovations[7] have been the starting of a digital library and the introduction of RFID.

Digitization: 707 very old books were digitized in Phase I and digitization has entered the Phase III now, with the digitization of old Gazettes. Users can access the collection through intranet and the library plans to make it available online soon.

RFID: With the introduction of RFID, manual labour has been reduced considerably and the staff time is utilized for providing better service to the users.

7.2.2 University Library in 2011

University Library[8] is on the path of modernization with the help of technology. It now has a LAN and CDROM Network. Rare collection of journals in microfilm, Internet and OPAC facilities are provided. The Library is today the major centre of study and research in the state and its collection of back volumes of social science periodicals is considered to be one of the best in South India.

A comparison between the status 2005 and 2011 is given in Table 12.4:

Table 12.4: University Library, Public Library & British Council Library in 2005 and 2011: A Comparison

Particulars	Public Library		University Library		BCL Trivandrum	
	2005	2011	2005	2011	2005	2011
Total no. of Members	30670	55002	42,304	–	8,804	Closed down in 2008
Total no. of books in collection	2,97,967	3,68,890	2,86,520	3,00,000	27,173	
Journals	139	210	369	478	43	

(Contd...)

Issues: Average book loans per day	640	800-850	750-615	700-750	750-850
Visitors per day	400	1000-1500	300-400	1000-1250	500-550
Newspapers	21	27	17	–	5 (British only)
Working hours	8.30 am – 11.30 am; 2-7 pm from Mon–Sat. 8 am–2 pm on Sundays	8 am– 8 pm	8 am – 8 pm on Mon-Sat. 2 – 8 pm on Sundays	8 am – 8 pm on Mon-Sat. 2 – 8 pm on Sundays	11 am – 7 pm Sunday Holiday

Table 12.4 shows that there has been an increase in the membership, collection and the number of visitors per day, especially in the case of the State Central Library, which has been indirectly attributed to the British Library's presence as a separate collection there.

In both the Public and the University libraries, it is true that the environment has changed for the better. Automation work has been given priority and most of the services have become IT-enabled. A recent study done in CUSAT Central Library[9] reveals that users also make use of the available ICT facilities and that the speed and efficiency of services has also increased.

8. Drawbacks

However when it comes to manpower majority of the University libraries in Kerala suffer from scarcity of staff. Besides, Vijayakumar[10] points out that the post of the University Librarian is lying vacant in many a University library in Kerala and this itself is a serious setback to the profession and library services. A proper leader is very essential for directing the manpower, especially when IT has brought in sweeping changes into the library field. According to him, the absence of the head will surely affect the planned and progressive growth of university libraries.

Moreover, there still exists a section-wise approach in the deployment of staff and this deprives one of a chance to explore and experiment. This problem is more keenly felt by those working in the University libraries and this affects staff performance to a great extent.

9. Solutions

Efforts are to be taken to instill professionalism into the present workforce. British Council Library had scored high on services and the professional attitude of the staff. This was made possible through their policy of providing continuous professional development. In the case of our libraries also both professionals and non-professionals need to be re-oriented and re-engineered along with new services. This is possible only if the organizational pattern of libraries is also re-structured. Water tight compartments will then disappear, only to be replaced by a rejuvenated workforce oriented towards adding value to whatever they do.

10. Conclusion

A flexible and dynamic structure which allows the freedom to alter the strategies when the priorities change and to change the priorities when the context changes; a re-aligned workforce which learns to adapt to changes and to gel as a team; task forces willing to take up new challenges through constant updating of skills and knowledge; an excellent physical environment conducive to learning and reading; excellent quality services that have the latest technological support; excellent staff who have the right attitude and efficiency—these were the factors that made the British Council Library more than a Public Library and brought it closer to a University Library. Our own public and university libraries will do well to take a leaf out of the BCL book.

NOTES

1. Lalitha, M. (2005). *An Investigation into the role of British Council Libraries in higher education in India*. Unpublished PhD thesis. University of Kerala.
2. Orr, R.H. (1973). Progress in documentation: Measuring the goodness of library services: A general framework for considering quantitative measures. *Journal of Documentation*, 29(3), 315-32.
3. www.britishcouncil.org (Accessed on 22nd January, 2005).
4. State Central Library. Annual Report 2005.
5. University of Kerala. Annual Report 2005.
6. www.britishcouncil.org/india-where-we-are.htm (Accessed on 25th March, 2011).
7. www.statelibrary.kerala.gov.in (Accessed on 25th March, 2011).

8. http://www.kulib.in (Accessed on 25th March, 2011).
9. Santha Devi Antharjanam and Sheeja, N.K. (2008). *Impact of ICT on library and information science: Major shifts and practices in CUSAT Central Library*. 5th International Caliber. University of Allahabad, 35-43.
10. Vijayakumar, K.P. (2008). University library manpower in Kerala: An analysis. *Annals of Library & Information Studies*, 55 (4), 300-07.

Automation of the Public Libraries in Kerala Using E-Granthalaya

13

A. Sudha

1. Introduction

Adopting new methods of delivery of information using different technologies is an essential part of the public library. The computer technology redefines the library services in the public libraries such as database creation, catalogue search, circulation and serial control. The IFLA/UNESCO guidelines (2001) state: "Public libraries must, whenever possible, make use of the new technologies to improve their services."[1]

The recent study on the public libraries in Kerala shows that only 20 per cent of the public libraries have computer sets. Of these libraries, a meagre number of libraries are using computers to make catalogue entry using locally developed library software and others use computers for DTP, CD browsing and to give computer training to the children. From these findings it can be concluded that computerisation of public libraries in Kerala is in initial stage.[2]

2. Role of Kerala State Library Council

Kerala State Library Council, the apex authority formed as per the Kerala Public Libraries (Kerala Granthasala Sangham) Act, 1989 is the nodal agent for the development of public libraries in Kerala. As per the State Library Council's record[3] there are 7191 public libraries affiliated to the State Library Council in 2010-2011, and they are classified into six grades from A to F based on standards formulated by the Council for the purpose of giving grants. It is the prime responsibility of the

State Library Council to take initiative for the automation of the public libraries in the State. In the budget estimate of Kerala State Library Council for the fiscal year 2010-11, an amount of Rs. 16 lakhs was earmarked for the computerisation of the public libraries in the State. The Council also allotted Rs. 25 lakhs for the e-collection in the selected libraries. For the retro conversion of the library catalogue the State Library Council allocated Rs. 10 lakhs to the libraries in 2010-11. The State Library Council recently provided training courses to the librarians of the selected twenty libraries in the library management software "E-Granthalaya". Kerala State Library Council is seriously thinking about the automation of the public libraries in the State.

3. Objectives of the Study

1. To look at the extent of computer use in the public library functions and services using the library software E-Granthalaya.
2. To find out the major problems hindering the automation of the public libraries in Kerala.

4. E-Granthalaya—The Library Management Software for Public Libraries

As described by National Informatic Centre (NIC), Government of India "E-Granthalaya is a digital agenda for library automation and networking". It was developed by NIC. Using this software the libraries can automate in house activities as well as user services. This software can be used both in stand-alone and in client-server mode. It facilitates LAN/Web based database creation and Web OPAC interface to public the library catalogue over Internet/Intranet.[4]

E-Granthalaya 3.0, network edition (eG3), is the latest version which is launched in 2007. This version manages the data entry in 10 Indian languages including Malayalam. It works in MS SQL 2005 DBMS and VB.NET/ASP.NET 2.0 platform. This software is provided to the public libraries on free of cost. NIC State/district centres also provide free support training to the libraries.

4.1 System Requirements

For Stand-Alone Mode (All the Components to be installed on a Single PC):

Hardware: PIV or above with backup device

OS: Windows XP with SP2 installed/Vista

DBMS: MS SQL Server 2005 (Express Ed)

Connectivity: LAN/Internet Connectivity

For Client-Server Mode:

Hardware: PIV or above with backup device

OS: Windows XP with SP2/Vista for Clients

OS: Windows Server 2003 for Server PC

DBMS: MS SQL Server 2005 (Standard Ed)

Connectivity: LAN/Internet connectivity

5. Automation of Public Libraries in Kerala using E-Granthalaya

Before using the eG3, the libraries must set language setting of their server PC. E-Granthalaya contains the following modules which help the automation of various public library services and functions.

1. Administration
2. Acquisition
3. Cataloguing
4. Circulation
5. Serial Control
6. Article Indexing
7. Budget Control
8. OPAC

5.1 Administration

Administration modules in E-Granthalaya provide space for adding/editing/deleting the information regarding the users who operate the software, bibliographic level, acquisition modes, countries, type of binding, currency codes, publisher details, vendor details, languages, text for reports, letters, etc. The public libraries can use this mode for the smooth functioning of their various services and functions.

5.2 Acquisition Modules

The public libraries in Kerala are purchasing mostly the Malayalam fiction from the local book vendors. Most of the libraries purchase books directly from the book shops without checking the duplicate titles or keeping any proper files. Using the acquisition module, the functions such as creation of vendor directory, check the duplicate titles, preparation of the list of books to be purchased, place orders, accessioning, billing and payment the acquisition process can be made systematic, proper, and easier.

5.3 Catalogue Module

The collection in the public libraries is not scientifically organised. A majority of the libraries do not classify or catalogue the books using a classification scheme or catalogue code. Most of the libraries (82 per cent) use ledger catalogue. In this local cataloguing method, the cataloguing details of the books such as serial number, author, and title are entered under the main subject headings such as novels, drama, History, and Science in a separate ledger or in loose sheets of paper. The studies show that 6.2 per cent of the public libraries use card catalogue and 10.3 per cent use other forms such as loose sheets of paper. Very recently a few libraries initiated the automation of library catalogue using a locally developed software. Only 5 per cent of the libraries use Dewey Decimal Classification scheme to classify the books. A vast majority use local method of assigning class numbers such as 'D' for drama, 'M' for Malayalam literature 'H' for History and so on.

Using the catalogue module in the E-Granthalaya library software, the catalogue information such as author, title, editor, publisher, volume number, ISBN and also accession number, class number and subject category can be entered in a standard format. This software also facilitates the bar coding of catalogue information of a book. It helps the stock verification in a proper and speedy way. The maximum utilisation is obtained from the stock of the library with the use of the computerised catalogue.

5.4 Circulation Module

A large majority of the libraries (89%) adopted ledger system for the circulation of books. In this method, in some of the libraries, the details of the books issued are recorded in a separate register serially under the date of issue, and in other, a separate page in the ledger is assigned for each member for recording the details of the books borrowed by them. While returning the books, it was marked against the corresponding items. Few libraries keep a membership card for each member with details of membership, and at the time of issue of books, the details of the books are noted on it and filed according to the membership number. In other few libraries, a book card with the details of books is prepared for each book and kept in the book themselves. While issuing the books, the details of the members are noted down on them and filed by the book number. When the books are returned, it is noted on the card and the book card is kept back in the books.

The circulation module supports the creation of membership database and the circulation of books. The details such as name, group, designation, address, gender, admission date and closing date can be entered to create membership database of a public library. This computerised database helps the public libraries to develop the user-statistics by gender, age-group, economic level, educational level and social status. It also helps to take issue statistics by the category of books, subjects, gender, category of members, etc.

5.5 Serial Control

Most of the public libraries subscribe to Malayalam weeklies and a meagre number of the libraries keep the bound volumes of some of the important periodicals. Half of the libraries lend periodicals to the members. The public libraries do not keep a proper record for entering the serial details and their receipts.

Serial module helps the public libraries to add details such as serials details, subscription information, automatic scheduling of missing issues, reminders for non-receipt of issues, and add bound volumes. The librarians can effectively control the subscription to the serials in the libraries by using E-Granthalaya.

5.6 Article Indexing Module

Article indexing is an important value added service to the members of the public libraries especially to the students and scholars. Article indexing module helps to create articles' database and populate it on web. The educational role of the public libraries can be fulfilled by offering this service.

5.7 Budget Control

E-Granthalaya facilitates public libraries in the works related to budget control such as to add budget details, add bill details, generate payment request form, etc.

5.8 OPAC

The library catalogue is one of the important services of the public libraries which enhance the optimum utilisation of their collection. The present practice of ledger catalogue is not an effective tool to find the books required by the readers. The OPAC is an innovative service which helps the members to find the books required by the fields such as author, title, class number, accession number and subjects.

6. Major Problems

The following are the major problems hindering the automation of public libraries in Kerala.

6.1 Lack of Trained Library Staff

Most of the librarians in the public libraries in Kerala are not professionally qualified and they have inadequate knowledge about the potentials of computers and their use in libraries. The lack of trained library staff is the main hindrance in the automation of public libraries.

6.2 Lack of Fund

Lack of adequate fund is one of the main obstacles in general and the libraries in particular in the automation of the public libraries in the State. The library authorities finance some of the libraries for the purchase of computers and also software and not for its maintenance and training.

6.3 Lack of Standardisation

Some of the public libraries in the State computerised in its own way using the locally developed software, not based on any national/international standards. It is seen that these softwares cannot meet all functions and services in the public libraries, that is, they are not comprehensive.

6.4 Under Utilisation

In the majority of the libraries the computers are used for replacing the clerical works. The libraries are under utilising the capabilities of this new technology such as automation of various functions and services in the public libraries and the provision of Internet.

7. Suggestions

The following suggestions are put forward for successful adoption of automation in the public libraries.

1. Kerala Government should allocate sufficient fund to support the automation of public libraries in the State.
2. Raja Rammohan Roy Library Foundation (RRRLF), the funding agent for the public libraries under the Union Government may show keen interest in the automation of the public libraries with the provision of more fund.
3. Kerala State Library Council should take leadership in the automation of the public libraries in the State and should select a suitable library management software which is flexible to the public library needs and to make accessible the regional language.
4. Kerala State Library Council should make necessary arrangements to provide training classes to the library personnels.
5. Kerala State Library Council should organise seminars and workshops to create awareness among libraries about the potential advantage of automation.

8. Conclusion

In future the public libraries will become attractive by the introduction of new services based on new technology. Libraries offering traditional services are likely to face increasing competition from new technology and new media. The computerised library services and operations will enhance the effectiveness and efficiency of library services and can provide value added services to the society. In the context of changing concept of public libraries, librarians should be qualified and skilled to handle automated libraries. IFLA/UNESCO (2001) state "public libraries have an exciting opportunity to help bring everyone into this global conversation and to bring what is often called the 'digital divide'. They can achieve this by providing information technology for public access by teaching basic computer skills.[5]

NOTES

1. IFLA/UNESCO (2001). *Public Library Service: IFLA/UNESCO guidelines for development*. Munchen: K.G. Saur.
2. Sudha, A. (2010). *Public Libraries in Malabar*. New Delhi: Serials.
3. Kerala State Library Council (2011). *Annual report and budget 2010-2011*. Trivandrum: Kerala State Library Council.
4. http: www.e-granthalaya.nic.in (Retrieved on 31st March, 2011).
5. IFLA/UNESCO (2001). *Public Library Service: IFLA/UNESCO guidelines for development*. Munchen: K.G. Saur.

PART V

INFORMATION USERS AND USER STUDIES

Information Need and Modern Information Retrieval

14

Khaisar Muneebulla Khan and *R. Pooja*

1. Introduction

The purpose of a library or an information system is to fulfill some needs for documents and information for users or potential users. Such needs may, for example, be related to educational activities, research activities, professional activities, recreation activities, cultural activities or personal development. It is important that need is not mistaken for demand. The demand for information or documents may be low, because the library is seen as inaccessible by the users. Still, the needs exist. An information need may be more or less recognized by the users.

Information needs are not "internal mental states". This is a mistaken understanding related to the subjectivity of the *cognitive view* and the concept of *ASK* ("Anomalous State of Knowledge"). A realist is quite different: If a person is in a problematic situation for which an effective solution exists, then the documents which inform about that solution are *relevant* whether the user recognizes this or not. The user needs the documents, but this need is not an individual mental state. It is something that a third part may recognize or claim is needed. To say that students have to learn mathematics, for example, is to claim that they will encounter situations in which mathematical knowledge is relevant and needed. This is the case whether or not the children recognize this need.[1]

1.1 Meaning and Definition

Information need is an individual or group's desire to locate and obtain *information* to satisfy a conscious or unconscious *need*. The 'information' and 'need' in 'information need' are inseparable interconnection. Needs and interests call forth information. Information needs are related to, but distinct from *information requirements*. An example is that a need is hunger, the requirement is food.[2]

According to Crawford[3] information needs depend on:

- Work activity
- Discipline / Field / Area of interest
- Availability of facilities
- Hierarchical position of individuals
- Motivation factors for information needs
- Need to take a decision
- Need to seek new ideas
- Need to validate the correct ones
- Need to make professional contributions
- Need to establish priority for discovery, etc.

The objectives of studying information needs are:

1. The explanation of observed phenomena of information use or expressed need;
2. The prediction of instances of information uses;
3. The control and thereby improvement of the utilization of information manipulation of essentials conditions.

Over time, the information field has developed a deepening understanding of the concept of information need and its role in information seeking and use. The view that information need motivates information behaviour is an embedded assumption of the user-oriented paradigm which focuses upon what people think, do and feel when they seek and use information. Observing and generalizing a concept of information need which exists in an individual's head as an inner motivational state is a challenge. One can only infer the nature of information need based on the behaviour that it engenders (information seeking and use), but, over time, information scientists have studied the complexities of this key concept.

1.2 Factors Affecting Information Needs

- The range of information sources available;
- The uses to which the information will be put;
- The background, motivation, professional orientation and other individual characteristics of the user;
- The social, political, economic, legal and regulatory systems surrounding the user; and
- The consequences of information use.[4]

1.3 Complexity and Problems Associated with Information Needs Identification

- Same information is perceived by different users differently as their information need (Value system of users differs due to the nature of work and it affects factors such as the information products and services);
- Researchers need original documents whereas planners need digests of 'point of view' / opinions);
- Information is put to different uses (R & D personnel, Application developers and Technicians all put information to different uses);
- Need is satisfied by having access to the identified information in a particular package and form, and at a suitable time;
- The flow of information and channels of communication are complex and add to the complexity; and
- Individual preferences and behavioural aspects add a further dimension.

Apart from the complexities mentioned above, there are problems due to individual behaviour too:

- A user may not like to reveal his/her need as s/he may like to show that s/he is above (any) requirements and that s/he knows his/her sources. To divert or mislead s/he may give or just because someone else is getting an information s/he may give a pseudo need to receive the same information. A super ordinate, to avoid a subordinate getting informed, may give it as a pseudo need and try to withhold the information received.

- Further, an interaction of all the above factors makes the process of identifying information needs akin to carrying out an investigation or detective work, and is one of the 'grey areas' of research in Library and Information Science for the past few decades.[4]

2. Information Retrieval

Information Retrieval (IR) is the science of searching for documents, for information within documents, and for metadata about documents, as well as that of searching relational databases and the World Wide Web. There is overlap in the usage of the terms data retrieval, document retrieval, information retrieval, and text retrieval, but each also has its own body of literature, theory, praxis, and technologies. IR is interdisciplinary, based on computer science, mathematics, library science, information science, information architecture, cognitive psychology, linguistics, and statistics. Automated information retrieval systems are used to reduce what has been called "information overload". Many universities and public libraries use IR systems to provide access to books, journals and other documents. Web search engines are the most visible IR applications.

2.1 Meaning and Definition

The meaning of the term information retrieval can be very broad. Just getting a credit card out of the wallet so that one can type in the card number is a form of information retrieval. However, as an academic field of study, information retrieval (IR) is finding material (usually documents) of an unstructured nature (usually text) that satisfies an information need from within large collections (usually stored on computers). As defined in this way, information retrieval used to be an activity that only a few people engaged in: reference librarians, paralegals, and similar professional searchers. Now the world has changed, and hundreds of millions of people engage in information retrieval every day when they use a web search engine or search their e-mail. Information retrieval is fast becoming the dominant form of information access, overtaking traditional database style searching.

2.2 Information Retrieval Process

An information retrieval process begins when a user enters a query into the system. Queries are formal statements of information needs, for example search strings in web search engines. In information retrieval a query does not uniquely identify a single object in the collection. Instead, several objects may match the query, perhaps with different degrees of relevancy. An object is an entity that is represented by information in a database. User queries are matched against the database information depending on the application the data objects may be, for example, text documents, images, or videos. Often the documents themselves are not kept or stored directly in the IR system, but are instead represented in the system by document surrogates or metadata.

Most IR systems compute a numeric score on how well each object in the database match the query, and rank the objects according to this value. The top ranking objects are then shown to the user. The process may then be iterated if the user wishes to refine the query. In order to fulfill the information needs of users there should be some effective information retrieval system with latest technologies. Information Retrieval deals with the representation, storage, organization and access to information items. The representation and organization of the information items should provide the user with easy access to the information in which he is interested.

2.3 History of IR

For approximately 4000 years, man has organized information for later retrieval and usage. A typical example is the table of contents of a book. Since the volume of information eventually grew beyond a few books, it became necessary to build specialized data structures to ensure faster access to the stored information. An old and popular data structure for faster information retrieval is a collection of selected words or concepts which have associated pointers to the related information (or documents). In one form or another, indexes are at the core of every modern information retrieval system. They provide faster access to the data and allow the query processing task to be speeded up. For centuries, indexes were created manually as categorization hierarchies. In fact, most libraries still use some form of categorical hierarchy to classify their volumes (or documents). Such hierarchies have usually been conceived by human subjects from the library sciences field.[5]

2.4 Modern Information Retrieval

Information Retrieval (IR) has changed considerably in the last several years with the expansion of the Web (World Wide Web) and the advent of modern and inexpensive graphical user interfaces and mass storage devices. As a result, traditional IR textbooks have become quite out-of-date which has led to the introduction of new IR books recently. The user information need cannot be used directly to request information using the current interfaces of Web search engines. Instead, the user must first translate this information need into a query which can be processed by the search engine (or IR system). In its most common form, this translation results a set of keywords (or index terms) which summarizes the description of the user information need. Given the user query, the key goal of an IR system is to retrieve information which might be useful or relevant to the user. The emphasis is on the retrieval of information instead of the retrieval of data.

In the past 20 years, the area of information retrieval has grown well beyond its primary goals of indexing text and searching for useful documents in a collection. Nowadays, research in IR includes modeling, document classification and categorization, systems architecture, user interfaces, data visualization, filtering languages, etc. Despite its maturity, until recently, IR was seen as a narrow area of interest mainly to librarians and information experts. Such a tendentious vision prevailed for many years, despite the rapid dissemination, among users of modern personal computers, of IR tools for multimedia and hypertext applications. In the beginning of the 1990s, a single fact changed once and for all these perceptions is the introduction of the World Wide Web. The Web is becoming a universal repository of human knowledge and culture which has allowed uninterrupted sharing of ideas and information in a scale never seen before. Its success is based on the conception of a standard user interface which is always the same no matter what computational environment is used to run the interface. As a result, the user is shielded from details of communication protocols, machine location, and operating systems. Further, any user can create his own Web documents and make them point to any other Web documents without restrictions. This is a key aspect because it turns the Web into a new publishing medium accessible to everybody.[5]

2.5 User-Retrieval System Interaction

The user of a retrieval system has to translate his information need into a query in the language provided by the system. With an information retrieval system, this normally implies specifying a set of words which convey the semantics of the information need. With a data retrieval system, a query expression (such as, for instance, a regular expression) is used to convey the constraints that must be satisfied by objects in the answer set. In both cases the user searches for useful information executing a retrieval task. Consider now a user who has an interest which is either poorly deed or which is inherently broad. For instance, the user might be interested in documents about medical subjects in general. In this situation, the user might use an interactive interface to simply look around in the collection for documents. But while searching, his attention may also be diverted into related topics like Medical Education, Patient Care, Knowledge about various diseases, drugs used, etc. In this situation, the user is said to be browsing the documents in the collection, not searching. It is still a process of retrieving information, but one whose main objectives are not clearly defined in the beginning and whose purpose might change during the interaction with the system.

Both retrieval and browsing are, in the language of the World Wide Web, 'pulling' actions. That is, the user requests the information in an interactive manner. An alternative is to do retrieval in an automatic and permanent fashion using software agents which push the information towards the user. For instance, information useful to a user could be extracted periodically from a news service. In this case, the IR system is executing a particular retrieval task which consists of filtering relevant information for later inspection by the user.

2.6 Role of Libraries in Information Retrieval

Libraries were among the first institutions to adopt IR systems for retrieving information. Usually, systems to be used in libraries were initially developed by academic institutions and later by commercial vendors. In the first generation, such systems consisted basically of an automation of previous technologies (such as card catalogues) and basically allowed searches based on author name and title. In the second generation, increased search functionality was added which allowed searching by subject headings, by keywords, and some more complex query facilities. In the third generation, which is currently being deployed, the focus is on improved graphical interfaces, electronic forms, hypertext features, and open system architectures.

2.7 Role of Web and Digital Libraries in Information Retrieval

The search engines continue to use indexes which are very similar to those used by librarians a century ago and three dramatic and fundamental changes have occurred due to the advances in modern computer technology and the advancement of the Web. First, it became a lot cheaper to have access to various sources of information. This allows reaching a wider audience than ever possible before. Second, the advances in all kinds of digital communication provided greater access to networks. This implies that the information source is available even if distantly located and that the access can be done quickly (frequently, in a few seconds). Third, the freedom to post whatever information someone judges useful has greatly contributed to the popularity of the Web. For the first time in history, many people have free access to a large publishing medium. Fundamentally, low cost, greater access, and publishing freedom have allowed people to use the Web (and modern digital libraries) as a highly interactive medium. Such interactivity allows people to exchange messages, photos, documents, software, videos, and to 'chat' in a convenient and low cost fashion. Further, people can do it at the time of their preference (for instance, you can buy a book late at night) which further improves the convenience of the service. Thus, high interactivity is the fundamental and current shift in the communication paradigm.[5]

2.8 Problems Associated with IR System

More recently, the advent of modern computers has made possible the construction of large indexes automatically. Automatic indexes provide a view of the retrieval problem which is much more related to the system itself than to the user need. In this respect, it is important to distinguish between two different views of the IR problem: a computer-centred one and a human-centred one. In the computer-centred view, the IR problem consists mainly of building up efficient indexes, processing user queries with high performance, and developing ranking algorithms which improve the 'quality' of the answer set. In the human-centred view, the IR problem consists mainly of studying the behaviour of the user, of understanding his main needs, and of determining how such understanding affects the organization and operation of the retrieval system. According to this view, keyword based query processing might be seen as a strategy which is unlikely to yield a good solution to the information retrieval problem in the long run.

2.9 Future Trends of Information Retrieval

In the future, three main questions need to be addressed. First, despite the high interactivity, people still find it difficult (if not impossible) to retrieve information relevant to their information needs. Thus, in the dynamic world of the Web and of large digital libraries, which techniques will allow retrieval of higher quality? Second, with the ever increasing demand for access, quick response is becoming more and more a pressing factor. Thus, which techniques will yield faster indexes and smaller query response times? Third, the quality of the retrieval task is greatly affected by the user interaction with the system. Thus, how will a better understanding of the user behaviour affect the design and deployment of new information retrieval strategies? Therefore the user needs a new technology which could answer all these questions.[6]

3. Conclusion

The drastic change in information environment calls for continual research to ensure that the needs of the information users are satisfactorily met and that the information professionals acquire the required expertise to cope with the operational management of the information resources and plan for the future. To ensure this, there is an urgent need to understand and grasp the complex process of 'identifying information needs', which is a very vital link in the chain of operations from information gathering to dissemination. Further, one might spend a lot of time, effort and money mining the various information sources and gather a great deal of sound information that does not answer the key questions of the users' decision-making/action taking process. Hence before initiating, building and developing any information centre/system, the relevance of information to be gathered must be checked thoroughly, this in turn depends entirely on the 'identification of information needs'. Moreover, the effectiveness of an information system depends on the extent to which the system's characteristics are in correspondence with the situation of the user and on how much the potential user of the system is willing and able to make use of the services provided by the information system. A careful identification, analysis and classification of the 'real' information needs of users (including all potential users and non-users as well) is an essential basis for the planning, implementation and operation of information systems. In fact, any lapse in proper identification of information needs will affect the efficiency and effectiveness of information systems and services. A very peculiar situation is faced perhaps only by the library and information professionals. They cannot prescribe the needed information to their clientele in the way the other professionals like physicians, lawyers, architects and engineers prescribe, where such prescriptions have a final say and authority, and which are gladly accepted by the clients. The prescription is authoritative mainly because the clients of physicians and other professionals are seeking advice in a field which they themselves are ignorant of, whereas the clients of information professionals are mostly specialists in the areas they seek information and professional advice. This is also the reason for the difficulties experienced by the information professionals in distinguishing the wishes/desires from the actual needs of the users. Hence the information professional has to prepare himself/herself in such a way as to create confidence in the users about his/her professional capabilities. Also, if the investigation of information needs is to be successful, it is important to bear in mind that the person chosen to be the Information Needs Identifier (INI) will need to be acceptable at all levels of users (and the management) and have credibility.

NOTES

1. Wilson, T.D. (1994). Information needs and uses: fifty years of progress, in: B.C. Vickery, (Ed.), *Fifty years of information progress: a Journal of Documentation review,* (pp. 15-51). London: Aslib. [Available at http://informationr.net/tdw/publ/papers/1994FiftyYears.html]
2. http://en.wikipedia.org/wiki/Information_needs (Retrieved on 3rd March, 2010).
3. Crawford, Susan (1978). Information needs and uses. *Annual Review of Information Science and Technology*, 13, 61-81.
4. Devadason, F.J. (1996). A methodology for the Identification of information needs of users, 62nd IFLA General Conference—Conference Proceedings, August 25-31.
5. Baeza-Yates, Ricardo (1999). *Modern information retrieval.* New York: ACM Press.
6. Frakes, William B. (1992). *Information retrieval data structures & algorithms.* New Delhi: Prentice-Hall.

Availability and Use of Socio-political Information on the Internet by the University Students in Kerala

15

V.K. Dhanyasree

> The sharp, compelling sense of humanity will have to be our weapon in times to come, when everything—our homes, our fields, our jobs, our rivers, our electricity, our right to protest, and our dignity—is being taken from us.
>
> Arundhati Roy[1]

1. Introduction

Information is one of the fundamental resources indispensable for development in all the vital spheres of the life of the civilized society. It is this realization, which has been largely responsible to inspire and encourage today the appropriately directed development initiatives at the national level all over the world.[2]

Information is an essential component for each and every human activity in the world. It is essentially needed by the policy makers, planners, scientists and technologists, economists, administrators, financial institutions, investors, entrepreneurs as well as analysis and decision makers involved in taking decisions affecting the society as whole because on the one side it provides the sound basis for taking gainful decision and on the other side it is an instrument of change which is essential for development in the fast changing societal needs. The type of information they need is also of considerable diversity. It includes socio-economic data and statistical information on current plans and issues, financial data, information on technologies, legal information, etc.[3]

In the present world of expanding communication facilities, information is an extremely important commodity.[4] Electronic medium is a powerful tool having vast and wide applications in the society. It has a pivotal role in information transfer and their efficiency and effectiveness. CD-ROM was the first to find application and later on online databases. Today the Internet with hypertext navigating tools like the World Wide Web (WWW) have opened opportunities for providing better information services.[5]

In recent years, telecommunications and computers, and in particular their combinations into integrated (convergent) systems have brought about great changes in the accessibility and processing of information. These systems now permit formal and informal information transfer worldwide on a massive scale, by satellite data transmission, video conferencing, electronic mail and the like, in addition to the conventional telephone and fax systems. Users can access remote databases on the other side of the world, select the information they require and download it into their own computer system for further processing and analysis. In the informal sector, Internet is the latest facility.[6]

Internet has made profound effect on the way in which people acquire, organize and disseminate information due to the astounding increase in the amount of information available at the information super highway and the diversity of tools available for managing information.[7]

There are vast resources of information available on the Internet on various topics and subjects including socio-political issues. There are several websites giving information about general socio-political issues and current issues. Besides this, a number of online newspapers and online news channels are available on the net from which users can access specific socio-political information.

There are hundreds of socio-political problems, big or small as the problems of poverty and dependency, crime and delinquency, sickness and physical handicap, unemployment and discontent, ignorance and superstition, war, population pressure and scores of other social ills that blight and mar the prosperity and progress of society. Some are obvious and clamour for remedial measures, and scores of social-work agencies, public and private, have been organised to remedy this one on that of these obvious social ills. Other problems are less obvious, and creep into the community and national life and sap the group vitality without being comprehended. Some problems respond quickly to the proper treatment, others require a programme of treatment extending over a generation or more.[8]

The Internet resources cover information on a wide range of socio-political issues such as environmental problems, gender inequality, terrorism, and violence, communalism, social justice, drug abuse, atrocities against women, child abuse, poverty, unemployment, population explosion, youth unrest, corruption, etc. at national level and even international level. All such information on the net is very up-to-date and is in pace with the fast moving information society.

Socio-political issues are of great importance in the modern changing world. Most of the problems faced by the world today are problems related to socio-political issues. The social evils such as dowry, female infanticide, atrocities against women, drug addiction, etc. and political issues such as terrorism, war, etc. are of much importance to the younger generations especially among the academic community. The younger generations are expected to fight against these evils in a more effective way. To fight against these problems, proper awareness about these problems is essential. The Internet being the medium of faster communication and a source of abundant information, the educated youths will be depending on Internet for getting up-to-date information on socio-political issues of the world.

2. Objectives of the Study

1. To find out the purpose of seeking socio-political information on the Internet by the students.
2. To understand the availability of socio-political information on the Internet.
3. To find out the category of socio-political issues on which students seek information on the Internet.

3. Methodology

The data were collected from 150 students undergoing different courses in university departments in Kerala using a structured questionnaire. All the questionnaires received back were not complete in every respect. Hence, the questionnaires which were complete in every respect were taken into consideration for the analysis. Thus the final sample consists of only 133 students.

4. Major Findings

1. Comparatively larger percentage of the male students (46.15%) and the majority of the female students (58.82%) seek socio-political information on Internet to have an awareness of current issues.
2. The availability of information on environmental pollution is average according to the majority of the male students (50.77%). The availability of information regarding crime and violence is also average in the opinion of comparatively larger percentage of the male students (41.54%). The majority of the male students opine that the availability of information on economic inequality related problems is average (53.85%). Comparatively larger percentage of the male students feels that the availability of information on drug addiction (38.46%), suicide (44.61%) and child marriage, divorce, etc. (47.69%) is average. It is also observed that the majority of the male students (56.92%) have the opinion that the availability of information on child labour is average.
3. The availability of information about environmental pollution is good according to the majority of the female students (51.47%). Comparatively larger percentage of the female students (42.65%) opines that the availability of information regarding crime and violence is good. The majority of the female students (52.94%) are of the opinion that the availability of information about economic inequality related problems is average. In the case of information about drug

addiction, comparatively larger percentage of the female students (39.71%) opines that their availability is average. Half (50%) of the female students feel that the availability of information on suicide is average. At the same time the majority of the female students (55.88%) opine that the availability of information on child marriage, divorce, etc. is also average. Comparatively larger percentage of the female students (42.65%) are of the opinion that the availability of information about child labour is average.

4. The majority of the male students (81.54%) and female students (75%) are of the opinion that socio-political information on Internet is moderately reliable.
5. In the opinion of the majority of the male students (72.31%) and female students (77.94%), information available on Internet is more current compared to that in print sources.
6. The majority of the male students (52.31%) seek information on terrorism and violence while the majority of the female students (61.76%) seek information on environmental problems.
7. The majority of the male students (92.31%) and female students (89.71%) often use Google for searching socio-political information. More than half of the female students (52.94 per cent) also use Yahoo. This reveals that the most often used search engine among students for searching socio-political information is Google.
8. The majority of the male students (55.85%) and half of the female students (50%) search for information on socio-political issues by giving keywords.
9. Comparatively larger percentage of the male students (43.08%) search information on problems in which they are interested. But comparatively larger percentage of the female students (47.06%) usually search information on current problems.

10. The majority of the male students (72.31%) and female students (69.12%) prefer general web information for getting information on socio-political issues.
11. The majority of the male students (63.08%) and female students (61.76%) feel that electronic sources are more easy to use than print sources for getting socio-political information.

5. Conclusion

It can be observed from the analysis that the most important purpose of seeking information relating to socio-political issues on the Internet is to have an awareness of the current issues. This shows that the students in Kerala are eager to know about the current socio-political issues. The availability of information is not so high. This calls for the attention of all the concerned to provide more information relating to socio-political issues through Internet. Information relating to environmental problems is the most important socio-political information sought by the female students. The most important information sought by male students is the information relating to terrorism and violence. Thus it can be observed that the students are concerned about environmental problems, terrorism and violence.

NOTES

1. Arundhati Roy (2005). *An Ordinary Person's Guide to Empire*. New Delhi: Penguin
2. Bhattacharya, G. (1996). Information: its definition for its service professionals. *IASLIC Bulletin*, 41(3), 97-112.
3. Bhatt, R.K., Srivastava, J.P. and Saleem Anwar (2003). Consortia based subscription to electronic resources for SCI-tech libraries: a practical approach towards effective use of financial resources. In Panday S.K. Sharma (Ed.), *Electronic information environment and library services: a contemporary paradigm*. Delhi: Indian Library Association, 214-21.
4. Pawar, S.S. (1996). Role of electronic and communication media in networks of libraries and information centres in India. In R.P. Kumar, Divya Srivastava and S.P. Gupta (Ed.), *Role of Libraries in National Development*. Delhi: Indian Library Association, 373-83.
5. Hanna Noor (2006). *Use of electronic information resources among the teaching faculty of Calicut University*. Unpublished MLISc Dissertation. University of Calicut.

6. Kaye, David (1995). Sources of information, formal and informal. *Library Management*, 16(5), 16-19.
7. Raman Nair, R. (2002). *Internet for Information Services*. New Delhi: Ess Ess.
8. Gillin, John Lewis et al. (1952). *Social problems*. Bombay: Times of India Press.

Need for Information Literacy Programmes in University Libraries

16

K. Anoopa

1. Introduction

The human race has progressed from a low productivity agricultural society through a more highly productive industrial society to a knowledge society of high productivity. In knowledge society people are receiving knowledge and adapting themselves to it. Education and training are the needs of the knowledge society to adapt to the changing environments and to gain more knowledge.

In modern times a library occupies a central service role in supporting the education system. The basic test of the quality of any library is its ability to get into the hands of the user, the information he wants at the exact time of the need. For this, a library acquires materials like books, CDs, maps, etc., processes them and makes them available for use. Now-a-days libraries are also providing Internet facilities. But in the modern era libraries are not expected simply to satisfy the information needs of the users but to create information needs by trying to create awareness of information sources and techniques.

2. University Library

University library forms the apex of academic libraries. The emphasis on research distinguishes the university library from college and school libraries. The major function of a university library is to support the educational policies of the university of which it is a part. Universities of India offer facilities for organized research in all subject fields in Science and Technology, Social Science, Humanities, Medicine, Engineering, etc., but the output of the research work are not very much utilized. The main reason for this is the lack of efficient and effective library services. As a result of present day knowledge explosion, there is an increase in the output of publications. So it is relatively impossible for the students, scholars and teachers to decide what he has to choose and where he has to find it. So library should plan to educate the user to enable him for maximum utilization of resources.

2.1 Need for Information Literacy Training

Information literacy can be defined as the ability of an individual to recognize the need for information and to locate, evaluate and use effectively the needed information. In the era of technological revolution and proliferation of literature, Information Literacy is of great importance. Information is now available through several media and most of the information available is unfiltered, making the choice and evaluation much complex.

ALA[1] defines information literacy as the ability to recognize when information is needed and the ability to identify, locate, evaluate and use information effectively. A person can be called as information literate when he is able to find, use and synthesis information by him. He may be prepared for lifelong learning. Bibliographic instruction, library orientation, and user education are the other terms used to denote the information literacy.

Today there is great emphasis on self-education. A student in higher education may have developed a logical, creative and critical approach to his subject. He needs the knowledge and skill to find out the needed information by him. The library becomes the centre of self-study. The instrument for independent use of the library is the programme of educating the library user. A trained user will be less dependent on library staff.

Most of the University libraries are either automated or are in the process of being automated. Implementation of IT requires some literacy for both user and staff. Now many of the books and periodicals can be accessed electrically via Internet. The Internet provides opportunity to extent learning outside space and time boundaries. So library should support users in the form of training to provide them with the skill needed for effective exploitation of resources.

Libraries have to teach the users how to search the OPAC. Instruction in the use of the computerized database, might lead to more sophisticated searches, thus becoming exposed to more information.

An IL programme will help the user to understand:

- The functions of the library.
- The form, format, location and access methods of information sources.
- How to use the library services and techniques.
- The use of IT based tools like OPAC, CD-ROM, internet, e-publishing, etc....

3. The Present Study

The present study is conducted among the users of University Libraries in Kerala to find out whether the users are information literate and to identify the need for Information Literacy Programmes in a university library setting.

4. Objectives of the Study

1. To find out the level of knowledge of the library techniques, sources, tools and services.
2. To know whether they can get the required document without any guidance.
3. To know the need for IL Programmes.
4. To suggest different methods or training programmes suitable for a university library.

5. Sample

The study was conducted on a sample of 80 postgraduate students in various university departments. Questionnaires were distributed to these students out of which 71 were filled and returned. Personal observation of library organization and services was also carried out. Among the 71 persons responded to the survey 35 were females and 36 were males.

6. Analysis

The data collected using the questionnaire is tabulated for further analysis and interpretation. Percentage method is used to derive findings.

Table 16.1: Awareness about Library Resources and Services (Males)

Resource/Service	Aware	Not Aware	Total
Collection	26 (72.22)	10 (27.78)	36 (100)
Service	16 (44.44)	20 (55.56)	36 (100)

Note: Figures in brackets show the respective percentages.

Table 16.1 shows that the majority of the male users (72.22%) are aware of the collection of the library. However, the majority of the male users (55.56%) are not aware of the services of the library.

Table 16.2: Awareness about Library Resources and Services (Females)

Resource/Service	Aware	Not Aware	Total
Collection	30 (85.71)	5 (14.29)	35 (100)
Service	4 (44.44)	31 (55.56)	35 (100)

Note: Figures in brackets show the respective percentages.

Table 16.2 reveals that the majority of the female users (85.71%) are aware of the collection of the library. However, the majority (88.57%) are not aware of the services.

Table 16.3: Method of Locating Books

Source	Male	Female	Total
From Catalogue	9 (25.00)	5 (14.29)	14 (19.71)
With the help of Staff	5 (13.89)	3 (8.57)	8 (11.27)
Directly from the Shelf	22 (61.11)	27 (77.14)	49 (69.01)

Note: Figures in brackets show the respective percentages.

It can be seen from Table 16.3 that the majority of the male (61.11%) and female (77.14%) users of the University library locate books direct from the shelf.

Table 16.4: Details about the Use of Different Sections

Section	Male	Female	Total
Maintenance	10 (27.78)	20 (57.14)	30 (42.25)
Reference	10 (27.78)	14 (40.00)	24 (33.80)
Periodical/e-journal	12 (33.33)	9 (25.71)	21 (29.58)

Note: Figures in brackets show the respective percentages.

It can be seen from Table 16.4 that only the maintenance section is used by the majority of the female users (57.14%). The use of all other section is comparatively less.

Table 16.5: Details about the Use of Collection

Collection	Male	Female	Total
Reference Books	32 (88.89)	29 (82.86)	61 (85.92)
Textbooks	10 (27.78)	13 (37.14)	23 (32.39)
Competition Books	8 (22.22)	6 (17.14)	14 (19.72)
Theses/Dissertations	3 (8.33)	2 (5.71)	5 (7.04)
Periodicals	10 (27.78)	2 (5.71)	12 (16.90)

Note: Figures in brackets show the respective percentages.

Table 16.5 reveals that among the collection of the library only reference books are used by the majority of the male (88.89%) and female (82.86%) users. The use of other materials is considerably less.

Table 16.6: Opinion about Library Tools and Practices

Opinion	Male	Female	Total
Confusing	30 (83.33)	31 (88.57)	61 (85.92)
User friendly	2 (5.56)	2 (5.71)	4 (5.63)
Helpful	4 (11.11)	2 (5.71)	6 (8.45)

Note: Figures in brackets show the respective percentages.

Table 16.6 shows that according to the majority of the male (83.33%) and female (88.57%) users, the library tools and practices are confusing.

7. Findings

The important findings of the study are the following:

1. The majority of the users are aware of the collection of the library. However, the majority of the users are not aware of the services of the library.
2. The majority of the users of the University library locate books direct from the shelf.
3. Only the maintenance section is used by the majority of the female users. The use of all other section is comparatively less. The use of all sections by the male users is less.
4. Among the collection of the library only reference books are used by the majority of the users. The use of other materials is considerably less.
5. According to the majority of the users, the library tools and practices are confusing.

8. Implications

The majority of the users are not aware of the services of the library. The use of library collection also is not high. The opinion of the users shows that the library tools and practices are confusing. It can be observed from the analysis that Information Literacy programmes are essential in the university library.

9. Conclusion

In the age of information explosion only information literate users can make the best use of the library. Hence, they should be trained well to find out and use information effectively. This will add value to the library profession as a whole. As the users are not much aware of the library services, tools and practices, the use of the library collection is not up to the mark. This calls for the introduction of Information Literacy programme among the university library users of Kerala.

NOTE

1. http://www.ala.org/ala/mgrps/divs/acrl/standards/informationliteracycompetency.cfm#ildef (Retrieved on 10th March, 2011).

Role of Information in Managerial Decision-making

17

Mehjabeen Aideed

1. Introduction

Information is a resource of immense economic and social value. It is vital for proper functioning of a democratic society, a crucial tool in a productive economy and an effective government, a central part of the growth and well-being of individuals. The ability of man in thinking and decision-making has given him the power to rule the universe. This power lies in gathering and addressing the relevant information relating to a particular problem. For taking a decision he has to gather the information from several sources. Information relating to trade and stock market industries, research, management of offices and homes, etc. is required in course of decision-making. As such information has become an indispensable resource to the individual. Information is required at the personal level and society level for the development and management of things.

Information is the knowledge derived from data that have been transformed to make them meaningful and useful. In effect, data are subjected to a value added process that yields meaningful information for decision-making.[1]

Good information is essential for effective operation and decision-making at all levels in businesses. Most managers would agree that good information is essential to the success of an organization. If an organization is to survive and prosper, it must understand both its own internal workings and the nature of the environment to which it has to adapt and respond. Good information improves decision-making, enhances efficiency and provides a competitive edge to the organizations. But in modern times information has acquired a new status and importance as an organizational resource.

Information plays a crucial role in planning and decision-making in organizations. Information-rich managers build up information networks actively and demonstrate an open-minded willingness to expose themselves to, and trade, information with others. They harness ideas and knowledge to policy and are characterised as being those decision-makers most implicated with framing policy. Theirs is information which goes beyond subject domain boundaries. They show awareness of semantic and psycho-social barriers in information acquisition and handling, and are motivated to adopt the utility-benefit approach to information in their company.

Information to have a real value to decision-making, it must be accurate, timely, relevant and complete. Information is a vital part of every manager's job. Managers use information to make decisions and conduct their work, and create new information used by others. Information has always been a key element in the performance of a business and the effectiveness of management, and information technology can now transform the use of this information to give managers substantial benefits in business planning and decision-making.

The part that information plays in making choices may not be understood in a number of distinct ways. The reality is that there is too much, rather than too little, information. Usually the valuable source of information for decision-making is intuition. But it may not be used because of over-emphasis on the importance of the rational decision-making. Judgment and hunch may be excluded from the decision process so effectively as to block the creative process of arriving at sound choices. There is also a need to recognize the extent to which information tends to be biased or non-objective. Confusion over handling and evaluating information can thus be another form of obstacle to decision-making.

Managers must consequently take a critical view about information. In recent years, micro processing technology has radically transformed the ability to acquire, analyse and produce information of various kinds, much of it in quantified form. Since decision-making is information-based the practicing managers must not merely understand the role of information for informing, instructing and motivating, but ensure that it contributes constructively to decision-making through being timely, relevant, available and intelligible.[2]

The role of information within management is in a state of dramatic transformation. Managers must grasp and act on the implications of this change if they are to maintain their competitive position both corporately and as individuals. Information technology continues to develop at an exponential rate. But it is only an extension of what has gone before, and should be understood and used in this light. Information relevant to managers is now accessible than ever before, particularly through the use of electronic databases and networks. Individual managers, whatever their function, must learn to take full advantage of the information resources available to them, and do so continuously as part of their management techniques. Organizations must develop an information strategy and corporate structure which ensures the fullest use of internal and external resources.

2. Objectives of the Study

The following are the important objectives of the study.

1. To find out the level of use of information by managers.
2. To assess the impact of information on the decision-making of the managers.

3. Methodology

The present study is conducted on a sample of 57 managers of small and medium size industries in Kerala who responded positively to the questionnaire distributed among higher, middle and lower level managers.

4. Analysis

The responses obtained from the managers are presented in the following Tables. Percentage method has been used for analysing the responses.

Table 17.1: Opinion about Role of Information in Decision-making

Opinion	Higher	Middle	Lower	Total
Very essential	31 (93.94)	15 (88.24)	3 (42.86)	49 (85.97)
Somewhat essential	1 (3.03)	2 (11.76)	4 (57.14)	7 (12.28)
Not essential	1 (3.03)	0 (0.00)	0 (0.00)	1 (1.75)
Total	33 (100.00)	17 (100.00)	7 (100.00)	57 (100.00)

Note: The figures in brackets show the respective percentages.

It can be observed from the Table 17.1 that the majority of the higher level and middle level managers are of the opinion that information is very essential for managerial decision-making. However the majority of the lower level managers have the opinion that information is somewhat essential for decision-making.

Table 17.2: Frequency of Using Information for Managerial Decision-making (Higher Level Managers)

Type of Information	Always	Sometimes	Never	Total
Information for product design and manufacture	23 (69.70)	7 (21.21)	3 (9.09)	33 (100.00)
Accounting and Tax information	15 (45.45)	17 (51.52)	1 (3.03)	33 (100.00)
Information on Human resource management	24 (72.73)	8 (24.24)	1 (3.03)	33 (100.00)
Sales and marketing information	24 (72.73)	7 (21.21)	2 (6.06)	33 (100.00)

Note: The figures in brackets show the respective percentages.

The in Table 17.2 the majority of the higher level managers always use information for product design and manufacture, information on human resource management and sales and marketing information for managerial decision-making. At the same time accounting and tax information is used sometimes by the majority.

Table 17.3: Frequency of Using Information for Managerial Decision-making (Middle Level Managers)

Type of Information	Always	Sometimes	Never	Total
Information for product design and manufacture	11 (64.71)	5 (29.41)	1 (5.88)	17 (100.00)
Accounting and Tax information	5 (29.41)	10 (58.82)	2 (11.77)	17 (100.00)
Information on Human resource management	12 (70.59)	5 (29.41)	0 (0.00)	17 (100.00)
Sales and marketing information	13 (76.47)	4 (23.53)	0 (0.00)	17 (100.00)

Note: The figures in brackets show the respective percentages.

Table 17.3 shows that the majority of the middle level managers always use information for product design and manufacture, information on human resource management and sales and marketing information for managerial decision-making. However, accounting and tax information is used only sometime by the majority of the middle level managers.

Table 17.4: Frequency of Using Information for Managerial Decision-making (Lower Level Managers)

Type of Information	Always	Sometimes	Never	Total
Information for product design and manufacture	3 (42.86)	3 (42.86)	1 (14.28)	7 (100.00)
Accounting and Tax information	2 (28.57)	5 (71.43)	0 (0.00)	7 (100.00)
Information on Human resource management	3 (42.86)	4 (57.14)	0 (0.00)	7 (100.00)
Sales and marketing information	5 (71.43)	2 (28.57)	0 (0.00)	7 (100.00)

Note: The figures in brackets show the respective percentages.

It can be seen from Table 17.4 that the majority of the lower level managers always use sales and marketing information for managerial decision-making whereas the majority of them use accounting and tax information and information on human resource management only sometimes for managerial decision-making.

Table 17.5: Time Spent to Collect Information for Managerial Decision-making

	Higher	Middle	Lower	Totals
Less than 2 hours	2 (6.06)	0 (0.00)	4 (57.14)	6 (10.53)
2 – 4 hours	5 (15.15)	8 (47.06)	2 (28.57)	15 (26.31)
4 – 6 hours	14 (42.42)	5 (29.41)	1 (14.29)	20 (35.09)
Above 6 hours	12 (36.37)	4 (23.53)	0 (0.00)	16 (28.07)
Total	33 (100.00)	17 (100.00)	7 (100.00)	57 (100.00)

Note: The figures in brackets show the respective percentages

The analysis in Table 17.5 shows that comparatively higher percentage of the higher level managers spend 4 to 6 hours to collect information for managerial decision-making. Comparatively larger percentage of the middle level managers spend less than 2-4 hours and the majority of the lower level managers spend 2 hours to collect information for managerial decision-making.

Table 17.6: Impact of Information on Decision-making (Higher Level Managers)

Areas	To a great extent	Somewhat	To lesser extent	Total
Product designing	23 (69.70)	7 (21.21)	3 (9.09)	33 (100.00)
Pricing	24 (72.73)	8 (24.24)	1 (3.03)	33 (100.00)
Distribution of products	17 (51.52)	15 (45.45)	1 (3.03)	33 (100.00)
Sales promotion	23 (69.70)	8 (24.24)	2 (6.06)	33 (100.00)

Note: The figures in brackets show the respective percentages.

Table 17.6 reveals that the majority of the higher level managers are of the opinion that information has great impact on product designing, pricing, distribution of product and sales promotion.

Table 17.7: Impact of Information on Decision-making (Middle Level Managers)

Areas	To a great extent	Somewhat	To lesser extent	Total
Product designing	12 (70.59)	4 (23.53)	1 (5.88)	17 (100.00)
Pricing	11 (64.71)	6 (35.29)	0 (0.00)	17 (100.00)
Distribution of products	7 (41.18)	10 (58.82)	0 (0.00)	17 (100.00)
Sales promotion	12 (70.59)	4 (23.53)	1 (5.88)	17 (100.00)

Note: The figures in brackets show the respective percentages.

The analysis in Table 17.7 reveals that the majority of the middle level managers are of the opinion that information affects to a great extent product designing, pricing and sales promotion whereas information affects only somewhat in the case of distribution of products.

Table 17.8: Impact of Information on Decision-making (Lower Level Managers)

Areas	To a great extent	Somewhat	To lesser extent	Total
Product designing	2 (28.57)	5 (71.43)	0 (0.00)	7 (100.00)
Pricing	4 (57.14)	3 (42.86)	0 (0.00)	7 (100.00)
Distribution of products	3 (42.86)	4 (57.14)	0 (0.00)	7 (100.00)
Sales promotion	5 (71.43)	2 (28.57)	0 (0.00)	7 (100.00)

Note: The figures in brackets show the respective percentages.

It can be seen from Table 17.8 that the majority of the lower level managers are of the opinion that information affects to a great extent pricing decisions and decisions on sales promotion. However, the majority of the lower level managers are of the opinion that information has somewhat impact on decisions on product designing and distribution of products.

Table 17.9: Areas in which Information has Impact on Product Designing

Area	Higher	Middle	Lower	Total
Improving quality	30 (90.91)	13 (76.47)	3 (42.86)	46 (80.70)
Colour and packaging decision	6 (18.18)	4 (23.53)	2 (28.57)	12 (21.05)
Getting raw material	5 (15.15)	3 (17.65)	0 (0.00)	8 (14.04)
Deciding method of production	9 (27.27)	5 (29.41)	3 (42.86)	17 (29.82)

Note: The figures in brackets show the respective percentages.

The result from Table 17.9 shows that the majority of the higher and middle level managers are of the opinion that information has impact on improving quality of products.

Table 17.10: Impact of Information on Pricing

Area	Higher	Middle	Lower	Total
To know the price of the competitive products	27 (81.82)	13 (76.47)	5 (71.43)	45 (78.95)
To know the demand for the product	26 (78.79)	13 (76.47)	5 (71.43)	44 (77.19)
To know the profit rate	25 (75.76)	14 (82.35)	7 (100.00)	46 (80.70)

Note: The figures in brackets show the respective percentages.

The analysis in Table 17.10 shows that the majority of the higher, middle and lower level managers are of the opinion that information has impact on pricing decisions in the areas such as to know the price of competitive products, to know the demand for the products and to know the profit rates.

Table 17.11: Information Required for Distribution of Products

Type of Information	Higher	Middle	Lower	Total
Transport information	16 (48.48)	3 (17.65)	2 (28.57)	21 (36.84)
Information about distributors/sellers	16 (48.48)	2 (11.76)	2 (28.57)	20 (35.09)
Information about marketing possibilities	12 (36.36)	17 (100.00)	4 (57.14)	33 (57.89)
Distance to market	4 (12.12)	3 (17.65)	0 (0.00)	7 (12.28)

Note: The figures in brackets show the respective percentages.

Table 17.11 reveals that all the middle level managers and the majority of the lower level managers require information about marketing possibilities. However, the level of requirement for other types of information is not found high.

Table 17.12: Required Information for Market Promotion

Type of Information	Higher	Middle	Lower	Total
Advertising agencies	13 (39.39)	4 (23.53)	4 (57.14)	21 (36.84)
Cost of advertising	6 (18.18)	5 (29.41)	0 (0.00)	11 (19.30)
Information about most suitable channel	14 (42.42)	9 (52.94)	2 (28.57)	25 (43.86)
Advertising pattern of competitive products	11 (33.33)	3 (17.65)	2 (28.57)	16 (28.07)

Note: The figures in brackets show the respective percentages.

It can be observed from Table 17.12 that the majority of the lower level managers require information about advertising agencies and the majority of the middle level managers require information about most suitable channel.

5. Result and Discussion

The analysis of the data collected from higher, middle and lower level managers reveal that information is very essential for higher and middle level managers for decision-making. It is true that more decisions are made by these categories of managers and hence they need more information. This is supported by the higher frequency of the use of information for managerial decision-making by the higher and middle level managers. The time spent to collect information also is high among the higher level managers. The managers who have to take higher level decisions feel that information has impact on all the areas of management.

6. Conclusion

Information is vital for managerial decision-making. Those who hold higher managerial positions need more information. The frequency of using information and the time spent for using information also are high among the higher level managers.

NOTES

1. Kesavan, R., Elanchezhian, C. and Ramnath, Vijaya B. (2004). *Principles of Management*. Chennai: Eswar Press.
2. Leigh, Andrew (1983). *Decisions, decisions!: a practical management guide to problem-solving and decision-making*. Germont USA: Gower.

Role of Electronic Information Sources in the Self-Development of Adolescents

18

Gayathri Madhusudan and *T.M. Vasudevan*

1. Introduction

Man has acquired technological expertise to store as well as disseminate all knowledge in a chip. The electronic information sources are competing and in some instances replacing the print based information sources which have been in place for centuries as the primary media for providing information.[1] The concept of Information Communication Technologies (ICTs) is nothing but a convergence of communication technology, through some electronic device, which can access and disseminate information very fast. The primary ICT sources familiar to the general public world wide include pictures, radio, sound recordings, video recording, streaming Internet content, etc. Information Technology has made information a commodity, which can be marketed through the electronic media.

Electronic information sources are often faster than consulting print indexes, especially when searching retrospectively, and they are straighter forward when wishing to use combinations of keywords. Related to these, Internet is used as a medium of expression to educate the learner, provide information needs at their desktop, and send hitch-free and cross-referenced data to the appropriate location. It can be said that improved data transmission facilities will go a long way to reduce the incessant hardship faced by young adults in the acquisition and generation of data which serves as the basis for research and academic performance improvement. This is because it seems the use of electronic information by students enhances their performance in academic activities. Among the electronic information system students use to get most of their information are: Internet, e-mail, electronic journal, bulletin boards, telephone, telex, CD-ROM databases and electronic books.[2]

Today's young people are coming to maturity in a rapidly changing complex society. At times, it seems, the only thing that is certain is change. Adolescents, who constitute a major part of society of today, have a wider spectrum of knowledge than their counterparts had in the past. They are fortunate to have access, to a variety of electronic information resources. Electronic information sources offer today's young people different opportunities for all their activities. They are increasingly expected to use electronic resources for studying as well as self-development. Adolescents constitute one part of the society who are fortunate to have access, at no cost to themselves, to a variety of electronic information resources. Universities use considerable proportions of their budgets to provide this technology for their students to assist in the learning process. Electronic information sources offer today's students different opportunities from their precursors. In order to utilize the growing range of electronic resources, young students must attain and apply the skills necessary to make use of them.

The period of young adulthood is primarily the period of education as well. In recent years, the use of electronic information has become prominent in the drive for making information and data transfer available to users, especially students. For the academic quest of the learning community, the information available on the Internet is unavoidable. Preparation of assignments, projects and other educational related activities need information available on the Internet. The Electronic information sources are of great help in the field of education. Teachers find that children who previously had no interest in verbal communication are learning to read and write through electronic media. The e-mail system has helped them to communicate with others. The children seem to grasp facts faster from the Internet than from their textbooks. The net provides a quick, efficient and sometimes colourful and graphically interesting way to share ideas.

Adolescents view the electronic information source as a useful resource tool for business and personal communication. It is a medium for socializing and creating an increased circle of new friends among different cultures. Since Internet connects many different people throughout the world who belong to different cultures, young adults could be influenced by each other. Therefore, youngsters could be linked to those foreign cultures and behave in the way their online friends behave. The problem is that those behaviours could be seen as being strange and do not conform to their actual culture restrictions and traditions. This confusing situation might be a direct source of having identity confusion since the adolescents do not know to what behaviours they should conform to.

At the same time electronic information sources enable adolescents to have close and meaningful interaction with peers which results in a positively self-esteem and well-being. Internet is considered as a technology, which may help the younger generation to build a strong personality. This can be true by taking into consideration the skills and successful training needed for extracting relevant and reliable information and getting rid of all spam and deleterious information. This can ensure a good learning by observing skill. Also, it can help the youngsters to develop by their own the required skills for looking for relevant and reliable information among a wide range of anonymous data. Besides, they can develop their sense of tolerance and respectful behaviour throughout the conversations they take part of with different people who have different mentalities all over the world. This constitutes an important way of developing interpersonal skills and broadening one's knowledge. Since young adults are at the phase of constructing their identity and building their personality, they are more fragile and are not ready for any failure. Hence, it can be assumed that the adolescents at this stage will be using electronic information sources extensively for self-development, extracurricular activities, for finding out suitable job, etc.

Man forwards through a series of developmental life stages that result in the gain of a character virtue. In the modern world, with its expanding culture and technology, racial and ideological conflicts, population explosion and increasingly complex social differentiation, man faces many difficulties in his quest for adjustment, maturity and happiness. Beliefs, attitudes, emotional responses and intellectual abilities change throughout man's life-span.[3]

It has been an extra-ordinary eventful century. The world passed through untold trials and tribulations, pangs and throngs, trials and errors to march on the road of progress. The journey of man from cave to microchip has been very impressive, eventful and enthralling. This is the age of Information Technology where knowledge is power and this knowledge is based on information. The new world of instant information and communication technology has overturned thinking and overthrown the old socio-economic order. Enterprises and organizations are transforming themselves, sometimes overnight. The whole world is plunged headlong in a scramble to keep up, to learn, to adapt, and to change. Those who learn fast enough and acquire the knowledge they need, will succeed.

Self-concept is the cognitive thinking aspect of self also related to one's self-image, the way we see ourselves in the mirror. Self-concept changes throughout life from how people look at a person and tells him what he is. Self-esteem is the affective or emotional aspect of self and generally refers to how a person feels about or how he values himself, or knows one's worth. Educators, parents, business and government leaders agree the need to develop individuals with healthy or high self-esteem characterized by tolerance and respect for others, individuals who accept responsibility for their actions, have integrity, take pride in their accomplishments, who are self-motivated, willing to take risks, capable of handling criticism, loving and lovable, seek the challenge and stimulation of worthwhile and demanding goals, and take command and control of their lives. In other words, the need to help foster the development of people who have healthy or authentic self-esteem because they trust their own being to be life affirming, constructive, responsible and trustworthy. Some have referred to self-esteem as merely "feeling good" or having positive feelings about oneself.[4]

2. Objectives of the Study

1. To find out the different areas of self-development influencing the adolescents by electronic information sources.
2. To find out the impact of the use of electronic information sources on the adolescents for self-development.

3. Methodology

The investigator distributed questionnaires to 150 adolescents in different schools in Kerala to collect the data. Out of the 150 questionnaires distributed 140 were returned completely filled. Hence, the actual study was on 140 adolescents in Kerala State.

4. Findings

1. Television is the most important electronic information source in developing writing skills (55.56%), conversational skills (59.72%), positive thinking (66.67%), appearance (65.28%), current awareness (54.17%) and social awareness (51.39%) of the majority of the male adolescents. At the same time Internet is the most influencing electronic source for socialization (38.89%) and for international events (48.61%) according to comparatively larger per cent and for career orientation according to the majority (66.67%).
2. Television is the most important electronic information source in developing conversational skills (52.44%), positive thinking (69.12%), appearance (77.94%), socialization (55.88%), current awareness (63.23%) and social awareness (60.29%) of the majority of the female adolescents and for international events according to half (50%). At the same time Internet is the most influencing electronic source for developing writing skills (69.12%) and for career orientation (54.41%) according to the majority.
3. In communication skill development electronic information sources have impact on developing

conversational skill according to the majority of the males (52.78%) and comparatively larger per cent of the females (42.65%).

4. In personality development, electronic information sources have impact on expanding knowledge according to the majority of the male (63.89%) and female (57.35%) adolescents.
5. In career orientation, electronic information sources have impact in choice of career according to half of the males (50%) and the majority of the females (57.35%).

5. Conclusion

The analysis of the data collected from the adolescents reveals that they are of the opinion that developing personality is essential. For self-development the adolescents mainly make use of Internet. The important areas of self-development influenced by television are writing skill, conversational skill, positive thinking, appearance, current awareness and social awareness in the case of male adolescents. At the same time, in the case of female adolescents the areas of self-development influenced by television are conversational skill, positive thinking, appearance, socialization, international events, current awareness and social awareness. The important self-development areas influenced by Internet are socialization, international events and career orientation in the case of male adolescents and, in case of female adolescents writing skill and career orientation. In communication skill development, the most important area influenced by electronic information sources is conversational skill. In personality development, electronic information sources influence the young adults in expanding knowledge. In the case of career orientation, electronic information sources have more impact on the choice of career. It can be seen that electronic information sources have great role in the self-development of adolescents. The electronic media from Television to Internet are helping the adolescents in the self-development.

NOTES

1. Cornish, G.P. (1997). *Collection Management for the 21st Century: A handbook for librarians*. Westport: Westport Press.
2. Tella, Adeyinko et al. (2007). *Self efficacy and use of electronic information as predictors of academic performance* (Retrieved January 5th, 2011 from http://southernlibrarianship.icaap.org).
3. Pikunas, Justin (1969). *Human Development: A science of growth*. New York: McGraw-Hill.
4. http://en.wikipedia.org/wiki/Personal development (Accessed on 8th January, 2010).

Utilization of E-book by the Researchers of Science Discipline in Kerala University, Thiruvananathapuram

19

N.R. Beegum Sarjoon and *S. Humayoon Kabir*

1. Introduction

E-books are gaining popularity and significance among libraries. Many higher education institutions around the world have provided e-book collections in their campus libraries and adopted e-books as learning material. E-books are not as popular as other types of e-publications, such as e-journals and e-newspapers. The possible reasons for this could be that the technology for creating/accessing e-books (both hardware and software) is not yet matured, the users' perspectives about e-books need to be changed and the awareness of e-books needs to be raised.

Digitization often has been a solutions to the 'library crisis'. E-books are high credible, most accurate, high reasonable and most supportive to the students, faculty members and research scholars. All the researchers depend upon e-resources without much of pain. The development of e-book technology that is revolutionizing the whole book publishing industry has started having an enormous impact on the society. E-books are changing the methods by which people read, as it is easy to use and are rapidly becoming a viable alternative. It is providing growing advantages over the traditional printed medium. Several companies all over the world are working towards making electronic publishing the rule rather than the exception.

University of Kerala has sixteen faculties and forty-one Departments of teaching and research. Teaching, Research and Knowledge extension are the mandate of the University

Departments. They primarily focus on postgraduate (Masters) programmes, M.Phil. programmes (1-year research degree) and doctoral research. There are ten science departments (Departments of Aquatic Biology and Fisheries, Botany, Biochemistry, Chemistry, Demography and Population Studies, Physics, Mathematics, Statistics, Geology, Zoology) and five applied science departments (Biotechnology, Computer Science, Environmental Science, Future studies, Optoelectronics) under University of Kerala.

2. Definition

An electronic book is a text and image based publication in digital form produced on, published by, and readable on computers or other digital devices. *The Oxford dictionary of English* defines e-books as "an electronic version of a printed book" but e-book can and do exist without any printed equivalent. E-books are usually read on dedicated hardware devices known as e-Readers or e-book devices.

3. Objectives

The main objective of the study are:

1. To find out the types of e-resources utilized by the research scholars of Kerala University.
2. To find out the awareness of e-book by the researchers of science discipline in Kerala University.
3. To find out the reasons and factors for using e-book.
4. To find out the purpose of using e-book.
5. To ascertain the frequency of using e-book by the researchers of Kerala University.
6. To find out the factors that hinder the researchers from utilizing e-books.

4. Methodology

A structured Questionnaire was used to collect information. The Questionnaire consists of two portions. In the first portion respondents were required to indicate their personal details. The second portion of the Questionnaire was formulated within the framework of accessing researcher's perception on e-books, reasons, purpose and factors for using e-book and the factors that hinder the utilization of e-books. This study adopts simple random sampling method to collect data. The Questionnaires were distributed to the 10 science and 5 applied science departments under University of Kerala. Ninety-six responses were received from the researchers.

5. Analysis

5.1 Personal Details of Respondents

Female respondents (75%) formed the majority of study sample. 48.96 per cent of the respondents are doing Ph.D. and 51.04 per cent of the research scholars are doing M.Phil.

Table 19.1: Personal Details of Respondents

Personal details	Category	Frequency	Percentage
Gender	Male	24	25
	Female	72	75
Qualification	M.Phil.	47	48.96
	Ph.D.	49	51.04

5.2 Types of E-Resources Used by the Research Scholars

Majority of the research scholars (88.54%) prefer to use e-journals. Next to e-journals researchers prefer to use e-books (81.25%) followed by e-thesis, e-magazines, e-map respectively. The e-resources like e-manuscript and e-data archive are comparatively used less.

Table 19.2 : Types of E-Resources Used by the Research Scholars

E-resources	Respondents	Percentage
E-journal	85	88.54
E-data archive	33	34.38
E-manuscript	28	29.17
E-map	40	41.67
E-book	78	81.25
E-magazine	48	50
E-thesis	64	66.67
www	53	55.21

5.3 Defining E-Book

When the respondents were asked to select the appropriate definitions of e-books from the given list. Majority of the respondents (77.08%) defined e-book as a combine package of e-text, e-book reading device and e-book software. 16.67 per cent of the respondents defined e-book as e-text.

Table 19.3: Defining e-book

Defining e-book	Respondents	Percentage
E-text	16	16.67
E-text+ E-book device + E-book software	74	77.08
E-book software	0	0
E-book reader	0	0
Don't know	6	6.25
Total	96	100

5.4 Modes of Reading E-Books

Majority of the respondents (81.25%) prefer to read e-book on screen. 13.54 per cent read it by printing a part of the book and e-book on e-reader (3.13%). 2.08 per cent of the researchers prefer to use the whole book.

Table 19.4: Modes of Reading E-Books

Modes of reading e-books	Respondents	Percentage
E-book on screen	78	81.25
E-book on e-reader	3	3.13
Print the whole book	2	2.08
Print a part of book	13	13.54
Total	96	100

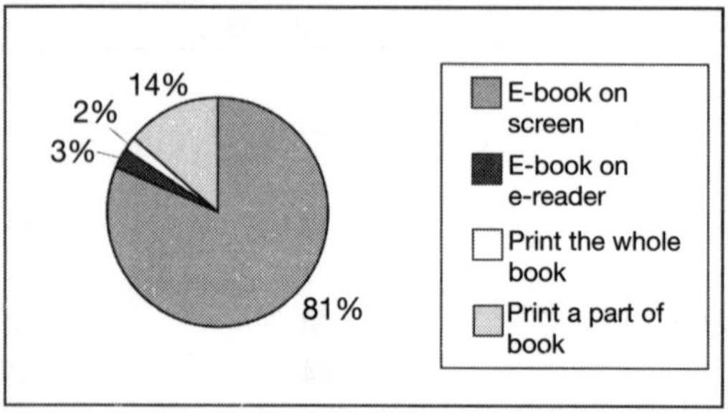

Fig. 19.1: Modes of Reading E-books

5.5 Reasons for Using E-Book

Easiness in using and more informative (37.5%) are the prior reasons for using e-book by the researchers. 23.96 per cent of the users use e-book because it saves time. Only 1.04 per cent of the respondents says that it is more useful.

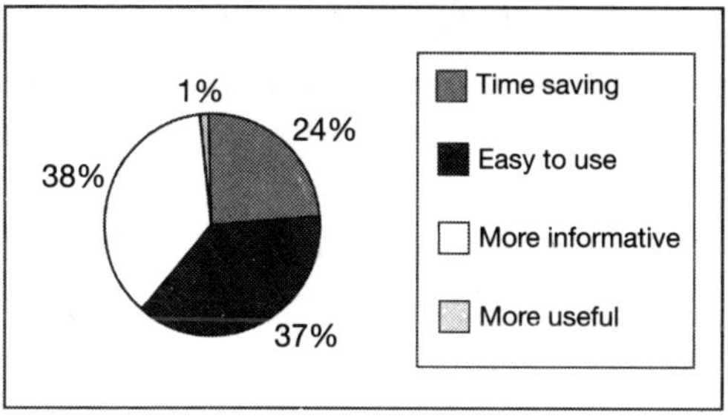

Fig. 19.2: Reasons for Using E-book

5.6 Factors for Using E-Book

Majority of the respondents reported that they use e-book because they are searchable (80.21%) and available round the clock. 50 per cent of the researchers indicate that e-book offer timely access. 39.58 per cent of the respondents use e-book because it allows easy navigation and save space.

Table 19.5: Factors for Using E-Book

Factors for using e-book	Respondents	Percentage
Available round the clock	63	65.63
Searchable	77	80.21
Allow easy navigation	38	39.58
Portable	27	28.13
No relevant paper book	18	18.75
Offer timely access	48	50
Helpful features	32	33.33
Save space	38	39.58
Allow e-archive	17	17.71
Save trees	12	12.5
Versatile	1	1.04

5.7 Purpose of Using E-Book

Respondents were asked to select the purpose of reading e-book. Majority of the research scholars (85.42%) use e-book to do their research. 69.79 per cent of the respondents indicate that they use e-book to find materials for their assignment. 32.29 per cent respondents are using e-books look up answers. 23.96 per cent of respondents are using e-book as textbook and only 8.33 per cent of respondent use e-book as their course book.

Table 19.6: Purpose of Using E-Book

Purpose of using e-book	Respondents	Percentage
Finding material	67	69.79
Research	82	85.42
Look up answers	31	32.29
Textbook	23	23.96
Course book	8	8.33
Leisure	0	0

5.8 Quantity of E-Book Usage

Majority of the researchers (65.63%) read 1 or 2 titles in past months. 16.67 per cent of the respondents read more than five titles followed by three or five titles (10.42%). The rest of the respondents do not remember or not read e-book.

Table 19.7: Number of E-Book Used in Past Months

No. of E-books	Respondents	Percentage
More than 5 titles	16	16.67
3 or 5 titles	10	10.42
1 or 2 titles	63	65.63
None	4	4.17
I don't remember	3	3.13
Total	96	10

5.9 Frequency of Using E-Book

Majority of the researchers (89.58%) use e-book sometimes and only 10.42 per cent of the researchers use e-book usually.

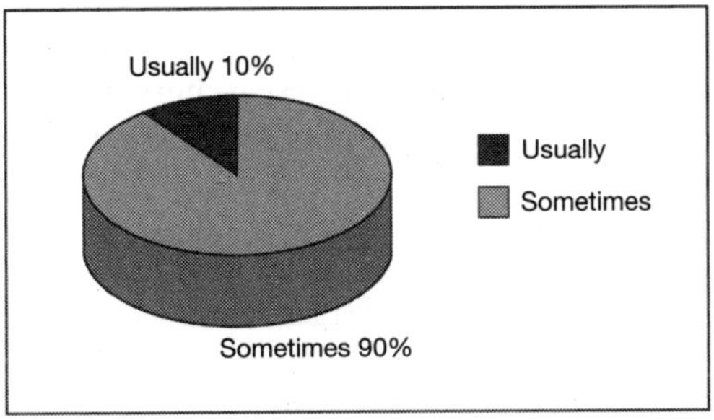

Fig. 19.3: Frequency of Using E-book

5.10 Awareness of E-reader

Majority of the research scholars (66.67%) are not aware of e-reader. Only 33.33 per cent of the respondents are aware of e-reader. Only three research scholars currently own e-reader. The rest of the researchers do not have e-reader.

5.11 Factors that Hinder the Utilization of E-Book

Cost is the major factor that hinders the respondents (61.46%) from using e-book. Difficult in accessing the computer or Internet (32.29%) and hard to read and browse (29.17%) is the next factor. Twenty-five per cent of respondents indicates enough printed books as a problem that hinder them from using e-book. Only 1 per cent of the respondents reveals that using e-book is not compatible, not confident with the technology and do not want to change.

Table 19.8: Factors that Hinder the Utilization of E-Book

Factors	Respondents	Percentage
Not familiar with the product	7	7.29
Difficult in accessing the computer or internet	31	32.29
Not compatible	1	1.04
Hard to read and browse	28	29.17
Not confident with the technology	1	1.04
Do not want to change	1	1.04
Enough printed books	24	25
Cost	59	61.46

5.12 Satisfaction with E-Book

81.25 per cent of the respondents are moderately satisfied with e-book. Ten per cent of the researchers are very satisfied. Some are not able to judge and neither satisfied nor dissatisfied with e-book.

Table 19.9: Satisfaction with E-Book

Level of satisfaction	Respondents	Percentage
Very satisfied	10	10.42
Moderately satisfied	78	81.25
Neither satisfied nor dissatisfied	3	3.13
Moderately dissatisfied	0	0
Unable to judge	5	5.21
Total	96	100

6. Findings

- The Survey revealed that female respondents (75%) formed the majority of study sample. 48.96 per cent of the respondents are doing Ph.D. and (51.04%) of the research scholars are doing M Phil.
- Majority of the research scholars (88.54%) prefer to use e-journals. Next to e-journals researches prefer to use e-books (81.25%).
- Almost all researchers are (77.08%) able to define e-book appropriately. It shows that all researchers knew what is an e-book.
- The survey found that most of the researchers are using e-book to find materials for their assignment and to do their research work (85.42%). On the other hand, only a few of the respondents are using e-books as their textbook and recommended course book. A large portion of the respondents (81.25%) like to read e-book on the screen.
- Easiness in using and more informative (37.5%) are the prior reasons for using e-book by the researchers. Most of the researchers like to use e-book because it is searchable, available round the clock and offer timely access.

- The study revealed that 65.63 per cent read 1 or 2 titles in past months and majority of the researchers (89.58%) use e-book sometimes.
- Majority of the research scholars (66.67%) are not aware of e-reader. Only three research scholars currently own e-reader.
- About (61.46%) of the researchers shows that cost is the major factor that hinders from using e-book.
- Most of the respondents are moderately satisfied with e-book.

7. Conclusion

E-book can promote better knowledge delivery/accessibility and long lasting knowledge repository, hence the researchers should make use of this facility to keep abreast with the e-book technology. Educational institutions should encourage scholars in the use of e-books. They should acquire more e-books and they should have a separate e-book collection. Sufficient funds should be allotted to purchase the same if not freely available. Free facilities should be provided to the researchers to view the e-books. The printed book will not disappear overnight. Continuing trend in the balance between print and e-books will definitely support the increasing number of researchers in various disciplines particularly in the University sector.

WORKS CITED

Anuradha, K.T. and Usha, H.S. (2006). Use of e-book in an academic and research environment—a case study from Indian Institute of Science. *Programme: Electronic Library and Information Systems,* 40(1), 48-62.

Chong, P.F. Lim, Y.P. and Ling, S.W. (2009). On the design preferences for e-books. (Retrieved December 12, 2010, from http://tr.ietejournals.org/text.asp?2009/26/3/213/50706).

Chu, H. (2003). Electronic books: Viewpoints and users and potential users. *Library Hi Tech* , 21(3), 340-46.

Ismail, R. and Zainab, A.N. (2005). The pattern of E-books use amongst undergraduates in Malaysia: A Case of to Know is to Use. *Malaysian Journal of Library and Information Science*, 10 (2), 1-23.

Letchumanan, Malathy and Tarmizi, Rohani Ahamad (2010). Utilisation of e-book among university mathematic students (Retrieved November

21, 2010, from http://www.sciencedirect.com).

Levine Clark, M. (2006). Electronic book usage: a survey at University of Denver Portal. *Libraries and the Academy*, 6(3), 285-99.

Nattar, S. and Selvakumar, M. (2009). Electronic books (e-Books): Current trends. *ILA Bulletin*, 45 (3-4), 27-30.

Nicholas, David et al. (2008). UK scholarly e-book usage: A landmark survey. *Aslib Proceedings: New Information Perspectives*, 60 (4), 311-34.

Wilkins, Valerie (2007). Managing e-books at the University of Derby: A case study. (Retrieved November 21, 2010, from *http: www.emeraldinsight.com/0033-0337.htm*).

Zheng, Liu and Tan, Sun (2009). E-books in China: Development and use (Retrieved November 20, 2010, from http://www.ifla.org/annual.conference/ifla75/index.htm).

PART VI

LIBRARY PROVISIONS AND ACCESS POSSIBILITIES

Remote Access Possibilities in Indian Academic Libraries: An Overview

20

V. Gopakumar and *V. Anuradha*

1. Introduction

Internet and the World Wide Web have brought a revolution in libraries. It has removed the barriers of time and space in information transfer. A number of new online library services were introduced and the existing services have gone through drastic change. Over a decade, the demands from the users have also changed. They now want to access the resources and the services of the library from wherever they want and whenever they want. The modern libraries have come out of their four walls to meet the users' demands by a new phenomenon called 'remote access' to library resources and services.

2. Meaning of Remote Access

Remote Access is the ability to log into a database on a computer or a network of an organization from an external location. Remote access is typically accomplished via a connection to the Internet or the intranet within a campus. Peters[1] has defined the term remote access as "any computer access to library resources and services from outside the physical confines of the library building". The distance education programmes of the universities and other academics are presently supported with Distance Learning Library Services which are essentially remote access to library resources.

We can divide the library users into three categories: on-campus users, off-campus users and distance education users. On-campus users are the ones who access library resources from classrooms, staff rooms, laboratories, the residences within the campus and the library itself. The off-campus user group belongs to student, faculty and staff members who access library resources from their homes or other locations which are away from the campus. The third category consists of members enrolled in distance education programme of the parent institution. They access library resources from faraway places and perhaps never visit the library.

Each of these categories of users has different needs regarding the type of information they look for and the type of assistance they seek from the library. So the library should use different methods to reach each group effectively. It is possible for the librarian to reach the on-campus users personally and look into his needs. Off-campus users and distant users are not so easy to reach. Most of their library needs have to be dealt with online. Librarians have to plan carefully which type of services to offer and how to offer them; within the limitations of time and money.

In early 1990s after the innovation of the Internet, the library scenario started changing. The earlier websites of libraries were static web pages which could provide information on the various resources and services of the library. During that period searching the catalogue was not possible, as databases were not integrated. Gradually, with the revolutionary evolution of Web 1.0, we could search the catalogue of libraries.

The evolution of Web 2.0 has brought in totally interactive websites for libraries too. OPACs of libraries have changed integrating the features of Web 2.0 like the RSS, Tagging, etc.

As the Internet became more popular, there came into existence digital sources of information in the form of e-books, e-journals and a number of online databases, both free and commercial. With e-resources, the demands of users changed. They wanted the information on their desk-tops with a click of a button. The libraries had to break their physical boundaries and reach out to the users wherever they are located. The remote access compels the modern libraries to provide appropriate support services in order to meet the needs of their users.

3. Advantages of Remote Access

The basic advantages of remote access are as follows:

- Information is available to a larger group. They need not even visit the library. Users can access information sitting anywhere.
- One copy published on the Internet is available to any number of users through remote access.
- Remote access has removed the physical limitations of library.
- Information can be accessed 24×7. The limitations of library timing are no more a matter of concern. After library hours the user need not wait for the library to open again so that he can use the resources.
- Dependency on library staff for locating the information is reduced. Much of the time of library staff was spent on locating a book or a journal issue. As the information is available in digital form through remote access, it can be easily located and accessed.
- Instant information promotes research and development. Information is delivered to the laboratories and the R & D divisions instantly.
- Providing electronic database information through library network can be economical for any institution. The library can purchase one subscription and through remote access make the service available to all its users.

4. Remote Access and Library Services

Libraries offer various services to satisfy the information needs of their users. Some of the services are designed in anticipation of the users' needs and some are served on demand. They include Reference Services, Current Awareness Programme, SDI, Interlibrary Loan, and Document Delivery Services. These traditional services of libraries have also got revolutionized through the demand for making them available remotely.

4.1 Methods of Remote Access

The methods by which the users access the resources of a library are many. Some of the important remotely available services and resources of a library are enlisted below.

4.1.1 OPAC (Online Public Access Catalogue)

OPAC is one of the major changes that are taking place in the library as a result of technology development. OPACs are like gateways to the resources of the library. They are the index to the holdings of library which is remotely available anytime. One can browse and locate information. They provide direct access to library's bibliographic database. It can be searched from a number of locations. Many libraries provide help in the form of instructions through OPAC. One can know the status of the document also from the OPAC. OPAC that is accessible through Internet is called as WebOPAC. It is available on the library website. Some ask for login ID and User Name and Password. Users can place request for document delivery and also view their own borrower accounts through Web-OPAC. They also provide cross references. Many Web-OPACs provide links to external resources like full text links, links to companies or scientific and research institutions, links to publishers, etc.

4.1.2 Access to Databases

Libraries subscribe to the databases (full text as well as bibliographic) maintained by aggregators and publishers. These subscribed databases are provided to the users of a library through proxy servers within the Intranet or the Internet.

In the case of Intranet the databases are made available to all those who get connected to it. But when it is provided over Internet for a wider audience the access is usually restricted with user names and passwords.

The escalating costs of such databases have forced libraries to have consortia arrangements for more bargaining powers. The INFLIBNET Centre of UGC in India is such an agency facilitating the access to e-journals through the nationwide network. The project is called 'Infonet'. The universities in India are very much benefited out of it.

4.1.3 Digital Reference Services

Reference Service is the direct personal assistance given to the reader either to find information or to answer his query. Users of a library now prefer to get their queries answered by the librarians online. They request for reading-lists, bibliographies and such other services through e-mails. Even the chatting facility is also used for this purpose. Internet technology supports the libraries to satisfy all these needs of the library users. Libraries design documentation bulletins, new arrival lists and such other current awareness bulletins and disseminate among the users through e-mail. These are services prepared expecting the use of the resources. Even library instruction programmes are also available online.

4.1.4 Online Information Literacy Programmes

With the implementation of modern technologies at every level in the functioning of the libraries, it becomes essential for the users to keep themselves updated with the new developments. This is a continuous process. Many libraries provide online information literacy tutorials to keep their users informed and trained.

4.1.5 Document Delivery Services

A library can e-mail a borne digital object or a created one through scanning, to a user who requires it. This is equivalent to the document delivery services existed/ing in traditional libraries. The present change is that as it has become digital, the transfer is instantaneous and multiple copies can be transmitted. For example, under the UGC Infonet scheme, there is a consortium called JCCC@inflibnet. This consortium has an index of all journals subscribed by the universities in India. It also has the index to the archival volumes of these journals. The JCCC website allows a user to find an article required by him through a keyword search. If it is available the user can send an e-mail request to the librarian for a copy of the same. The librarian has to oblige to this request by sending a digital copy to the user's e-mail.

The new integrated library software packages allow libraries to send e-mail alerts, SMS alerts to the users about the new arrivals, overdue of books, etc. Library Blogs and integrated RSS facilities inform the latest developments in a library to its users.

4.1.6 Digital Libraries and Institutional Repositories

The digital libraries and Institutional Repositories are extensions of libraries available to users over the Internet. Digital libraries are organized collection of digital documents usually held in the servers of libraries. The documents can be searched using the keywords and metadata. Most libraries make them available to the uses who want to make use of them from remote locations. Similarly, many institutions offer online locus for collecting and indexing digital documents that originate from that institution. They are called as Institutional Repositories. These collections are also available to the users for access from remote locations. Electronic Theses and Dissertations (ETD) are another new development in the services that are extended from the libraries. Many universities have started digitizing their research output in the form of theses and dissertations and make them available to users for open access. The Sodhaganga project of the INFLIBNET Centre, Ahmedabad and the Vidyanidhi project at the Mysore University are some of the examples. The Mahatma Gandhi University in Kerala has hosted their ETD under the URL:www.mgutheses.org, which is functioning very well and offers open access to their thesis anywhere on the globe.

4.1.7 Current Awareness Services

Many libraries give current information like the list of new arrivals, newly added journals arrivals of latest issue of the journals, faculty publications and others through Remote Access. They put this information on digital Bulletin Boards or give a link on the library websites or simply send a mass-mail to their users. Library notices are also uploaded form time to time. Some libraries also come out with a documentation bulletin in digital form wherein they index all the articles of the journals subscribed by the library. The Goa University Library has started such a service.

4.1.8 E-Selective Dissemination of Information

In most of the academic and R & D institutions, because of tight schedules of teaching and research, their faculty members and researchers find no time to visit the library. To facilitate these people many libraries started SDI service to provide information in the area of user interest to their desktops. The profiles of users and the information in electronic databases are searched periodically and e-mails are sent to the respective members.

4.1.9 Internet Subject Gateways

A number of European libraries are developing Internet subject gateways on remote access. These are subject specialized entrances or gateways to quality assessed Internet resources. They act as an alternative to the Internet search engines and web directories. They are like electronic special libraries. A very popular subject gateway is 'PINAKES'.[2]

5. The Indian Scenario

From 1970s onwards the use of IT in the field of libraries started becoming popular in India. Libraries started taking steps towards automation and also started accessing and subscribing to digital resources. However Remote Access to library resources is no longer a dream now. Libraries of well-established institutions like IISc, IITs, IIMs and major universities are now providing online access to the library resources to their users. This is facilitated through the library websites. Access to e-books, e-journals and a number of e-databases, and multimedia products is provided by these libraries. They also maintain electronic databases of theses and dissertations. They support electronic submission of thesis and dissertations by postgraduate and doctoral students and maintain full text database of the same. Most of these libraries also have set up an archive of publications brought by the faculty of the institute. Very few libraries have uploaded their institutional archives on the Internet. Most of the resources are on the Intranet where in the access is restricted to the campus. As the service is restricted to the registered members of the library, a simple authentication in the form of login, username and password is necessary to access the resources.

6. Conclusion

Remote access to library services and electronic resources round the clock is one of the most challenging development of contemporary librarianship. Libraries are taking full advantage of the Internet and web facilities. However a point to be noted is that, in the enthusiasm to provide remote access, the traditional library services should not be neglected. Remote access services should complement the existing services. The traditional ways of personally meeting the needs of the users should be used to promote remote access and at the same time remote access should be utilized to promote conventional library services. Ultimately remote access is only a means to reach out to the library users and it is up to the libraries how best they can exploit it to their advantage.

NOTES

1. Peters, Thomas A. (1998). Remotely familiar: Using computerized monitoring to study remote use. *Library Trends*, 47 (Summer), 7-20.
2. http://www.hw.ac.uk/lib/WWW/irn/pinakes/pinakes.html (Retrieved on 15th January, 2011).

Intelligence Generation Capabilities of the University Libraries in Kerala

21

V.M. Vinod

1. Introduction

The very essence of the modern library profession is built around the idea of user orientation. Perpetrators of this modern profession have been urging the practicing information professionals to orient themselves and their institution on this line. The concept of user orientation has got universal acceptance, thanks to the pragmatic efforts of marketing pandits like Philip Kotler and Peter Drucker. However, this is nothing new to the information professionals in India. The father of Indian library science, Dr. S.R. Ranganathan has laid the philosophical base for this user centred approach way back in 1928, when he published the "Five Laws of Library Science" and its implication may reveal the close proximity with modern marketing management theories, as both expect to bring glory to the respective institutions through its satisfied customer/user. Though the concept of user orientation has been forming a significant portion in the curriculum of library science schools in the country, the practical application remained far from the expected lines. But the 'LPG effect' (Liberalisation, Privatisation and Globalisation) provided the much needed impetus for adopting the user centric approach to the management of libraries and information centres in India.

The university libraries always enjoyed a pivotal position in the higher education sector as the prime disseminators of information in assisting, teaching and research. The survival and continuation of these noble institutions will depend a great deal on their ability to win back the confidence of their targeted users. The user oriented institutions are the end result of a long march. As the Chinese proverb states, 'a thousand mile journey starts with a single step', knowing the user interests , preferences and their psychology leading to the utilization on the products or services, is the primary and perhaps the most difficult task for any one trying to become user oriented.

2. User Intelligence

Intelligence is a term with wider ramification. Formally it was associated with psychology and military operations. From the psychological point it is the ability to adapt effectively to the environment, either by making a change in oneself or by changing the environment or finding a new one. Intelligence in military operation is concerned with collection, analysis and evaluation of information concerning the strength, activities and probable courses of action of foreign countries. With the growing competition, business as well as service organizations all over the world began to use this concept, especially when they have to know their customers better than their competitors. From the information professional's point of view, it involves gathering of data regarding the need and preference of the actual and potential user, their information seeking behaviour, access to alternative information sources, use patterns, scope for application of the accumulated information, etc.

3. Intelligence Generation

Intelligence generation is a process undertaken by organizations to verbalise the needs and preferences of their customers. It also includes an analysis of exogenous factors that influence those needs and preferences. Service rendering organizations like libraries and information centres have been using this technique, may be under a different name from the days of Dr. S.R. Ranganathan, the father of Indian Library Science. The growing influence of globalisation and liberalisation has reiterated the need for this pragmatic approach to survive in the highly competitive and strategically important information market. The study has been designed in this context to analyse the intelligence generation capabilities of the university libraries functioning in the educationally and socially advanced state of Kerala.

4. Objectives

- To assess the intelligence generation capabilities of the university libraries functioning in the Kerala state.
- To measure the magnitude of variations, if any, in the intelligence generation capabilities.
- To identify the weaker areas in the intelligence generation methods of the university libraries.
- To suggest remedial measures for improving intelligence generation capabilities of the university libraries.

5. Methodology

Intelligence generation capabilities of the university libraries in Kerala is a qualitative study based on the primary data collected from the eight hundred and thirteen users belonging to different categories like teachers, students, research scholars and others (include all other type of members who cannot be included in the first three groups) who are utilizing the services offered by the seven university libraries disseminating information in the higher education sector in the state of Kerala. The universities thus included under the scope of the study are Kerala University Library, Mahatma Gandhi University Library, Cochin University Library, Sree Sankaracharya University Library, Kerala Agriculture University Library, C.H. Mohammed Koya Library, University of Calicut and Kannur University Central Library. Required data was collected by using a five-point Likert type questionnaire consisting of fifteen statements. The statements included in the questionnaire covered areas like user segmentation and the ways and means by which the university libraries are expected to assess user needs and preferences formally and informally. The data was consolidated by using the spread sheet package 'Excel' and later subjected to quantitative analysis with the statistical package 'Statistica'.

6. Analysis

The intelligence generation capabilities of the university libraries were analysed from four different angles namely, time spent for information retrieval, subject background of the user, gender of the user and category of their membership. Arithmetic mean was used to condense the user perceptions regarding the intelligence generation capabilities. The dispersion in the perceptions was measured with the help of standard deviation. Based on the mean score, the level of user perceptions were rated by comparing with a grading table where the scores ranging from 1 – 2 were rated as Poor, 2 – 3 as Low, 3 – 4 as Moderate and 4 – 5 as High. The statistical significance of variation in the mean sores based on the classificatory variables was tested with the help of ANOVA. The weaker areas in the intelligence generation activities were identified by analyzing each statement in the questionnaire independently. The result of the analysis is presented in four Tables (21.1 to 21.4).

Initially the intelligence generation capabilities of the university libraries were analysed according to the average time spent by the users during a week for information retrieval. Time spent wise analysis of intelligence generation is carried out to know the difference in the perceptions of the users based on the time they spent in the library for information retrieval.

Table 21.1: Intelligence Generation – Time Spent-wise

Time Spent in Hours	Frequency	Mean	Standard Deviation	p-value
Less than 1	39	3.18	0.36	
1 – 3	373	3.51	0.45	
3 – 5	174	3.47	0.36	0.00000
5 – 7	132	3.50	0.34	
More than 7	95	3.32	0.34	
Aggregate	813	3.46	0.40	

From Table 21.1 it is seen that the level of intelligence generation in the university libraries of Kerala varies between 3.51 and 3.18 in a scale where the maximum and minimum scores are five and one respectively. The aggregate mean score is 3.46 with a standard deviation of 0.40. This indicates the existence of a moderate level of intelligence generation in the university libraries in Kerala. The Table also reveals that, majority of the university library users on an average are spending around 1 – 3 hours in the library during a week. Incidentally highest rating (mean score = 3.51) for the intelligence generation activities of the university libraries has come from this group. The lowest mean score of 3.18 is shown against those spending less than one hour in the library. It is also worthy to note that the entire mean scores are above 3-point mark. It shows that, in general, the whole groups are moderately satisfied with the intelligence generation activities of the university libraries. Test of statistical significance shows that p-value, zero is significant at one per cent level. Hence it can be concluded that the opinions of users relating to intelligence generation differ significantly according to the average Time Spent by them in the university libraries during a week.

The data relating to intelligence generation is further classified according to Department/Subject background of the use and is presented in Table 21.2. The subject wise analysis may help to compare the level of perceptions of users belonging to Social Science, Humanities, Language and Literature, Science and Technology, Commerce and Management and Other Subject categories. The criterion followed by the University of Calicut for identifying faculty is used as a base for the classification of users according to their Department/Subject background.

Table 21.2: Intelligence Generation – Department/Subject-wise

Subject	Frequency	Mean	Standard Deviation	p-value
Social Science	141	3.33	0.42	
Humanities	151	3.47	0.34	
Language & Lit.	165	3.45	0.39	
Science & Tech.	229	3.47	0.41	0.000401
Commerce & Mgt.	75	3.54	0.49	
Other Subjects	52	3.59	0.38	
Aggregate	813	3.46	0.40	

Data presented in Table 21.2 clearly exhibits that according to the Department/Subject background of the users, the intelligence generation in the university libraries in Kerala varies between 3.59 and 3.33. The highest mean score of 3.59 is shown against the users who belong to Other Subjects (Subjects other than Social Science, Humanities, Language and Literature, Science and Technology and Commerce and Management). It is followed by users belonging to the Commerce and Management stream with a mean score of 3.54. The least mean score of 3.33 is recorded against those belonging to the Social Science group. In this case also the entire mean score is above the 3-point mark. The variance analysis carried out to test the statistical significance of the difference of the mean scores of intelligence generation indicates that the variation is significant at one per cent level as the p-value is 0.000401.

Table 21.3: Intelligence Generation – Gender-wise

Gender	Frequency	Mean	Standard Deviation	p-value
Male	419	3.42	0.39	
Female	394	3.50	0.42	0.003253
Aggregate	813	3.46	0.40	

Supplementary classification of data based on the Gender of the user is furnished in Table 21.3. The Gender-wise analysis of Intelligence Generation reveals that the female users (Mean Score = 3.50) feels the Intelligence Generation activities of the university libraries more than their male counterparts (Mean Score = 3.42). As the p-value 0.003253 is significant at one per cent level, it can be concluded that there is significant difference in the opinion of Male and Female users regarding the Intelligence Generation activities of the university libraries.

The category-wise analysis recorded in Table 21.4 may help to compare the level of perceptions of Teachers, Research Scholars, Students and Other members regarding the Intelligence Generation activities in the university libraries.

Table 21.4: Intelligence Generation Membership Category-wise

Category	Frequency	Mean	Standard Deviation	p-value
Teacher	183	3.42	0.43	0.136688
Research Scholar	181	3.42	0.42	
Student	246	3.49	0.39	
Others	203	3.48	0.38	
Aggregate	813	3.46	0.40	

Membership Category-wise presentation of Intelligence Generation in Table 21.4 shows that, among the user community, the Students (Mean Score=3.49) feels these activities more than the other groups. It is closely followed by Other category of users with a score of 3.48. Teachers and Research Scholars occupy the bottom position with a mean score of 3.42 apiece. However, the analysis of variance indicates that the p-value 0.136688 is not significant at five per cent level. It shows that the variation in the mean scores of Intelligence Generation according to the Category of Membership is not significant.

7. Implications and Suggestions

Achieving the status of marketing oriented institution is a quintessential aim for all institutions in the modern era. Generation of customer intelligence systematically and periodically is a prerequisite for achieving marketing orientation. In this context the analysis of date relating to Intelligence Generation shows that the university libraries in Kerala are generating customer intelligence at a moderate level. Hence they are in the right path towards introducing marketing orientation in their institutions. It is worthwhile to note that, not even in a single case, the mean score attributed to this integral part of marketing orientation is below the three-point mark. So it can be inferred that the factor Intelligence Generation is indeed one of the strong component contributing towards the marketing orientation of the university libraries in Kerala. However there are some areas which have the potential for immediate improvement. Independent analysis of the statements included in the questionnaire revealed the need to diversify the method of

Intelligence Generation. This can be achieved by organizing user group meeting at regular intervals, informal discussions regarding the information requirements of the users whenever possible, making user surveys at regular intervals a mandatory affair and by creating an atmosphere where the users can interact with the professionals working in the nonservice sections (Acquisition, Technical, etc.). The study further exposed that the classification of user based on the Category of Membership is not significant as this factor caused little a variation in their perceptions regarding the Intelligence Generation in the university libraries in Kerala.

WORKS CITED

Bora, Khageswar (1996). Application of marketing analysis in library and information services. In H.S. Chopra (Ed.), *Information Marketing*. Jaipur: Rawat.

Deshpande, Rohit (1999). Introduction. In Rohit Deshpande (Ed.), *Developing a Marketing Orientation*. New Delhi: Sage.

Vinod, V.M. (1997). A study on the use of marketing techniques by Calicut University Library in information dissemination. Unpublished. M.L.I.Sc. dissertation, University of Calicut, Kerala.

Webb, D., Webster, C. and Kreppa, A. (2000). An exploration of the meaning and outcomes of a customer defined market orientation. *Journal of Business Research*. 48(4), 101-12.

Expansion of E-journals Access to Universities and Colleges: Usage and Its Effect on Academicians

22

B.K. Vishala

1. Introduction

A technical innovation in academic libraries has changed the ways in which library users are finding and using information today. There is a need for the librarians to review their skills to ensure that they are well-versed and have thorough knowledge of electronic journals, to maximise the benefit of using electronic journals for their academic purposes.

Electronic journals are considered one of the main vehicles used by the researchers for scholarly communication. They play a significant role in the creation and transmission of knowledge. Though Vennevar Bush first described the "e-journal" in 1967 as a part of MEMAX proposal only in 1990's, most of the e-journals came into the market and a few important ones were Psycholoco, Online Journal of Current Clinical Trail (OJCCT).[1] Though Psycholoco was launched in around 1990, the first peer -reviewed electronic, full text e-journal including graphics was OJCCT which was launched in 1993 when technology was beginning to support the use of graphics.[2] The other document reveals that the first electronic journals appeared during 1970s. However, they were not available to a large number of users; and this was one of the reasons, why they were not widespread.[3] With the increase in the use of Internet and personal computer; the number of electronic journals rapidly grew. Until 1995, this number was rather low, but then it started to rise.

Now-a-days major publishers like American Chemical Society, American Institute of Physics, American Physical Society,

Annual Reviews, Wiley-Blackwell Publishing, Cambridge University Press, Elsevier Science, Emerald, Institute of Physics, J-STOR, Oxford University Press, Royal Society of Chemistry, Springer Link, Taylor and Francis and the rest offer electronic versions of their journals. 48th edition of Ulrich's Periodical Directory 2010 contains more than 2,00,000 regular and irregularly serials publications and also adds more than 14,000 new publications and the list of serials and databases available on CD-Rom and Online and also complete information on magazines and newspapers.[4] Recently the open access initiatives are gaining momentum and the availability of the number of open access journals are increasing enormously.

In a Higher Education System libraries function as a vital integral element and are centred round by the teaching, research, and scientific activities of the academic institution. The digital notion is mounting the very nature of teaching and learning. Considering the importance of Scholarly journals, the libraries throughout the world have joined together to form library consortia to negotiate licenses that provide information access to group of institutions. Libraries of developed countries like USA, UK, Germany, France, etc. have successfully implemented the electronic journals consortia. Some of the leading Consortia like OHIO-LINK, HEAL-Link, Georgia's Gelilio and Virginia's VIVA, Korea Electronic Site License Initiative (KESLI), London Higher Education Consortium, North West Universities Association (NWUA), Scottish Confederation of University and Research Libraries (SCURL), SEUL (South East University Librarians), West Midlands Higher Education Association, Yorkshire University Library and Information Services (YULIS), HELLENIC Academic Libraries Link are gaining importance throughout the world.

In India Consortium of E-Journal is a quite recent development. Though several consortia like Forum for Resource Sharing in Astronomy and Astrophysics (FORSA), Indian Digital Library of Engineering Science and Technology (INDEST) Consortium, CSIR Consortia, IIM Library Consortium and Health Science Library Network Consortium (HELINET) are materialised for Technical, Scientific and Research Libraries, very few consortia were formed for academic libraries.

At present the University libraries in India are facing challenges due to reduced budget and devaluation of rupee and escalation in cost of publication. Realising the need for scholarly e-journals for scholarly communication, University Grants Commission (UGC) in India has set up an ambitious project known as UGC INFONET E-Journals Consortium in the year 2003 which facilitates free access to scholarly journals literature and databases to the Indian Universities. In the year 2004 the access was provided to 5500 plus electronic journals and 9 databases from 23 publishers. At present the project covers more than 7000 plus core and peer-reviewed journals and 10 Bibliographical databases from 26 publishers in various disciplines. Access is provided to current as well as archival issues. At present out of 181 that come under the purview of UGC, 160 Universities have been provided access to subscribed journals.

2. Study-1

The research study had been undertaken to investigate in the year 2006 the then current state of the use of electronic journals and its impact on the academicians on their academic development of various universities of Karnataka state. The research study also determined how the use of e-journals has influenced teaching and research activities. Hence to investigate the use of electronic journals and their influence on academic community, the survey method has been adopted for the research study.

A survey was administered to the entire teaching staff and the research scholars of selected departments. The criterion applied to select the departments from each university was that the electronic journals relevant to that subject area were included in UGC-InfoNet e-journals consortium. The departments were grouped into 5 broad disciplines as (1) Arts and Humanities, (2) Social Science, (3) Physical and Chemical Science, (4) Life Science, and (5) Mathematics, Computer Science and Statistics.

2.1 Findings

In total, out of 1,367 responses only 979 were usable, thus resulting in a response rate of 71.62 per cent. Out of 979 respondents, 492 (50.26%) were faculty and 487 (49.72%) were research scholars.

The total strength of such academic communities of various departments, who were considered for the study and the questionnaire distributed and responses received are shown in Table 22.1. It depicts that the largest population (313) was from University of Mysore. It also reveals that the highest response, out of 178 respondents 170 (95.51%), was collected from Mangalore University.

Table 22.1: Questionnaires Distributed and Responses Received

Sl. No.	University	Questionnaire Distributed	Response Received	Percentage
1.	Karnatak University	246	176	(71.54)
2.	Bangalore University	264	177	(67.05)
3.	Mangalore University	178	170	(95.51)
4.	University of Mysore	313	199	(63.58)
5.	Gulbarga University	216	135	(62.50)
6.	Kuvempu University	150	122	(81.00)
	Total	1367	979	(71.62)

The literature reviewed identified the response rate for the survey of e-journals use as usually low. The response rate for the present study was 71.62 per cent which is above the normal response to e-journal user survey.

Table 22.2 reveals that out of 979 responses 783 (80%) reported using e-journals and 196 (20%) reported they had never used e-journals. Among the faculty—382 (76.9%) and among the research scholars—401 (83.2%) reported using e-journals. Among the non-users of e-journals, the faculty respondents—115 (23.1%) was more than the research scholars—81 (16.8%).

Table 22.2: E-journals Use by Faculty and Research Scholars

Use of e-journals	Faculty	Research Scholars	Total
Yes	382 (76.9)	401 (83.2)	783 (80.0)
No	115 (23.1)	81 (16.8)	196 (20.0)
Total	497 (100)	482 (100)	979 (100.0)

Note: Percentages are shown in parentheses.

Table 22.3 depicts that out of 979, only 544 (55.57%) respondents confirmed that they used the UGC-InfoNet e-journals and 239 (24.41%) respondents reported that they used general e-journals which were available freely on the Internet and which were not offered through UGC-InfoNet e-journals consortium project. One hundred ninety-six (20.02%) respondents reported that they had never used electronic journals. Hence the study revealed that out of 979 respondents only 544 (55.57%) had used UGC-InfoNet e-journals and the remaining 435 (44.4%) had never used the journals provided through UGC-InfoNet.

Table 22.3: Users of e-journals and UGC-InfoNet e-journals

Respondents	Frequency
Number of respondents using UGC-InfoNet e-journals	544 (55.57)
Number of respondents using e-journals but not using UGC-InfoNet e-journals consortium	239 (24.41)
Number of respondents not using e-journals	196 (20.02)
Total	979 (100.0)

Note: Percentages are shown in parentheses.

The very purpose of conducting this research study was to investigate the impact on the users and non-users of UGC-InfoNet e-journals in their academic development.

Out of a total of 979 respondents, 196 who reported that they had never used electronic journals at all were excluded and the responses of remaining 783 were analysed to study the impact of using e-journals on academics. The responses of 783 e-journal users were further categorized into responses of faculty and research scholars who used UGC-InfoNet e-journals and those who did not use the said facility. Two hundred thirty-nine (117 faculty and 122 research scholars) respondents were identified as non-users of UGC-InfoNet e-journals project and 544 (265 faculty and 279 research scholars) were identified as users of UGC-InfoNet e-journals consortium project.

There are certain criteria to measure the impact of e-journals usage. The number of readings is also one of the measures of journal usage.[5]

The study revealed that out of 783 respondents who used e-journals, 544 (69.5%) were using UGC-InfoNet e-journals, 167 (21.33%) were not using UGC-InfoNet e-journals. There were 44 (5.6%) respondents who knew the existence of UGC-InfoNet e-journals but were not using and 28 (3.57%) respondents did not know the existence of the journals offered through UGC-InfoNet project.

The break-up of the results of the use of UGC-InfoNet e-journals according to the discipline revealed that, 164 (81.6%) physical and chemical scientists were the highest users of UGC-InfoNet e-journals and 27 (49.1%) from Arts and Humanities were the least users of UGC-InfoNet e-journals.

The comparative analysis between the UGC-InfoNet e-journal users and non-users revealed that the faculty members who used UGC-InfoNet e-journals read 19,506 articles at an average of 74 articles as against 4,543 articles at an average of 39 read by those who had not used the project journals in the past two years. It was observed that 54,971 articles reading at an average of 197 was recorded by the research scholars who used UGC-InfoNet e-journals and 6,519 article reading at an average of 53 was recorded by non-users of UGC-InfoNet e-journals.

Both users and non-users of UGC-InfoNet e-journals mentioned that the primary purpose of reading or using e-journal articles was for conducting research (96% of faculty and 97% of research scholars who used UGC-InfoNet e-journals and 75% of faculty and 80% of research scholars who did not use UGC-InfoNet e-journals). The purpose of reading e-journals was similar to both the users and non-users of UGC-InfoNet e-journals.

As far as the extent of use of e-journals helped in achieving the purpose for which it was used is concerned, the same ratings (50%-75%) were given by both—users and non-users of UGC-InfoNet e-journals regarding the "improvement in the results", "saving time" and "helped in completion of the work". But a higher rating—Above 75 per cent was offered for the options: "it broadened, changed focus", "inspired new thinking/ideas", "resulted in collaboration work", "resolved technical problems" by the users of UGC-InfoNet e-journals than the non-users of the project journals.

The publication by the users and non-users of UGC-InfoNet e-journals revealed that both faculty (1,769 articles publication at an average of 7) and research scholars (276 articles at an average of 1) who used UGC-InfoNet e-journals authored more articles in "international journals" than the faculty (215 articles at an average of 2) and research scholars (35 articles, 0.28 average) who did not use UGC-InfoNet project journals.

The number of articles authored by both the faculty—1,390 at an average of 5.25 and by research scholars—180 at an average of 0.65 in "referred and non-referred Indian journals" was more than that of the faculty (284 articles at an average of 2.43) and researchers (39 articles at an average 0.32) who did not use UGC-InfoNet project journals.

Faculty who used UGC-InfoNet e-journals recorded 471 publications at an average of 1.78 and research scholars recorded 73 publications at an average of 0.26 in "chapters in books, proceedings", where as only 92 publications at an average of 0.79 by faculty and 11 publications at an average of 0.09 by research scholars were recorded by the non-users of UGC-InfoNet e-journals.

Publication of books was more by faculties—(103 at an average of 0.39) who used UGC-InfoNet e-journals than the faculty—(26 at an average of 0.22) who did not use the project journals. But it is also revealed that among research scholars, books publication was recorded more by the non-users of UGC-InfoNet e-journals (8 books at an average of 0.07) than the users (5 books, at an average 0.02).

It is evident from the study that the number of publications in international journals, national journals, chapters in books or proceedings is more by the users of UGC-InfoNet e-journals than the non-users.

It is also recorded that users of UGC-InfoNet e-journals have received more awards or recognition for their work than the non-users.

It is recorded that only 24.2 per cent of faculty and 31.9 per cent of research scholars used BIOSIS bibliographical database. It is discouraging to note that other bibliographical databases were not exploited by the respondents. Gateway Portals are also not profoundly used by the respondents. Among the faculty only 21.5 per cent reported using J-Gate Gateway Portal and among research scholars 28.3 per cent recorded using Ingenta Gateway Portal.

The study disclosed that among the faculty, the first highest—136 (51.5%) usage was recorded for "Elsevier database" and among research scholars the second highest—166 (59.5%) was recorded for "Elsevier Science Database". This particular information indicated that though a very few (34) full text journals from Elsevier publisher were covered in the UGC-InfoNet Project, both faculty and research scholars used them extensively. It is also found out by the personal discussion with the respondents that they used the Elsevier database to access abstract of articles. It is also reported that the highest usage by the research scholars was "Springer Link/Kluwer Online" (63.1%) database than the Elsevier Science database (59.5%).

Opinion about the level of satisfaction by using the project journals revealed that the majority of faculty (43.8%) and research scholars (48.2%) were "Moderately Satisfied".

The majority of faculty, 196 (74%) and research scholars, 221 (79.2%) confirmed to have orientation.

It was noticed that the majority of the faculty, 143 (54%) and research scholars, 184 (66%) had encountered problems while accessing the project journals. The main reason identified by the majority of faculty 101 (70.62%) and 121 (65.76) research scholars was "problem with connectivity". This was followed by "limited number of systems" to use e-journals which was felt as a problem by 68 (47.55%) faculty and 103 (47.55%) research scholars.

A similar study was conducted in the year 2008 to assess the usage of open access journals by the faculties of Autonomous Colleges affiliated to Mangalore University.

The enormous growth of literature on the one side and the increased subscription cost of the journals on the other enforced the libraries to put their academic community on their back feet. Open access concept or open access journals facilitated the academicians who were searching for an alternative source of information.

According to Peter Sober—Open-access (OA) literature is digital, online, free of charge, and free of most copyright and licensing restrictions.[6]

3. Study 2

Though the e-journal access was given to the Universities of India through the UGC-InfoNet Project in the year 2003, such benefit was not extended to the colleges till 2010. A literature search on Library and Information Science Abstracts Plus (LISA Plus), and scanning of journal articles, convention volumes revealed only a few general surveys on e-journals use and such studies have not been extensively done in Indian general libraries, especially in college libraries regarding e-journals usage. Therefore a research study has been undertaken to know the current state of the use of open access journals in Autonomous colleges and to assess the impact of the use of open access journals by the academic communities of Autonomous colleges in Dakshina Kannada districts. The main objective of the study was to investigate whether the users are aware of the open access journals and to investigate the impact on the users of open access journals on their academic development.

The result of the study would provide documentation indicating the awareness and usage of existing open access journals by the faculty members of Autonomous Colleges in Dakshina Kannada. These studies serve as an indicator to assess how frequently readers use open access journals so that steps can be taken to provide awareness to the non-users.

The research study also determines how the use of open access journals has influenced teaching and research activities. This study would provide library professionals and academics with some clear insights into the benefits of using open access journals. Survey method was used to collect data for the survey.

The academic communities covered under the study are the faculties of five Autonomous colleges in Dakshina Kannada district. These colleges are St. Agnes, St. Aloysius, Roshni Nilaya: The School of Social Work, St. Ann's from Mangalore and Sri Dharmastala Manjunatheshwara College of Ujire. In total structured questionnaires were distributed to 200 teachers of selected departments of all five colleges. Out of the total of 200 questionnaires distributed 147 respondents returned filled in questionnaires. The response rate therefore accounts for 73.5 per cent. Thus, the rest of the analysis is based on the 147 coded filled in questionnaires.

The total strength of such academic communities of various departments, who were considered for the study and the questionnaire distributed and responses received are shown in Table 22.4. It reveals that the highest response, out of 70 questionnaire distributed 57 (76%) was collected from St. Aloysius College. The response rates from St. Aloysius and SDM were almost equal, i.e 76 per cent and 73 per cent respectively. It was also identified that the number of faculty members who were working on permanent basis at Roshni Nilaya and St. Anns Colleges were comparatively less than the faculty members of St. Agnes, St. Aloysius and SDM College.

Table 22.4: Questionnaires Distributed and Responses Received

Sl. No.	Colleges Distributed	Questionnaire Received	Response	Percentage
1.	St. Agnes	45	30	67%
2.	St. Aloysius	70	57	76%
3.	Roshni Nilaya	25	18	72%
4.	St. Anns	15	09	60%
5.	SDM	45	33	73%
	Total	200	147	73.5%

3.1 Findings

3.1.1 Awareness about Open Access Journals

Electronic journals provide many opportunities to the academicians to develop in their area. The researcher was keen in knowing whether the academicians are aware of open access journals which are gaining momentum these days. Table 22.5 reveals that out of 147 respondents the majority—133 (90.5%) were aware of the e-journals and 14 (9.5%) were unaware about the electronic journals.

Table 22.5: Aware of Open Access Journals

Awareness	Frequency	Percent
No	14	9.5
Yes	133	90.5
Total	147	100.0

3.1.2 Use of Open e-journals

Response received from the users regarding the usage of e-journals is shown in Table 22.6 which reveals that out of 147 responses 74 (50.3%) reported using e-journals and 73 (49.7%) reported they had never used e-journals.

Table 22.6: Use of Open Access Journals

Usage	Frequency	Per cent
No	73	49.7
Yes	74	50.3
Total	147	100.0

It is evident from the study that 57 (77%) faculty who used open access journals primarily for "Teaching" purpose followed by 56 (75.7%) who used it for "Research".

As far as the extent of use of e-journals facilitated in achieving the purpose for which it was used is concerned, the same ratings (50%-75%) were given by the majority of users of open access journals for the options like "It improved the results", "It broadened/changed focus", "It inspired new thinking/ideas", "it resulted in collaboration joint research", "It resulted in faster completion". The higher rating "Above 75 per cent" was given by the majority of the users for the option "it saved time". Majority of the faculty opined that there was a greater impact and academic development by the usage of open access journals. The respondents also felt that Open access initiative is a boon to the academicians and they should use the journal articles available freely on the Internet for their teaching and research and other academic activities.

The study disclosed that among the open access journals users the first highest, 26 (43.3%) usage was recorded for "Use of Free Full Text directory" followed by the second highest, 24 (40%) for "PubMed Central directory". It is only 13 (21.7%) respondents recorded usage of open access journals offered through DOAJ Directory.

The reason "Not familiar with e-journals" was identified as the main reason by the majority of faculty, 21 (28.8%) for not using e-journals. These were followed by 20 (27.4%) faculty who identified that they "not familiar with electronic journals and needed training".

Among the 36 respondents who reported facing problem while accessing e-journals, the majority of the faculties, 24 (32.4%) identified "problem with connectivity" as the main problem. "Do not understand the process involved", "limited number of systems" and "inconsistent power supply" were identified as the second main problem in using e-journals.

The result revealed that out of 74 e-journals users, the majority of the faculty, 57 (77.03%) expressed the idea that they were in need of orientation program to use e-journals.

3.1.3 N-LIST Project

Recently in the year 2010, the project entitled "National Library and Information Services Infrastructure for Scholarly Content (N-LIST)", was implemented jointly by the UGC-INFONET Digital Library Consortium, INFLIBNET Centre and the INDEST-AICTE Consortium, IIT Delhi.[7] The access was provided to selected resources of INDESTAICTE to universities and selected resources of UGC-INFONET Digital Library Consortium to technical institutions (IITs, IISc, IISERs and NITs) and access to selected e-resources is also provided to 6,000 Government/Government-aided colleges. "As on Jan. 15, 2011, a total number of 1581 colleges have registered themselves with the N-LIST program including 1,060 Government/Government-aided colleges covered under the 12-B Act of the UGC. Log-in ID and password for accessing e-resources have been sent to the authorized users from these 1,060 colleges. All e-resources subscribed for colleges under the N-LIST Project are now accessible to these 1,060 colleges through the N-List website. INFLIBNET acts as a monitoring agency for colleges and evaluates, promotes, imparts training and monitors all activities involved in the process of providing effective and efficient access to e-resources to colleges." It is a golden gift especially to the colleges who were deprived of the UGC-Infonet facility.

4. Conclusion

E-journals Consortia and open access initiatives are gaining momentum these days. The paper provides some insight into the importance of usage of journals subscribed through consortia and open access journals. Findings of both the studies were consistent that positive results have been observed. It is fascinating to note that both the studies revealed that there is an increased acceptance of journals by the academicians of academic libraries. The percentage of usage differs between the users of college and university libraries. It is evident from the study that the usage is more among the university academicians than the faculty of colleges. The purpose of using e-journals by the academicians of universities was for "Research" whereas by the faculty of Autonomous Colleges was for "Teaching". Therefore, in the college environment the research culture among faculty and students should be improved to enhance the usage of e-journals. The respondents have indicated that e-journals have changed the way research is done and the information obtained through electronic form has greatly improved the result of the research. More and more resources must be made available under the program based on the survey report it is felt by the researcher that awareness raising activities by the libraries will have greater impact on the usage of e-journals. The respondents also consider that the print journals will not disappear in future and e-journals will not replace the print ones completely.

UGC and INFLIBNET Centre are supporting universities and colleges in India which is praiseworthy. Usage of e-journals by the academics will not improve unless the due importance is given to infrastructure development of universities and colleges. The lacuna in infrastructure was the major bottleneck for using e-journals. The researcher experienced that the proper infrastructure facility provided by the University and College authorities will definitely enhance the usage of e-journals. The administrators of universities and colleges should realize the need for the development of infrastructure facility which would facilitate easy accessing and using e-journals. Cooperative work always brings good result. The administrators, university and college libraries should work together to enhance the usage of e-journals. There is no doubt that the usage of scholarly literature will bring about a qualitative change in the education, research and development. The expectations of the users are also depending on the experience in the usage of e-resources. There is a transformation in the expectation of the users regarding the library. They anticipate required information instantly within their finger tip. Therefore towards building knowledge society there is a need for the library to act as a catalyst for management of e-resources. The library should be the bridge between the resources and the end users. The librarian should adapt to change and accept the role of intermediaries between the e-journals and the users and has to play a greater role in making the users aware of the available journals by an effective promotional implementation. The e-journal service needs continuous input and feedback from the users. Ultimately optimum utilisation and exploitation of these resources is possible only with the shared vision of and responsibility of the entire academic community.

NOTES

1. Chakraborty, H.K. and Chakraborty, B. (2002). *E-journal: coming of age.* Paper presented at the Internet Engineering for Libraries and Information Centres: 1st International Convention Caliber 2002, Ahmedabad: Inflibnet.
2. Keyhani (1993). The online journal of current clinical trials: an innovation in electronic journal publishing. *Database,* 16, 14-23.
3. Tenopir, C. and King, D.W. (2000). Electronic journals: realities for scientists, librarians, and publishers. *Psycoloquy,* 11.
4. *Ulrich's Periodicals Directory* (2010). (Retrieved January 20, 2011, from http://www.bowker.com/index.php/component/content/article/2/487).
5. Tenopir, C. and King, D.W. (2000). Electronic journals: realities for scientists, librarians, and publishers. *Psycoloquy,* 11.
6. Suber, Peter. Open access overview: Focusing on open access to peer-reviewed research articles and their preprints (Retrieved December 12, 2010, from http://www.earlham.edu/~peters/fos/overview.htm).
7. http://nlist.inflibnet.ac.in/about.php (Retrieved on January 18, 2011).

An Overview of Library Provisions for the Differently-abled Students in India

23

V.S. Midhula Soman and *K.G. Sudhier*

1. Introduction

Access to information is a major problem for the differently-abled in India. There are quite a number of challenges faced by the visually and physically challenged persons in accessing the library services. Education is for all, therefore the accessibility to the library services should be accessible to all. The available facilities in the libraries are not sufficient to meet the information needs of the physically challenged children. They are not able to access information directly from the libraries like other children. So the libraries should start new services to meet their information needs, as they have the same right to information as other children. They also have equal rights to education and to information. The libraries need to be committed to ensure full access to their range of services and facilities to their user community. Disabled persons should get equal access as compared to their counterparts. But in reality they are ignored from our society.

Different types of disability require different types of specialised services. Library services for the blind must enable them to have access to equipments such as Braille printers, Braille embosser and tape duplicators, etc. For the physically challenged the library must be barrier free to wheel chairs and other mobility devices and ensuring that all devices including door handles are designed for easy manipulation. In order to create an efficient and effective library programme for the disabled, libraries need managers who are up-to-date and are aware of the latest developments that are likely to have profound effect on their services. It is their collective responsibility to promote quality services by gaining a good insight into the problems faced by the disabled. Library staff must recognize that some disabled persons have no control over their behaviour and must be competent enough to handle difficult situations. They must be prepared to give individual attention so as to understand their strongest communication mode. Therefore, the following aspects are essential to develop a model library programme for them by way of:

- Training the library staff
- Developing user assistance schemes
- Offering special services.

The entrance to any inaccessible built environment should plan to have ramps that will be designed and built to enhance the imposing frontage that will attribute that it will be welcoming to people with acute impairments. The physically challenged persons varies from mild to acute impairment. The library building should be friendly to the physically challenged persons, so that they can access books directly from the library itself.

Library needs an online catalogue which is accessible to both visually and physically challenged persons with speech synthesizer. Visually impaired can access the catalogue and able to select independently what they require from the library. The library should be accessible to all. Visually and physically challenged persons should be provided with good environment and books in the form that they are comfortable in reading. Eg: Braille, large print, etc. All print books in the library should have the same copies in Braille for the visually challenged persons. The library should have a talking computer for use by the visually challenged persons in accessing the database. Qualified Braillists should be assigned to the library. The library should have a recording studio to record books used by the visually challenged persons.

2. Previous Studies

A lot of studies were made about the information needs of visually and physically challenged students mainly in foreign countries. The review of literature shows that there have been very few studies on this area in India.

Varatharajan and Chandrasekhara[1] described software and hardware, facilities and services for the visually challenged users at IGM Library, University of Hyderabad. A study report[2] summarises the recommendations of a group of experts on how UNESCO could assist its member states in facilitating social inclusion of persons with disabilities through Information and Communication Technologies (ICT). Angadi and Koganuramath[3] studied the state of the art ICT facilities and services made available at M.K. Tata Memorial Learning Centre. They made a brief description about the concept of disability, services and learning resource centre, library services for visually impaired people, etc.

Koganuramath and Chaukimath[4] contributed a paper suggesting Learning Resource Centre (LRC) for the visually impaired students in the universities to foster inclusive education. In the paper the views and concerns about achieving the goals of inclusive education in the Indian higher education system through the computer and assistive technologies of a learning resource centre for the visually impaired students was presented. Maina[5] made a study about the problems and solutions faced by visually and physically challenged persons in accessing library services and lecture halls in Kenya. He pointed out that the physically and visually challenged persons face a lot of problems in getting access to the library and lecture halls. The lack of pure physical ground space available to library makes physical access difficult to achieve.

Roy and Bandyopadhyay[6] conducted a study offering suggestions about designing barrier free services for visually challenged persons in the Academic libraries in India. The paper aims to design a barrier free environment in University libraries by procuring proper equipments, technologies and providing proper infrastructural facilities and need based services for the visually disabled. Pillai[7] in her paper tried to analyze the need for a centralized resource centre for visually handicapped in India. The author gives details of some of the technologies and the barriers to access them. The paper also talks about legislation and the need for a better legislation in India at par with other countries. Technology is a boon for visually handicapped in India. She says that, people who are handling them should be trained and should utilize the maximum resource available so that a visually impaired will not be a burden to the society.

Davies[8] presented an overview of internationl research into the library and information needs of visually impired people. Williamson[9] contributed an article on information seeking by blind and sight impaired citizens: an ecological study, in which the information seeking by blind and sight impaired people, with particular emphasis on the role of the internet is described.

Alemna[10] presented a brief overview of the existing library provision for the blind in some African countries. He explained that there are signs of improvement in the educational and social services for the blind, various challenges faced by the librarians in their attempts to provide services for the blind are outlined, and the implications of these challenges are also discussed. Thomsen[11] narrated that visually challenged people all over the world should be given the same opportunities for education, vocational training and employment as well as for taking active part in the general cultural and political debate in the society as their sighted peers.

3. Problems Faced by the Visually Challenged in Libraries

Blindness and sight impairments are common disabilities in all countries of the world. India is now home to the world's largest number of sight-disadvantaged people. Out of the 37 million people across the globe who are blind, over 15 million are from India.Visually impaired people have the same library and information needs as everyone else, although they may require adaptations in the form of service. Access to information is a major problem for the visually challenged in India. Visually challenged persons have problem in accessing books in the library. All books are in print and a blind person is not able to read. The mode of communication is in Braille which is read the raised dots by touch. Literacy means more than just being able to read and write. It means being able to communicate at different levels. These cannot be achieved without having access to Braille books in the library. The visually challenged persons are left with no alternative but to seek assistance from Braille transcribers and other persons who would like to volunteer to read to them during free hours. The lack of access to the Braille books has been a source of tremendous frustration to the students with disabilities for a number of years. As the books in the libraries are all in print, visually challenged persons feel frustrated when they do not get books in the form they want like their peers.

Library is the factory of knowledge and as such, everybody is supposed to have access to it. Less number of course books in Braille, less number of books for competitive exams in Braille or audio are some of the major problems faced by visually challenged students in libraries. For a visually impaired person, library service is a critical channel and often the only source of reading material. While a sighted person has not only access to the public library but the local book store, news-stands and book clubs as well, a blind person cannot expect to get recorded or Brailled literature from these sources. Thus library plays a great role in fulfilling the information and educational needs of the visually impaired people. Therefore efforts need to be done for improving the library and information services. Attention has been drawn to the still very insufficient library services available so that steps can be taken up to improve and develop new services to fill up the lacunae in providing information services to the visually impaired people. Therefore, serious efforts need to be done by the libraries/institutions/NGOs for these neglected groups of special people in fulfilling their information needs.

4. Problems Faced by the Physically Challenged in Libraries

The entrance to the library is always an obstacle to the physically challenged persons. It does not have a ramp or lift to enable persons with disabilities access to the library using wheel chairs. The entrance to any inaccessible built environment should plan to have ramps that will be designed and built to enhance the imposing frontage that will attribute that will be welcoming to people with acute impairments. The physically challenged persons vary from mild to acute impairment. The library building should be friendly to the physically challenged persons, so that they can access books directly from the library itself. The institution should ensure that disabled students are able to access academic text necessary to their studies and thereby avoid serious prejudice. The institution should ensure that all new construction work carried out in respect of the built environment is physically accessible to all. If fairness is supposed to be seen, it is the role of the institutions architecture to enforce any party contracted in support of new construction work with consultative support regarding the needs of people with disabilities in general. The institutions should be commended on doing as much as it is possibly can under difficult circumstances to achieve reasonable access.

5. Library Provisions—International Status

Developed countries like USA, Canada, UK and many European nations have started their initiatives to facilitate the persons with disabilities much before. Most of the universities and the institutes in these countries are providing access to information to the disabled persons by way of enacting the law, by formulating the national policies and funding the libraries and information centres. They have state-of-the-art technologies to assist in the information access. All such institutes have disabled person-friendly infrastructure, information communication tools, facilities and services and trained man-power. The government departments, institutes, libraries, corporate houses, foundations and NGOs have disability friendly websites and portals.

5.1 Indian Scenario

India is not left far behind in empowering its disabled citizenry. It has provided all possible support to the persons with disabilities either by enacting a special Act, or by executing a 'National Policy for Persons with Disabilities', or by way of providing reservations in education, employment, government schemes and programmes or establishing institutes and organizations and many more. In addition to the legal framework, extensive infrastructure has been developed including the 'National Institute of Visually Handicapped (NIVH), Dehradun'.

In India many organizations like NAB (National Association for the Blind); NIVH (National Institute for the Visually Handicapped), NFB, (National Federation for the Blind), etc. are working in the field of disseminating information and providing guidance, training, etc. Indian scenario seems to be much encouraging and supportive. Even though the situation in India is not as developed as in foreign countries; there are some kind of developments to support the differently-abled; mainly by some University libraries.

Academic library services for the differently-abled are not adequate. According to the web based survey, only some Indian universities have taken initiative to establish specialised library services for the differently-abled. Some of the universities are:

5.1.1 Bharathiar University Tamil Nadu

It has introduced a Talking Book Library. Rotary Club has provided help to form the library. The library has started functioning with 1,000 books in the form of CDs and audio cassettes.

5.1.2 Jammu University

Jammu University has opened a Resource Cell for the visually disabled users. A separate software JAWS (Job Access with Speech) has been installed to convert hard copy to voice.

5.1.3 Delhi University

Extended its existing Braille library for multipurpose use. The Braille library is established in the Central reference library. The ABRC (Audio Book Resource Centre) provides recorded cassettes to the visually impaired students. There are three recording studios in the ABRC which is located next to the Braille library in the Central library. ABRC makes an effort to identify the books students might need most and undertakes to record them. It has a collection of several hundred books available for use.

5.1.4 Panjab University

Panjab University has established a special section in the library for visually impaired users where facilities for listening to the contents of books are available by using some special software.

5.1.5 Jawaharlal Nehru University (JNU)

Jawaharlal Nehru University (JNU) has also established a separate section called 'Hellen Keller Unit for Visually Challenged Students'. The unit has twenty computers with special software like Kurzweil, JAWS, etc. These are two screen reading software which allows users to hear text, as it appears on screen.

5.1.6 Lucknow University

Lucknow University has established an exclusive library for visually disabled students (Dr. Manohar Lohia Library).

5.1.7 University of Calcutta

University of Calcutta with the collaboration of National Association of the Blind (NAB) is going to open a state-of-art 'Digital Braille Library and Audio recording workstation', in the 2nd floor of the Central Library, college street, where all modern learning equipments for visually disabled persons will be available.

5.1.8 The U.P Jagadguru Rambhadracharya Handicapped University

This institution was established to provide higher and professional education to persons with disabilities.

These are some of the Universities in India, which give facilities for the differently-abled students to access information from the libraries. But, we can see that, all these libraries are providing facilities or they are focusing only on visually challenged students. And from this it is clear that, there is no University library which provides information to all kind of differently-abled students. Thus, it is essential to rethink and reconsider academic libraries in every aspect, for designing buildings to developing information resources and to structuring information services. This research is unique of its kind in India and sheds light on special groups of users who are forgotten in academic libraries of India. From the above descriptions it is clear that no library in India fully satisfies the information needs of differently-abled students.

6. Suggestions to Improve Library Provisions

Some of the suggestions to improve the facilities for the differently-abled in libraries are:

- Differently-abled students should be provided with good environment and books in the form that they are comfortable in reading. Eg: Braille, large print, ordinary print, etc.
- All print books in the library should have the same copies in Braille for the visually challenged students. Alternative formats of resources like enlarged print, embossed print and spoken word, etc. should be available to these users.
- Qualified braillists should be assigned to the library. The library should have a braille embosser. Give the visually impaired more books to read by making the production of braille books more efficient.
- The library should have a recording studio to record books used by the visually challenged students.
- There should be a talking zone where formal reader service can be provided. Trained library professionals can read out the relevant information to the visually disabled users whenever needed. Here these special users can also use different audio media to access the resources.
- Library professionals should be specially trained to provide proper services to the differently-abled. They have a big role to know about different grades of disability and to develop skills that will enable them to deliver library services to this special group. In-service training is needed for library professionals for this.
- Modern computer technology helps in modifying existing software/hardware as well as developing new software/hardware, etc. to enable people with disabilities to work independently. This is often called adaptive or enabling technology. The reduction in price of these technology devices is offering a great opportunity for all libraries to satisfy the needs of the disabled persons without involving much expenditure.

- Besides being equipped with different types of adaptive technology, academic libraries should establish a formal reader service section to increase the accessibility of their library. As all documents are not available in their technology like Braille or talking book and some books are rarely needed by these users. At this point Reader service is the only way to provide 'right information to the right user at the right moment'.
- For the physically challenged the library facility must be barrier free to wheel chairs and other mobility devices ensuring that all devices including door handles are designed for manipulation.
- Academic libraries should modify their existing buildings to accommodate these special users.
- Services should be introduced/developed according to the needs of the library users.
- Awareness programmes on regular basis is required.
- Promotion/marketing of services is also needed.
- Services/facilities are to be monitored.
- Representatives from the users should be there in the managerial decision-making committees.
- Provide access to the academic information sources.
- Explore the utilisation of 'Assistive Technologies'.

7. Conclusion

The present facilities are not sufficient to meet the information needs of the differently-abled students in our country. Access to information is a major problem for the differently-abled in India. There are quite a number of challenges faced by the differently-abled persons in accessing library services. The government and authorities should consider them like other children and their information needs should be met as their counterparts. If the authorities are ready to consider their information needs and if they are met in a proper way it will provide a new life to them.

NOTES

1. Varatharajan, N. and Chandrasekhara, M. (2010). Library services and the visually challenged users in the digital environment: a case study. Proceedings of the International conference on Innovation Driven Librarianship: Expectations of *Librarians and library users (ICIDL-2010)*. SRM University, Tamil Nadu.
2. http://www.ada.gov (Retrieved on 12th December, 2010).
3. Angadi, Mallikarjun and Koganuramath, Muttayya (2009). ICT facilities and services at M.K. Tata Memorial Learning Centre for visually challenged. *Proceedings of 7th International CALIBER*, INFLIBNET Centre, Ahmedabad.
4. Koganuramath, Muttayya and Chaukimath, Puttaraj A. (2009). M-Learning resource centre for the visually impaired students in the Universities to foster inclusive education (Retrieved January 17, 2011, from crl.du.ac.in/ical09/.../ical-104 215 458 2 RV.pdf).
5. Mania, Christopher K.A. (2009). Problems and solutions faced by visually and physically challenged persons in access in library services and lecture halls (Retrieved January 26, 2011, from www.ctevh.org/conf2009/.../braille%20address7.doc).
6. Roy, Chanda Protap and Bandyopadhyay (2009). Designing barrier free services for visually challenged persons in the academic libraries in India (Retrieved February 17, 2011, from crl.du.ac.in/ical09/papers/index files/ical-105 241 602 1 RV. pdf).
7. Pillai, Priya R. (2008). Knowledge for all: Opportunities and challenges for visually handicapped people in India for higher education. *International conference on knowledge for all role of libraries and information centres*, 12-15 Nov. 2008.
8. Davies, J.E. (2007). An overview of international research into the library and information needs of visually impaired people. *Library Trends*, 55 (4), 785-95.
9. Williamson, Kirsty (2000). Information seeking by blind and sight impaired citizens an ecological study: *Information Research*, 5 (4) (Retrieved January 22, 2011, from http://information.net/ir/5-4/paper79.html).
10. Alemna (1991). The provision of Library services for the blind in Africa (Retrieved January 17, 2011, from http://forge.fh-potsdam.de/IFLA/INSPEL/93-4alan.pdf).
11. Thomsen, Paulli (1985). The establishment of a library service to visually handicapped people in African developing countries. *IFLA journal*, 11 (36), 1985 (Retrieved February 20, 2011, from http://sagepub.com/cgi/reprint/11/1/36).

PART VII

THE OPEN SOURCE PHILOSOPHY

Application and Usage of Open Source Software in Libraries

24

N.K. Sheeja

1. Introduction

Applications of Information and Communication Technologies (ICTs) in library services and functions have been an area of focus for librarians all over the world for the past several years. Along with the use of computers and related hardware, librarians were also concerned with the use, application and evaluation of a range of software specifically designed to suit diverse library operations. But computer software were not commonly applied by all libraries owing to finance, human resource, infrastructure, training and knowledge. As library software packages were generally proprietary in nature, purchase and use of them required huge financial investment. The trained manpower was essential to manage the environment. Librarians needed education and knowledge in these areas. The process of maintenance and updating of software was also complicated involving cost and related issues. All these factors hindered the practice of use and application of software in libraries. The advent of Free and Open Source Software (OSS) and their applications in libraries are becoming important area of study and discussion in this context.

Free and Open Source Software (F/OSS) are computer software that are available free of cost with their source code and with many freedoms attached with it; to use, change, and improve the software, and to redistribute it in modified or unmodified form. The attitude behind OSS is mutual sharing of knowledge, expertise, and skills. It is widely used by organizations and industries worldwide. It is not necessarily cost-free, but is free to use, free to modify, and free to share.

The name of Open Source Software was given in 1998 by a group of leaders in the free software community. Since then, the F/OSS movement has become a revolution in software development. The Free Software Foundation (FSF)[1] maintains a formal definition of free software. It identifies four aspects of freedom, from the software users' perspective:

- The freedom to run the program, for any purpose (freedom 0).
- The freedom to study how the program works, and change it to make it do what you wish (freedom 1). Access to the source code is a precondition for this.
- The freedom to redistribute copies so you can help your neighbour (freedom 2).
- The freedom to improve the program, and release your improvements (and modified versions in general) to the public, so that the whole community benefits (freedom 3). Access to the source code is a precondition for this.

The OSS differs from the proprietary software in terms of many aspects. Proprietary software may only be obtained by some form of payment, either by purchase or by leasing. The major difference between the two is the freedom to modify the software. In proprietary software, only the original developer or designates can make changes. Its source code is not distributed to customers and users may not have the freedom to share, resell, or further distribute software. In open source software, source code is available to anyone that uses the software and it can be modified and redistributed. A wide range of free and open source software are available today including the Linux operating system, the Apache web server, Perl programming language and MySQL database management software.

The library and information science (LIS) community first started to take note of OSS in 1999, when Daniel Chudnov, founder of the Open Source Systems for Libraries project, wrote an introductory article in Library Journal. According to Chudnov[2] there are three factors pushing the use of OSS in libraries:

- F/OSS licenses allow libraries to cut budget on software and use it to other issues needing more funds.
- F/OSS product is not locked into a single vendor. Thus even if a library buys an open source system from one vendor, it might choose to buy technical support from another company or get it from in-house experts.
- The entire library community might share the responsibility of solving information systems accessibility issues.

There are a number of benefits associated with OSS applications. The low start-up cost associated with using OSS is frequently mentioned as its main attraction. OSS has many attractions for developing economies. OSS is a useful and significant tool that can be helpful to solve many problems faced by the librarians of developing countries. The low cost, anti-piracy campaign, security, and technological independence are the main factors behind the expansion of OSS in the developing world.[3] OSS licenses mean that software can be run on multiple machines (or at home or on laptops) with no extra licensing fees. However, this is not its only advantage. OSS is also seen as a solution to the issues many libraries experience with commercial integrated library system software that is slow to evolve and expensive to upgrade. The expected benefits of OSS approach would also include more flexibility and a better match to libraries' requirements. Poynder[4] commented that OSS also has reduced vulnerability to viruses. It is also technology neutral, meaning that applications will run on more than one platform (such as Windows, Linux, Unix, and MacOS X). This is true when they are written in languages such as Perl and PHP that are available for a number of platforms. Bretthauer[5] remarked that vendors of proprietary software can "withdraw the product, discontinue its support, go out of business, and/or can be acquired by another vendor who can do any of the above", and notes that this is not a risk when using open source software. OSS removes the requirement to constantly upgrade hardware in order to be able to run newer, more sophisticated software being promoted by commercial organizations.

2. Scope of the Study

This paper aims to explore open source application in libraries. There are many open source library applications available today, and each satisfies a particular need. Open source library software is available for automating the library services and functions to build their digital libraries and manage the knowledge produced by the institutions' community. They help libraries save library budget and serve more users online. Besides automation, institutional repository and digital library software, open source software packages are used in other areas like content management, inter library loan applications, etc. Even though there are a number of OSS available in LIS field this paper concentrates on application and usage of KOHA, DSpace and Greenstone-three commonly used open source software packages under three headings namely, Open Source Integrated Library System, Open Source Institutional Repository Software and Open Source Digital Library Software.

3. Design

This study is purely a web-based one. The open source software packages were recognized by scanning the available literature on the topic, visiting the websites of respective OSS initiatives and through Internet search.

4. Findings

4.1 Open Source Integrated Library System

Since a Library Management System (also called Integrated Library System) plays a momentous role in supporting business and technical functions of a library, it is a critical part of any software solutions for libraries. A typical library management system includes several modules: acquisition, cataloguing, circulation, and administration. It also provides an online public access catalogue (OPAC) that can be searched by users through a Web browser.

Some currently known open source Library Management Systems are Koha, Avanti, Openbiblio, Evergreen, and Emilda.

Of these projects, the New Zealand-based Koha is probably the most active and complete one. Including modules for circulation, cataloguing, acquisitions, serials, reserves, patron management, branch relationships, and more, Koha has been declared as a true enterprise-class Library Management System, comparable to those commercial ones, Koha includes a full catalogue, OPAC, circulation and acquisitions system. It is used in hundreds of libraries including academic, public, school, and religious, and has demonstrated good scalability (from 1 to 8 branches and from 1,000 to 300,000 items).

4.1.1 Koha

Koha is the first open source fully featured Integrated Library System (ILS) that was originally developed by Katipo Communications Limited of Wellington, New Zealand for the Horowhenua Library Trust (HLT), a regional library system located in Levin. Development of Koha, began in 1999, funded by a group of libraries in rural New Zealand that found proprietary software expensive and lacking needed features. Koha is currently maintained by a team of software providers and library technology staff from around the globe. Some of the key features of Koha are listed below:

- Web based.
- Copy cataloguing and z39.50.
- MARC21 and UNIMARC for professional cataloguers.
- Manage online and off-line resources with the same tool.
- RSS feed of new acquisitions.
- E-mail and/or txt patron's overdue and other notices.
- Print your own barcodes.
- Serials management module.
- Web based OPAC system.
- Simple, clear search interface for all users.
- Simple and comprehensive acquisition options.[6]

There has been a high level of interest in Koha internationally, and it is currently being used in many countries including India. The Koha project uses a number of channels to allow members of its community to communicate with each other — there is a general mailing list, as well as separate ones for developers, Windows users, French-speaking Koha users/developers, and German-speaking Koha users/developers. In addition, the developers use Internet Relay Chat (IRC), a real-time message facility for scheduled meetings and less formal conversations. More information about Koha is available at http://www.koha.org. Figure 24.1 is a screen shot of Online Public Access Catalogue interface of CUSAT library using Koha ILS.

Fig. 24.1: Online Public Access Catalogue Interface of CUSAT Library

4.2 Open Source Institutional Repository Software

The contents produced in a particular institution as part of teaching, learning, research and collaboration are known as institutional knowledge. DSpace was actually created for capturing this knowledge and providing access to it with facilities for long time preservation. When an institution needs to capture and disseminate data created outside the institution but required by its members, it can be called as digital library. Hence the DSpace software can be effectively used for both institutional repositories and digital libraries. DSpace can be downloaded from http://sourceforge.net, the open source software repository. Instructions for installations can be achieved from various sources including online community support.

4.2.1 DSpace

The concept of institutional repositories became popular with the advent of DSpace. DSpace is developed in 2002 by MIT Libraries and Hewlett Packard (Hp) Labs. DSpace is the most popular OSS across the world for building institutional repositories/digital libraries to capture, store, index, preserve, and redistribute the intellectual output of a university's research faculty in digital formats. Key features of DSpace are:

- Authentication
- Authorization
- Ease of Access
- Faster Search and Retrieval
- Hierarchy to manage contents
- Import and Export
- Statistics
- Supporting large number of digital formats
- Customization
- Standards Compliance
- Optimized Search (dspace.org).[7]

DSpace is a platform that allows capturing items in any format—in text, video, audio, and data. It distributes it over the web. As it indexes the work, users can search and retrieve the items. It preserves the digital work over the long-term. More information about DSpace is available at http://dspace.org/. Figure 24.2 is a screenshot of an institutional repository run on Dspace platform.

4.3 Open Source Digital Library Software

Digital libraries are composed of collections of digital objects, including text, image, video, and audio, along with methods for access and retrieval, and for selection, organization and maintenance of the collection. Some major OSS projects for building and managing digital collections are DSpace, Fedora, and Greenstone.

Fig. 24.2: Screenshot of an Institutional Repository of CUSAT

4.3.1 Greenstone

The Greenstone Digital Library Software (GSDL) is promoted by the New Zealand Digital Library project research group at the University of Waikato, headed by Dr. Ian H. Witten, and is sponsored by the UNESCO. Greenstone provides a new way of organizing information and publishing it on the Internet in the form of a fully-searchable, metadata-driven digital library. It is open-source, multilingual software, issued under the terms of the GNU General Public License. Greenstone runs on all versions of Windows, and Unix/Linux, and Mac OS-X. Greenstone is highly interoperable using contemporary standards, it incorporates a server that can serve any collection over the Open Archives Protocol for Metadata Harvesting (OAI-PMH), and Greenstone can harvest documents over OAI-PMH and include them in a collection. The Greenstone digital library software includes a web interface for searching and viewing digital collections, and a librarian's interface for building and managing collections. Since the Greenstone Librarian Interface (GLI) is developed with Java, the Java Run-time Environment (JRE) is required to run the program. The JRE package is free for download from Sun Develop Network. Some features of Greenstone are:

- standard digital formats
- metadata-based browsing facilities
- runs on a wide variety of platforms

Fig. 24.3: Screenshot of IIMK's Digital library

5. Usage of Open Source Software in LIS

OSS methodology is making slow but stable progress within the library community. Currently available Open Source library-related applications include not only integrated library management systems but also a range of innovative functionality, such as Greenstone (Digital library system), DSpace (digital library/Institutional Repository system), etc. The OpenDOAR-Directory of Open Access Repositories[8] lists 25 Greenstone installations around the world. As per DSpace wiki[9] there are 1059 libraries which use Dsapce software around the world.

6. Discussions

The OSS software world is growing steadily. Libraries are in the forefront of applying OSS in libraries for various services and functions. However, the success of OSS application is depending upon the factors like: organizational culture, intensive training, dedication, documentation, expertised human resources and finance i.e. finance for hardware and human development.

7. Conclusion

The adoption of OSS in libraries is an important area for exploration. OSS helps librarians to meet their functions without investing on software. OSS gives them freedom to access and modify the software according to their needs. The involvement of large number of professionals in the development, use, and modification of OSS offers great potential for librarians to learn and exchange knowledge and skill. The OSS model also gives them an opportunity to be actively involved in development projects, to improve their expertise and to employ a wide range of technological applications. However, the adoption of OSS on a wide scale will largely depend on long-term commitments by the organizations. Libraries and library professionals need to empower themselves with needed technological skills, and address conceptual, social, financial, technical, human issues in a collaborative manner for greater efficiency and cost savings.

NOTES

1. http://www.gnu.org/philosophy/free-sw.html (Retrieved on 15th July, 2010).
2. Chudnov, D. (1999). Open source software: the future of library systems. *Library Journal*, 124 (13), 40-43.
3. Rajani, N. (2003). Free as in education: significance of the free/libre and open source software for developing countries (Retrieved 15th July, 2010, from http://www.itu.int/wsis/docs/background/themes/ access/ free_as_in_education_niranjan.pdf).
4. Poynder, R. (2001). The open source movement. *Information Today*, 18 (9), 66-67.
5. Bretthauer, D. (2001). Open source software in libraries. *Library Hi Tech News*, 18 (5), 8-9.
6. http://koha.org/about/features (Retrieved on 10th March, 2010).
7. http://www.dspace.org/ (Retrieved on 10th March, 2011).
8. http://www.opendoar.org/ (Retrieved on 10th March, 2011).
9. http://www.dspace.org/whos-using-dspace/Repository-List.html (Retrieved on 14th March, 2011).

Development of Library Automation Systems in Open Source Software Mode: Opportunities and Challenges for Libraries in India

25

V. Vimal Kumar and *Thomas Abraham*

1. Introduction

Open source is becoming a trend setter in libraries. Lots of Open Source software packages are available for various automation purposes in libraries. Open source digital library and institutional repository software packages are very popular among the librarians. But such software packages are mainly used to preserve and disseminate scholarly literature and other digital content. Digital libraries and institutional repositories have relevance only in big library systems. Circulation, cataloguing, acquisition and serial control are common basic functions in all types of libraries. Automation of basic housekeeping operations is the first priority of most of the libraries. Open source ILS (Integrated Library Systems) help to make automation of basic library functions affordable.

Due to financial recession, libraries in developed countries began to think about various possibilities to reduce the cost involved in library automation systems. Small and medium size libraries feel that automation of housekeeping operations as a financial burden due to the high price of proprietary Library Management Systems. As part of cost cutting strategy, many libraries in the United States and Canada recently migrated from their legacy automation systems to open source library management systems. Libraries in developing countries also show interest in open source ILS because of its economic feasibility; i.e. free availability. Open source library management systems give effective way to automate their library operations without much financial investment. Principles and practices of open source software are very similar to the principles and practices of modern librarianship both value free and equal access to data, information and knowledge. Both strive to promote human understanding and to make our lives better. Both make effort to improve society as a whole.[1]

2. What is Open Source ILS

An integrated library system, or ILS, is an enterprise resource planning system for a library. An ILS is designed to coordinate and automate such library functions as the online catalogue, the circulation system, and the acquisitions system.[2] An ILS improves the efficiency of housekeeping operations and library services. Use of ILS requires only the one time entry of the data (bibliographic and user) and the same can be made use for all other purposes. Proprietary ILS is costly and protected by copyright and has strict restrictions on use and distribution. Open source ILS is a free alternative to proprietary integrated library management system. Libraries can obtain open source software freely and can use for the automation purposes. Open source software packages are available with source code and if necessary libraries can make changes in software. There is no much difference between the features and functions of commercial and open source ILS. The fundamental difference is visible in the development processes and distribution methods. Group of people or institutions contribute resources (time, money and skill) into the development of open source library management system for their library automation. Open licenses are adopted for the free distribution of software. Most of the open source ILS projects are licensed under GNU (General Public License). Koha, Evergreen, PMB, Newgenlib, Senayan and OpenBiblio are the popular open source integrated library systems. They are available free and offer good control on library automation.

3. Who is Doing It

Open source software packages are developed for the goodness of the community and the ownership rest with the public. Openness and cooperation at all stages of software development expands opportunity for collaborative work. So professionals and users are being attracted to open source software projects and make use their spare time for creative contribution.

Most of the Open Source ILS were initially developed as stand-alone library automation system. At later stages, they moved to open source platform and released software in public domain. Koha ILS was developed in 2000 by Katipo Communications for Harovenua Library Trust and later released under open source license. Koha gained rapid attention among library professionals and software developers because of its open source nature. Now Koha development activities are lead by community members from various countries. NewGenLib is another mature open source ILS developed in India released in public domain in 2008. Kesavan Institute of Information and Knowledge Management and Verus Solutions Pvt. Ltd. started NewGenLib as proprietary initiative and they gained substantial user base. They adopted General Public License, popular free software license with the hope of getting more customers and to ensure community participation in development.

In certain instances, a group of libraries with similar functional requirements developed ILS for their consortium operations. Evergreen library management system was developed in 2006 for the use of PINE (Public Information Network for Electronic Services) consortium of 544 libraries in Georgia State, United States. Member libraries in the consortium can pool their resources including technology, money and human resource for the development and maintenance of their own ILS without buying commercial ILS. In such cases they can also save a significant amount of money for library automation. In addition, it is easy to establish good connectivity between libraries and can share their resources for the benefit of member libraries.

4. How Does it Work

Development and maintenance of open source software project is the responsibility of the public, especially the concerned user group. Always software projects in public domain start as a solo initiative. OpenBiblio developed by Frédéric Descamps for the automation of a school library where his wife worked.[3] Later more people joined with the OpenBiblio project and contributed to the development process.

Libraries, programmers and funding agencies jointly take part in the various activities of the software development. Online communication tools like wiki, online discussion forums, and blogs are used for the interaction between members in the software community. Users and developers interact through discussion forums to report errors, giving suggestions and to clear doubts regarding the operation of software. Open source ILS projects ensure the end users participation in the preparation of technical documentation, language translation and user manuals. Day by day request for new features are received from libraries and they are trying to incorporate into these existing software with the help of community members. Active open source projects usually have regularly updated web pages and busy development e-mail lists. They usually encourage the participation of those who use the software in its further development. If everything is quiet on the development front, it might be that work has been suspended or even stopped.[4]

5. Why is it Significant

The main attraction of open source ILS is that it charges no license fee. Investing in a proprietary library ILS is a never ending process. In addition to huge initial investment, libraries are compelled to shell out money to retain the ILS service. Purchase of a proprietary ILS does not mean that library have full control over the software. Ownership of the software will rest with the company and libraries should be continuing as mere users. If libraries dare to stop the service of commercial ILS, they will face the severe consequences including loss of control over bibliographic data. In such cases companies may charge a good amount to give bibliographic records back to libraries.

Local technical support can be sought for the installation and maintenance of open source software in libraries. Technical specifications and other details are available for public and it helps to deploy open source ILS with the help of technical service providers either from library or locally available. It ensures access of technical help for the trouble shooting of ILS without any delay. Most of the open source ILS projects make use open standards and tools for software development. MySQL, Perl, PHP, Zebra and Apache are the favourite tool kit for the development of popular open source ILS. Z39.50, SRU/W, OpenNCIP, OpenSearch, and XML are the examples of open standards utilized by open source ILS projects for data exchange and retrieval. "We needed the freedom to change things, to change the code if necessary, because the types of things we want to do are not going to appear in commercial library software for years."[5]

6. Where is it Going

We can observe that popular open source ILS projects started with minimum functional features. Consecutively more features are added to existing software receiving the contributions from developer and user community. For example, MARC support, z39.50 server and NCIP modules in Koha were developed initially for Nelsonville Public Library, US. Later these modules were made available with the main software release. The Crawford County Libraries in Pennsylvania chose to support the integration of the Zebra XML storage and retrieval environment into Koha. The Westchester Academic Libraries Director Organization (WALDO) contracted to introduce many features into Koha required for academic libraries. Contributions from many libraries to the software development have led to the expansion of Koha from a very simple ILS to one with a competitive set of features suitable for many small and medium-sized libraries.[6]

Open source ILS projects are expanding their features list receiving the advantages of innovative technology and growing number of users. Each successive version of open source ILS tries to manifest user requirements based on suggestions. Koha and PMB adopted web 2.0 technology to enhance the user experience. Latest version of Koha has provisions for RSS, federated searching, tagging and reviews by users. It also adopted zebra plug-in for efficient text indexing and retrieval from large bibliographic record collection. Open source ILS have to achieve the capability to handle digital content in near future. They were initially developed to handle the automation purpose of libraries with small collection. Now they are in progress on the way to take place in the list of enterprise class library automation systems.

7. What are the Selection Criteria

Selection and evaluation of open source software is different from proprietary programs. A key difference for evaluation is that the information available for open source programs are usually different than from proprietary programs; source code, analysis by others of the program design, discussion between users and developers on how well it is working, and so on.[7] Open source ILS is free and libraries can try full version of the software. It is possible to install and test more than one open source ILS to find the suitability against the library requirements. All types of technical information related with open source ILS are available for free access. Technical documentation, bugs information, users queries in discussion forums are open for public and it provides valuable information for ILS selection and maintenance. Certain features or functional modules essential for day-to-day work may not be available with the initial development stages of open source ILS. In such cases, libraries have to purchase additional modules from open source service providers or making use the in-house expertise to build the required features. It is essential to read release notes of latest version and software road map to know which features are already available and are expected in future. Ensure the availability of standards (e.g. MARC, Z39.50, NCIP, etc.) which are essential for data exchange.

8. What are the Downsides

Even though open source ILS are available free, it is not ready to use. Many features in ILS are generalist and must be either customized before use or adjust with existing features. Open source ILS are available with standardized features, majority of libraries required.

If technical expertise for installation and maintenance are available in the library itself, open source ILS is free from initial investment and other ongoing expenses. Otherwise, library has to hire technical support of software service provider for services such as installation, data migration and maintenance. Initial investment on open source ILS is probably less than the annual maintenance of commercial ILS. Many libraries simply do not have the in-house expertise to support open source software development, and also do not have the ability to train staff on the use of the new technologies.[8] Libraries should make a good home work before the adoption of open source library management system.

Lack of awareness and knowledge in open source technology and software among library professionals restrict widely adoption of open source ILS in libraries. Marshal Breeding says "support is a significant impediment to the implementation of open source software. The software license fees represent only one component of the overall costs that a library bears in its automation effort. The personnel required for the initial implementation and system administration is a major consideration."[9] Knowledge in Linux administration is essential for effective deployment of open source ILS in a live library environment. In the Indian context majority of the library professionals lack the facility for training in Linux operating system and related application softwares. In such cases, commercial open source service providers can help libraries to host ILS and provide continuous support. In India, very few companies provide commercial support for open source solutions in libraries. Price of the services from commercial Open Source ILS is not affordable by most of the Indian libraries.

9. What is the User's Commitment

Open source software is highly depended on its users for its development and maintenance. In a typical open source project, community members have varying levels of participation, ranging from passive users to core developers. Library professionals and software developers are involved in the open source ILS projects. High involvement of library professionals is necessary to fulfill the functional requirements of an ideal ILS. So efforts and expenses of open source ILS are equally distributed among the user community. Open source software projects expect user participation in the following areas[10]:

1. To find bugs,
2. To find usability problems,

3. To suggest new features,
4. To review and inspect source code,
5. To submit source code,
6. To offer project administration assistance, and
7. for documentation.

Direct investment of money for the development of entire software packages is not necessary in the context of open source software project. Libraries can pay money to develop additional features required by the library and missing in current software release. Next release onwards, newly developed features will be available with main software distribution. With commercial software a big portion of the license fee goes to research and development over which the library has no control, while with open source that same money can be funded for the development of the software modules that the library really wants.[11] Open source software projects opened up wide range of options for user contributions and participation in software development process.

10. Open Source ILS in India

Earlier, adoption rate of Open Source ILS in India is comparatively slower than other developed countries due to lack awareness among library professionals. Compared with other Open Source ILS, Koha is more popular in India due to its active users community in India. Many prestigious library automation projects in India adopted Koha due to its capability to handle Indian languages. Delhi Public Library began to use Koha in 2007. The library collection consist of 15 lakh books. In the initial stages a significant portion of records migrated from CDS/ISIS database to Koha. Delhi Public Library consists of a central library, a zonal library, three branch libraries, 26 sub-branch libraries and 6 community libraries. Online Public Access Catalogue catalogue (www.dpl.gov.in) is integrated with library website and provides information regarding library resources. Granthalaya (www.granthalaya.org) is another prestigious automation project using Koha Open Source ILS. This project envision a union catalogue of of public libraries in Konkan region Maharashtra, India. Central Library and other Department libraries in Cochin University of Science and Technology adopted Koha and is fully functional from 2009.

The Government of Kerala, has made a decision in principle to make Koha as its official software for computerization of libraries under Government control.[12] Educational institutions under Institute of Human Resources Development has adopted Koha in their libraries and is providing in-house training for library professionals. IHRD is an autonomous body under Government of Kerala and it owns about 50 educational institutions.

The University Library of Central University of Kerala, Kasaragod which is a newly established central university in Kerala has automated its in-house operations using KOHA. They are also providing webOPAC through the university website (www.cukerala.ac.in). The webOPAC of the university library of Central University of Kerala is also available through its blog www.cuklibinfopage.blogspot.com.

Installation of Open Source ILS was difficulty for library professionals because of its complex installation procedure. Many learning and installation aids for Open Source ILS are now available for the help of library professionals. They make librarians to install Open Source ILS in the library without the help of a Linux expert. Dr. A.R.D. Prasad, DRTC, Bangalore developed a live CD (http://sourceforge.net/projects/liblivecd/) suitable for learning purpose and installation. Koha, Dspace and other helpful applications also included in the live CD.

Lot of misunderstandings exist among library professionals regarding the use and maintenance regarding Open Source ILS. A very sad situation is that library professional organizations and library science schools in India still follow head in sand approach towards giving awareness and training in Open Source library management systems.

11. Conclusion

Impact of open source movement made positive effects in libraries in India. Library professionals are recognizing the impact of open source softwares and began to adopt in library automation purposes. Open source culture empowers libraries to try innovative technologies in their working environment. In addition, libraries have started to develop their own tools such as meta search and social functionality tools to integrate with open source ILS. This practice helps them to develop solutions to solve their technology related problem within the walls of libraries.

In a certain extent, open source library management system helps to solve common problems faced by libraries such as fewer budgets for proprietary ILS, management of increasing number of records, large number of members, and lack of powerful administration over all modules in library. Open source library management systems provide access to libraryowned data and provide much more flexibility for your library than commercial ILS.[13] It is necessary to make awareness among library professionals about the advantages of open source software. Then only libraries can attain tremendous savings on library automation and to achieve increase in performance at the same time.

NOTES

1. http://infomotions.com/musings/biblioacid/ (Retrieved on 20th December, 2010).
2. http://en.wikipedia.org/wiki/Integrated_library_system (Retrieved on 20th December, 2010).
3. http://openbiblio.sourceforge.net/indexeng.html (Retrieved on 20th December, 2010).
4. www.osswatch.ac.uk/resources/tips.xml (Retrieved on 21st December, 2010).
5. http://www.athenscounty.lib.oh.us/koha_questions.html (Retrieved on 21st December, 2010).
6. Breeding, Marshall (2008). The viability of open source ILS. ASIS&T Bulletin (Retrieved on December 21, 2010, from http://www.asis.org/Bulletin/Dec-08/DecJan09_Breeding.html).
7. www.dwheeler.com (Retrieved on 21st December, 2010).
8. http://liblime.com/welcome.html (Retrieved on 21st December, 2010).
9. Breeding, Marshall (2002). An update on open source ILS: Marshall Breeding reviews three open source projects. *Information Today*, 19 (9) (Retrieved December 24, 2010, from http://www.infotoday.com/IT/oct02/breeding.htm).

10. Zhao, Luyin and Fadi P. Deekv (2004). User collaboration in open source software development. Electronic Markets 14 (2), 89-103.
11. www.myacpl.org/about/koha/qa (Retrieved on 1st January, 2011).
12. http://koha.org/news/government-of-kerala-decides-to-use-koha (Retrieved on 5th January, 2011).
13. http://infopeople.org/training/webcasts/webcast_data/354/index.html (Retrieved on 10th January, 2011).

Open Source Bibliographic Citation and Reference Management Tools: A Review

26

Trupti D. More

1. Introduction

Publishers and academic institutions generally specify their requirements about the document format to be submitted, including the reference lists and the citations. In this case the collection and formatting of bibliographic data, which includes author and publication details, for works cited in a document becomes tedious, monotonous, and error driven task. It becomes time consuming too particularly when one has to later change the styles, as it often involves the manual entry of these details into a database. An automated bibliographic application simplifies this process faster. It allows a user to forget about these hidden details and focus on writing. These applications help researchers to manage their thousands of references and to create formatted citations lists in required style format.

2. Open Source Bibliographic Citation and Reference Management Tools

Open source software is available free under open source license terms and conditions where source code of the software is available free to the end user for any developments, redistribution, and customization. This software can be freely used, copied, studied and modified by anyone who obtains the copy.

"Citation management tools enable researchers to capture bibliographic information about research materials, create bibliographies, add footnotes, and manage research collections.

Some citation management tools make it easy to share references with other researchers."[1]

Bibliographic Citation Management software is software developed for scholars and authors to use it for recording, utilizing and managing their bibliographic citations. Once a citation has been recorded, it is used time and again in generating bibliographies, such as lists of references in scholarly books and research articles.

There are several open source bibliographic citation management tools available, which are free, easy to use, and beneficial in research and academic disciplines. For example, Aigaion, Bebop, Bibus, BibDesk, Connotea, JabRef, Jumper 2.0, KBibTeX, Pybliographer, Refbase, RefDB, Referencer, Wikindx, Zotero, etc. These software packages normally consist of a database in which full bibliographic references can be entered. It has a system for generating selective lists of references in the different formats as required by the publishers. Some reference management packages are integrated with word processors so that a reference list in the appropriate format is produced automatically as an article is written and it reduces the risk that a cited source is left to include in the reference list. They also have a facility for importing the details of publications from online bibliographic databases.

3. Benefits of Using Open Source Bibliographic Citation and Reference Management Software

(a) Open source citation management tools are free, very powerful and easy to operate. They help to collect, organize, cite and share the references.

(b) They allow taking books, articles, and web pages allowing its citation, then organize, annotate those items, and allow exporting citations into variety of citation style formats.

(c) They not only allow to manage all references as per different categories but also allow to upload the full text files along with each reference and these full text files get indexed so that search inside the PDF files can be possible.

4. A Review of Open Source Bibliographic Citation and Reference Management Software

The open source bibliographic citation management software packages are available under the terms of the GNU General Public License and free BSD license, which are free for use and can be modified as per requirement. They are categorized as web based and application based software packages. Most of these software packages have capacity to work on a variety of operating systems.

4.1 Aigaion

Aigaion is web-based reference management software. It is a HP/MySQL based multi-user system for managing annotated bibliographies. It allows the users to order publications in a self-chosen topic structure, offers BibTeX and RIS import and export and has an intuitive user interface. Formatted export to txt, html or rtf in common citation styles is possible in Aigaion. It is platform independent and it offers multi-language support.[2]

4.2 Bebop

Bebop is web-based software that creates a web interface to a list of publications stored in a BibTeX file and allows browsing by author, year, document type, topic and keywords using PHP, Java script and XML technologies. It can be mainly used by institutes for self-archiving and creating institutional repositories. It is suited for single source publishing of bibliography information as it uses one single BibTeX file as its database; therefore no database server like MySQL is needed. The BibTeX entries for publications can be annotated with more information by using research area, keywords, abstract, file link, and presentation and poster keys. AJAX-based interface allows displaying abstract, BibTeX entry and links to Digital Object Identifier, full text, slides and poster files. RSS feeds and Permanent links are available per year, research area, keyword and document type. Adding new publications can be done via an online form or by directly editing the BibTeX file. Bibliographic entries can be exported as BibTeX through UnAPI, making it compatible with Zotero.[3]

4.3 Bibus

Bibus is bibliographic and reference management software. It allows one to search, edit, and sort bibliographic records. It is designed for multiuser environments. It gives facility to insert references and format bibliographies into LiberOffice.org, OpenOffice.org and Microsoft Word. Since it has foreign language support through Unicode, it is available in English, Chinese, Czech, French, German, Hungarian, Portuguese, Slovenian, and Spanish. It works on most modern platforms like GNU/Linux with LiberOffice.org and OpenOffice.org and Windows98/2000/XP with LiberOffice.org, OpenOffice.org and Microsoft Word. It Interfaces seamlessly with PubMed Entrez and with eTBLAST. It has ability to create custom styles for bibliographies.[4]

4.4 BibDesk

BibDesk is an open-source reference management software package for Mac OS X, used to manage bibliographies and references when writing essays and articles. It offers a front-end for creating, editing, managing, and searching BibTeX databases, with integrated connectivity to external databases including PubMed, the U.S. Library of Congress, Web of Science, and any other databases searchable via the Z39.50 or Entrez protocols. It enables one-click importing of references to articles and books listed in these databases and library catalogues. It imports unformatted references from websites or documents without requiring that they be re-typed. It permits articles residing on a user's computer to be linked to their BibDesk database entries via dragand-drop, and will auto-file linked PDFs or other copies of articles in desktop folder. It can also export citations formatted in any given citation style in plain text, RTF, HTML, and RSS. It does not itself contain citation styles, but through its integration with LaTeX it can automatically produce citations in any of the basic BibTeX styles, and can when used with BibTeX style-files replicate nearly any citation format.[5]

4.5 Connotea

Connotea is a free online reference management service for scientists, researchers, and clinicians. It is a social bookmarking tool, where users can save links to their favourite websites. It recognizes a number of scientific websites and automatically collects metadata for the article or page being bookmarked, including author and publication names. It is also possible to add non-recognized web pages, by manually entering information. An alternative method of adding an article is to retrieve the Connotea form and add the Digital Object Identifier (DOI) for the article. The system recognizes users who are bookmarking the same papers or using the same keywords, and alerts them to potentially related material. It allows completely free tagging. It provides RSS feeds, allowing users to keep track of articles posted under interesting tags or by users with similar interests. It has the capacity to export the references in RIS format to a citation manager program.[6]

4.6 JabRef

JabRef is reference management software that uses BibTeX as its native format. It provides an easy-to-use interface for editing BibTeX files, for importing data from online scientific databases, and for managing and searching BibTeX files. It is released under the terms of the GPL license. This application is programmed in Java, and is maintained for Windows, Linux and Mac OS X. It allows direct search and download from PubMed, IEEEXplore, CiteSeer and ArXiv. It links to URL, DOI number, PDF, PS, DjVu or other file types, which can be opened with a single click. It has Cite-as-you-write functionality for external applications such as LyX, Kile, Emacs, WinEdt, Vim and LaTeX Editor. It also has Plug-in system based on Java Plug-in Framework supporting new import/export filters, cite-as-you-write functions, and export formatters.[7]

4.7 Jumper 2.0

Jumper 2.0 is an open source web application script for collaborative search and knowledge management. It was publicly released under the GNU General Public License and was made available free to download. It is enterprise web-infrastructure for tagging and linking information resources. It lets to search and share high-value content, media, or data across remote locations using knowledge tags to capture knowledge about the information in distributed storage. It collects these tags in a tag profile. The tag profiles are stored in an interactive knowledge base and search engine. The software represents a fundamentally new approach to searching structured and semi-structured data using a Web 2.0 front-end. It is an interactive, user-submitted recommendation engine which uses peer and social-networking principles to reference any information located in distributed storage devices, either inside or outside the firewall, and capture the collective knowledge about that content, media, or data. This web application is written in PHP and Javascript. It runs on any industry standard web server such as Apache, Microsoft Internet Information Services, or Zeus Web Servers. It by default supports storing of the tag profile and associated knowledge tags within MySQL. It can easily be configured to support Oracle database, IBM DB2, and Microsoft SQL Server as the back-end database. In addition, it can be integrated with LDAP for user and group management. Users can access it via any industry standard browser; including Windows Internet Explorer, Mozila Firefox, Apple Safari, Google Chrome, and Opera.[8]

4.8 KBibTeX

KBibTeX is reference management software primarily for BibTeX which is typically used in conjunction with TeX/LaTeX. Beyond normal editing capabilities, it offers searching and importing new references from Google Scholar or BibSonomy. It is written using the KDE framework.[9]

4.9 Pybliographer

Pybliographer is a reference management software tool that deals with bibliographic databases, used for viewing, editing, searching, and reformatting bibliographies. It is written in Python and licensed under GNU General Public License. It provides a scripting framework of classes and functions, which makes it extendable to many other applications. In addition to the scripting environment, it provides a graphical GNOME interface called Pybliographic, allowing many customizable viewing and editing possibilities. The interface can also be used to insert references directly into LyX, Kile or OpenOffice, direct queries to Medline, and more. File formats supported—BibTeX, ISI, Medline, Ovid, and Refer.[10]

4.10 Refbase

Refbase is web-based institutional repository and reference management software which is often used for self-archiving. It is licensed under the GPL and written in PHP and uses a MySQL backend. It can import and export a variety of standard bibliographic formats, including BibTeX, Endnote, RIS, ISI, MODS XML, PubMed, Medline, RefWorks, and Copac. It can generate formatted bibliographies and citations in LaTeX, RTF, HTML, and PDF. It also has advanced search features and can generate RSS feeds from searches. Links using DOIs and URLs can be added, as can links to files. It supports the Search/Retrieve via URL (SRU) and OpenSearch web services as well as COinS and unAPI metadata.[11]

4.11 RefDB

RefDB is a client/server reference database and bibliography tool for markup languages like SGML, XML, and LaTeX. It is suitable for standalone use for the purpose of self-archiving, but can be used as an institutional repository as well. Data storage proper is done in one of several supported SQL database engines. It runs on a variety of Unix-like operating systems (Linux, FreeBSD, NetBSD, Mac OS X, and Solaris) and on Windows/Cygwin. RefDB is licensed under the GPL. It supports a variety of bibliographic formats, including BibTeX, Endnote, RIS, ISI, MODS XML, PubMed, MARC, and Copac and can create output in these formats, or as TEI, DocBook, HTML, or XHTML documents. Text editor extensions are provided for Emacs and for Vim to integrate editing, searching, and citing references as well as transforming documents into XML, SGML, or LaTeX authoring environment. RefDB ports or packages are available for a variety of operating systems.[12]

4.12 Referencer

Referencer is a GNOME application to organize documents or references, and ultimately generate a BibTex bibliography file. An automatic acquisition of bibliographic information for some kinds of documents via Internet is possible in it. Upon adding a PDF file to a Referencer library file, it will automatically be searched for key identifiers such as a DOI code or arXiv identifier. It imports from BibTeX, Reference Manager and Endnote. It automatically retrieves arXiv, PubMed and CrossRef metadata for PDF documents which have arXiv ID or DOI code. With the Python plug-in support the Python scripting language can be used in it. It is translated into many languages.[13]

4.13 Wikindx

Wikindx is a free bibliographic and quotations/notes management and article authoring system (Virtual Research Environment) works on a variety of operating systems and designed for multi-user collaborative use across the internet. It provides functionality to write notes and entire papers. It is developed under the GNU GPL license. It supports non-English multi-byte character sets. It allows multiple attachments for each bibliographic resource. It can export a bibliography in various citation styles. It allows users to edit or create bibliographic styles through a graphical interface. It can import and export other bibliographic formats including BibTex and EndNote format.[14]

4.14 Zotero

Zotero is a Firefox browser extension which can be used for storing bibliographic data and related research materials, such as PDFs, while browsing. Notable features include web browser integration, online syncing, generation of in-text citations, footnotes and bibliographies, as well as integration with the word processors Microsoft Word and OpenOffice.org. Zotero was the first to adopt the Citation Style Language, and maintains the Zotero Style Repository. Users can generate citations and bibliographies through the word processor plug-in, or directly in Zotero.[15]

5. Bibliographic Citation and Reference Management Experiment with Zotero

Before start working in Zotero, one has to install Mozilla Firefox Web Browser in their system, which is again totally free for download. Since it is an extension of Mozilla Firefox, its icon always appeared down at the right-hand corner of the browser. By clicking that icon one can start building their bibliographies working in the web browser itself. Further one can install word processor plug-in of Zotero and have facility to work in Microsoft word also. The recorded data in the Zotero library in browser as well as in word processor plug-in can be operated offline also. A brief practical introduction to Zotero is given with the help of following snapshots:

- On many websites such as online library catalogues, Google Books, Amazon.com, Wikipedia, and publisher's websites, Zotero shows an icon when a book, article, or other resource is being viewed. By clicking this icon, the full reference information can be saved to the Zotero library (See Figs. 26.1 and 26.2).

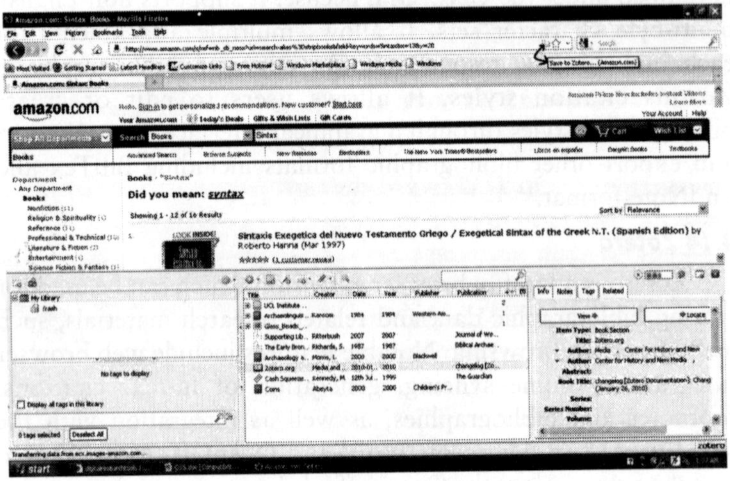

Fig. 26.1

Fig. 26.2

- Zotero has facility to save a copy of the webpage as well as to save a copy of full text PDF also (See Figs. 26.3 and 26.4). Users can then add notes, tags, attachments, and their own metadata.

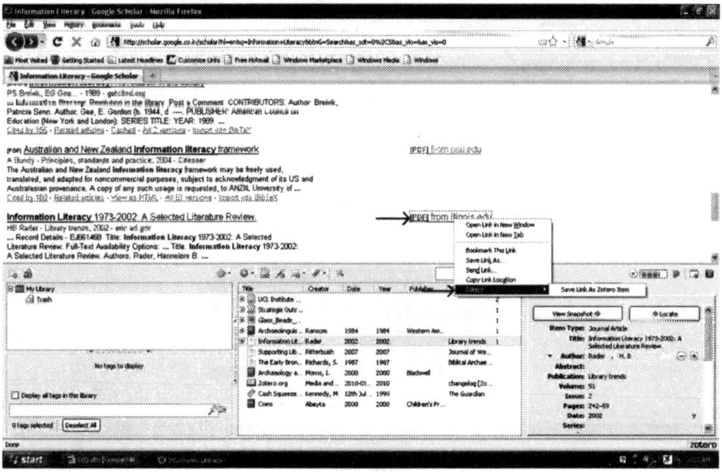

Fig. 26.3

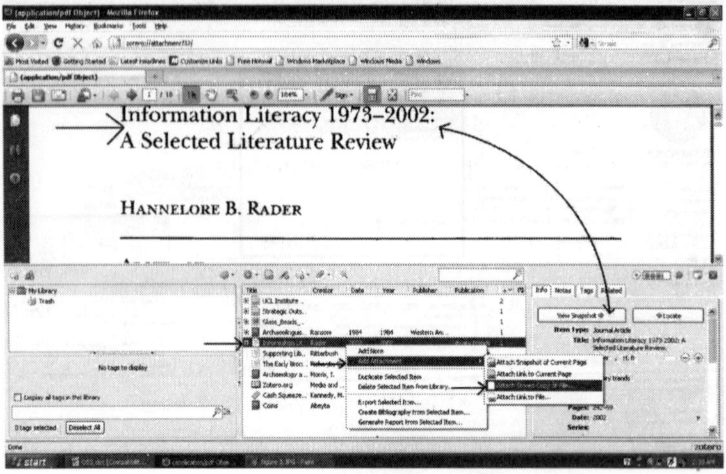

Fig. 26.4

- Selections of the local reference library data is possible to be exported as formatted bibliographies in selected citation style format (See Figs. 26.5, 26.6 and 26.7).

Fig. 26.5

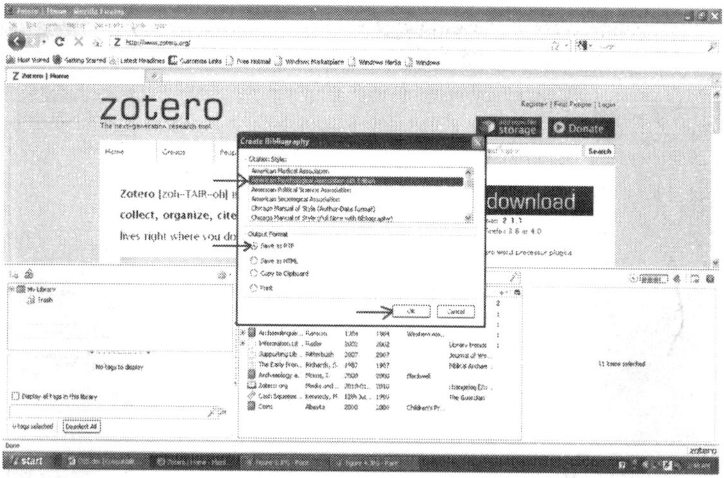

Fig. 26.6

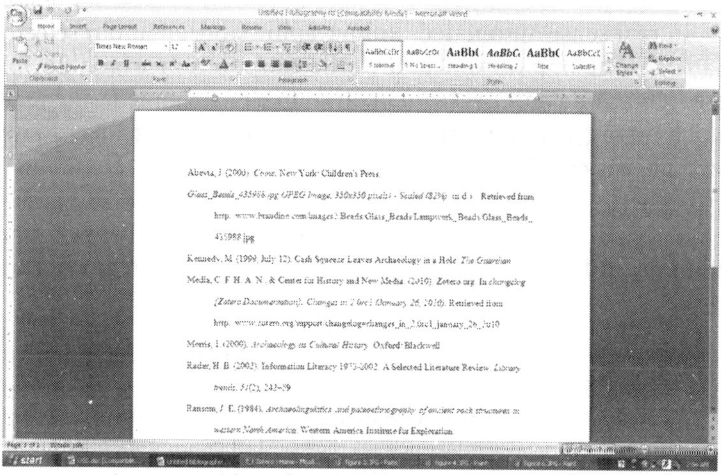

Fig. 26.7

- Users can generate citations and bibliographies through the word processor Zotero plug-in, simultaneously while writing a paper (See Fig. 26.8).

Fig. 26.8

6. Conclusion

In real sense automated bibliographic citation and reference management application is an efficient solution available for researchers and authors from open source environment, through which many activities related to resource management have become easier, time saving and even error-free. These help researchers easily to gather, manage, store and share all types of references from online libraries and databases as well as generate citations and bibliographies automatically in different citation styles.

NOTES

1. Matei, Sorin Adam (2009). What's new in the world of citation Management? (Retrieved March 21, 2011, from http://matei.org/ithink/2009/05/15/whats-new-in-theworld-of-citation-management/).
2. http://www.aigaion.nl/ (Retrieved on 28th March, 2011).
3. http://bebop.sourseforge.net (Retrieved on 28th March, 2011).
4. http://bibus-biblio.sourceforge.net (Retrieved on 28th March, 2011).
5. http://bibdesk.sourceforge.net (Retrieved on 28th March, 2011).
6. http://connotea.org/ (Retrieved on 28th March, 2011).
7. http://jabref.sourceforge.net/ (Retrieved on 28th March, 2011).
8. www.jumpernetworks.com (Retrieved on 28th March, 2011).

9. http://home.gna.org/kbibtex/ (Retrieved on 29th March, 2011).
10. www.pybliographer.org (Retrieved on 29th March, 2011).
11. http://www.refbase.net (Retrieved on 29th March, 2011).
12. http://refdb.sourceforge.net (Retrieved on 29th March, 2011).
13. http://icculus.org/referencer (Retrieved on 29th March, 2011).
14. http://wikindex.sourceforge.net (Retrieved on 29th March, 2011).
15. http://www.zotero.org/ (Retrieved on 29th March, 2011).

List of Contributors

Anoopa, K., Professional Assistant, Kannur University Central Library, Kannur-670 002. E- mail: anoopavarma@yahoo.com

Anuradha, V., Librarian, BITS Pilani, K.K. Birla Goa Campus, Goa. E-mail: anuradhav@bits-goa.ac.in

Archana, S.N., Professional Assistant, Cochin University of Science and Technology, Cochin, Kerala.
E-mail: niharikamanakkil@gmail.com

Beegum Sarjoon, N.R., Research Scholar, DLIS, University of Kerala, Trivandrum- 695 034. E-mail: sarju.bsnr@gmail.com

Beena, C. (Dr.), Assistant Librarian (Sen. Gr.), Cochin University of Science and Technology, Cochin, Kerala.
E-mail: beenacherukuth@gmail.com

Biju, R., Greenstone Support for South Asia, Center for Development of Digital Libraries (CDDL), Indian Institute of Management, Kozhikode (IIMK).

Bulu Maharana, Sr. Lecturer, P.G. Department of Library & Information Science, Sambalpur University, Jyoti Vihar-768019, Orissa. E-mail: bulumaharana@gmail.com

Dhanyasree, V.K., Research and Teaching Assistant, IGNOU, New Delhi-110 068. E-mail: vk.dhanyasree@gmail.com

Dineshan Koovakkai (Dr.), Assistant Librarian, Central University of Kerala, Kasargod, Kerala-671 123. E-mail: dineshank@gmail.com, Blog: www.dineshkoovakkai. blogspot.com

Gayathri Madhusudan, Librarian, Bharatheeya Vidya Bhavan, Kozhikode. E-mail: gayathrimadhusudan@gmail.com

Gopakumar, V. (Dr.), University Librarian, Goa University, Goa. E-mail: librarian@unigoa.ac.in

Gopikuttan, A. (Dr.), Associate Professor & Head, DLIS, University of Kerala Trivandrum-695 034. E-mail: agopikuttan@yahoo.co.in

Humayoon Kabir, S. (Dr.), Associate Professor, DLIS, University of Kerala Trivandrum-695 034.
E-mail: humayoonkabirs@gmail.com

Jayasree, V., Professional Assistant, Cochin University of Science and Technology, Cochin, Kerala. E-mail: jayasreernair@gmail.com

Joshy Kuriakose, Greenstone Support for South Asia, Center for Development of Digital Libraries (CDDL), Indian Institute of Management, Kozhikode (IIMK).

Khaisar Muneebulla Khan (Dr.), Reader, DLIS, Mangalore University, Mangalore. E-mail:: khaisarmk@yahoo.com

Lalitha, M. (Dr.), Librarian, SCERT Kerala, Trivandrum.
E-mail: rlsshome@gmail.com

Mehjabeen Aideed, Junior Research Fellow, DLIS, University of Calicut, Kerala-673 635. E-mail: mahjabeenhabeeb@gmail.com

Midhula Soman, V.S., Research Scholar, DLIS, University of Kerala, Thiruvananthapuram-695 034.
E-mail: midhula_soman@yahoo.com

Mohamed Musthafa, K., Research Scholar, DLIS, Aligarh Muslim University, Aligarh, India. E-mail: musthafa.lis@gmail.com

Naushad Ali, P.M. (Dr.), Chairman, DLIS, Aligarh Muslim University, Aligarh, India. E- mail: naushadali.amu@gmail.com

Pooja, R., Senior Librarian, Kasturba Medical College, Mangalore-575 001. E-mail: poojabhat_2003@yahoo.com

Rehana Ummer, Library Assistant, ISRO HQ Library, Bangalore.
Email: rehana@isro.gov.in

Rekha Rani Varghese (Dr.), Assistant Professor, Department of Library and Information Science, Pondicherry University.
E-mail: rekhatvm@gmail.com

Sabitri Majhi, Junior Research Fellow, P.G. Department of Library & Information Science, Sambalpur Universty, Jyoti Vihar-768019, Orissa. E-mail: sabitriindia@gmail.com

Santhosh Kumar, G., Senior Lecturer, Department of Computer Science, Cochin University of Science and Technology, Cochin, Kerala. E-mail: san@cusat.ac.in

Sheeja, N.K. (Dr.), Assistant Librarian, University Library, Cochin University of Science and Technology, Cochin-22. E-mail: sheeja@cusat.ac.in

Sreejaya, P., Greenstone Support for South Asia, Center for Development of Digital Libraries (CDDL), Indian Institute of Management, Kozhikode (IIMK).

Sreekumar, M.G. (Dr.), Greenstone Support for South Asia, Center for Development of Digital Libraries (CDDL), Indian Institute of Management, Kozhikode (IIMK). E-mail: mgsree@iimk.ac.in

Sudha, A. (Dr.), Deputy Librarian, Kannur University CentraLibrary, Kannur. E-mail: sudha.azhikodan@gmail.com

Sudhier, K.G. (Dr.), Assistant Professor, DLIS, University of Kerala, Thiruvananthapuram-695 034, Kerala. E-mail: kgsudhier@gmail.com

Suguna, L.S., Research Scholar, DLIS, University of Kerala, Trivandrum-695 034. E-mail: sugunals@yahoo.co.in

Sunitha, T., Greenstone Support for South Asia, Center for Development of Digital Libraries (CDDL), Indian Institute of Management, Kozhikode (IIMK).

Surendran Cherukodan, Junior Librarian, School of Engineering, Cochin University of Science and Technology, Cochin, Kerala. E-mail: csura@cusat.ac.in

Susan Mathew, K., Assistant Librarian (Sr. Scale), University Library, Cochin University of Science and Technology, Cochin-682022. Email: susankarott@gmail.com

Thomas Abraham, Open Knowledge Society, Kottayam, Kerala. E-mail: tomuhs@gmail.com

Trupti D. More, Librarian, Deccan College Post Graduate and Research Institute, Pune. E-mail: moretrupti02@gmail.com

Vasudevan, T.M., Associate Professor, DLIS, University of Calicut. E-mail: amandev44@yahoo.com

Vimal Kumar, V., Library Assistant, Mahatma Gandhi University, Kottayam, Kerala. E-mail: vimal0212@gmail.com

Vinod, V.M. (Dr.), Assistant Librarian, CHMK Library, University of Calicut Kerala-673 635.
E-mail: vinodvmvinod@rediffmail.com

Vishala, B.K. (Dr.), Selection Grade Librarian, St. Agnes Centre for Post Graduate Studies and Research, (Autonomous), Bendore, Mangalore-575 002.

Website: http://drvishala.synthasite.com,

E-mail: bk.vishala@gmail.com , vishalrajbk@yahoo.co.in

Index